The Lighter Side Of Cruising Part One

Cruising, Volume 1

Stephen Barker

Published by Stephen Barker, 2024.

While every precaution has been taken in the preparation of this book, the publisher assumes no responsibility for errors or omissions, or for damages resulting from the use of the information contained herein.

THE LIGHTER SIDE OF CRUISING PART ONE

First edition. May 22, 2024.

ISBN: 979-8224344970

Written by Stephen Barker.

Table of Contents

The Lighter Side Of Cruising Part One

Steve Barker

Foreword

Welcome aboard, intrepid traveller! Or should I say, future cruise enthusiast? Whichever you are, you're about to embark on a voyage through "The Lighter Side of Cruising" with me, Steve Barker, your self-appointed cruise comedienne and master of maritime mischief. Don't worry—I promise not to hit you with a life preserver or make you walk the plank. Well, unless you're into that sort of thing.

This book is a delightful concoction of helpful hints, cheeky anecdotes, and laugh-out-loud moments, all centred around the wonderful world of cruising. Think of it as your personal guide to the high seas, minus the seasickness and awkward captain's dinners. It's a blend of practical advice and humorous escapades, giving you the tools to navigate your cruise with a smile on your face and a cocktail in hand.

Now, if you're here for a serious, no-nonsense guide to cruising, you've taken a wrong turn at the buffet line. This book is about seeing the cruise experience through my eyes, as it happens, in all its chaotic and hilarious glory. From the joys of finding the best deck chair (tip: it's not the one next to the screaming toddler) to the perils of overindulging at the midnight chocolate buffet, I'm here to share it all.

So, whether you're a seasoned sailor or a cruise virgin, I hope that this book will inspire you to book your next adventure on the high seas. And if it doesn't, well, I'll just have to take the Travel Director aside and give him a good talking-to. After all, finding the perfect cruise is a personal mission of mine, and I take my duty very seriously. Seriously funny, that is.

Get ready to laugh, learn, and maybe even snort your piña colada out of your nose. Welcome to the lighter side of cruising!

Bon voyage!

Baltic Cruise: A Solo Adventure

Day 1 - Home to the Ship and the first day

As I lay there, snug as a bug in a rug in the distance, I heard the sound of a Sparrow Fart, so with an outreached hand, I grabbed the nearest timepiece to check on the timage; it was indeed daft o'clock. Time to get my lazy butt out of bed and make way to London Heathrow for the flight to Copenhagen, where I would meet the Norwegian Star and start the long-awaited cruise.

Well, I did not think much of the SAS Airplane, but never mind, I suppose it is only an air taxi and one-and-a-half-hour flight. I was glad to see the cabin crew was not dressed in a one-piece black jumpsuit and wearing balaclavas. I suppose the letters SAS printed on the aeroplane do not stand for an elite British fighting unit but a Scandinavian airline company instead. I was glad about that as I didn't fancy bailing out over Copenhagen as someone from the Cabin crew shouted Go, Go, Go.

Getting through the formalities at Copenhagen was straightforward, taking only about ten minutes or so before entering the main arrivals hall. The airport seemed hectic, with no precise control, but it must work. After searching for what seemed like ages, I managed to locate the NCL guide, who had been cleverly hidden next to a big sign with NCL proudly displayed, ingenious, was soon on my way to the coach and transfer to the Ship.

I started to talk to a charming young lady who was also making her way to the coach, suitcases and all. Friendly banter was exchanged with the young woman in question, too, the coach. While chatting, it was discovered that she was joining the Norwegian Star as one of the crew. So it goes to prove that staff-friendly behaviour starts before you even arrive at the Ship. Well played, NCL.

So, there I was, strolling into the Port, fully prepared for the classic waiting game before setting foot on the Ship. But oh boy, was I in for a surprise! Instead of lounging around for an hour, I found myself caught up in a whirlwind of health questionnaires and check-ins faster than you can say, "anchors aweigh." All designed to make me question my decision to embark on this adventure.

And just when I thought I had escaped the madness, I had to navigate through what can only be described as a gauntlet of Pack hounds, or as NCL likes to call them, " photographers." They were prowling around, just waiting to pounce on unsuspecting passengers like a scene out of a wildlife documentary. But fear not, I managed to pull off some top-tier stealth moves and slip past them like a ninja in the night.

I chuckled to myself as I watched them redirect their attention to a group of poor souls who unwittingly stumbled into their clutches, positioned perfectly in front of a suspiciously green screen. Ah, the joys of embarkation day!

While waiting for my cabin to be free, I decided to make the most of the Beverage Package I had already purchased and headed for the Red Lion bar for a well-earned cold beer—OK, several. After checking with the helpful Barman on what was included in the package, I sat down with the foresaid beer.

Feeling as sprightly as a caffeinated squirrel, I decide it's high time for a little nibble at the Market Kitchen. A quick snack, I tell myself. But oh, the folly of such intentions! Surrounded by an abundance of delectable delights, my snack quickly morphs into a full-blown three-course extravaganza.

With each dish expertly crafted and beckoning to be devoured, who am I to resist? Surely this feast will tide me over until dinner, I naively declare to myself. But alas, my stomach has other plans. It roars with laughter at my feeble attempt to curb its voracious appetite.

But hey, who needs a diet when you're on holiday? I chuckle at my own folly and surrender to the culinary delights before me. After all, calories don't count when you're having this much fun, right?

It was time to look around this great Ship and locate all the essential places, not just the bars but also other areas. The Ship was seen, and the obligatory photos of the vessel were taken. It was off to find my stateroom and unpack.

I strut into my room like a conquering hero, ready to claim my temporary kingdom aboard this NCL ship. Lo and behold, the housekeeper has gone above and beyond, even tucking my bag into its rightful place. NCL's customer service strikes again, leaving me feeling like royalty... or at least a slightly pampered court jester.

With my bags unpacked in record time, I embark on the next great adventure: mastering the art of the bathroom ballet. After a valiant struggle against the rebellious toilet seat (spoiler alert: it keeps losing the battle), I emerge victorious, albeit slightly bewildered. Note to self: toilet seats are not meant for interpretive dance.

Now, with bladder control skills honed to perfection, it's time to tackle the true challenge of the evening: making a sizable dent in my beverage package. I gallantly venture forth to explore a new watering hole, eager to discover what delights await within. But alas, the Solo Travelers Club proves to be a solo affair indeed, with yours truly being the sole member in attendance.

Undeterred by the lack of company, I raise a glass to my own camaraderie and decide to join myself for a beer. Suitably refreshed, I saunter off to the theatre, ready to be entertained by whatever spectacle awaits. After all, who needs a crowd when you've got front-row seats to the greatest show on the high seas?

Well, slap my flip-flops and call me entertained! That opening night show was a real barnstormer. I've been around the cruise block a few times, hobnobbing on so-called five-star liners, but let me tell ya, the Norwegian Star's entertainment blew 'em all out of the water, and not just 'cause we're on a ship!

They had it all, folks. Singers belting out tunes like they were auditioning for Broadway, dancers busting moves that'd make Fred Astaire jealous, magicians pulling rabbits outta hats like it's their day job (which, I guess, it kinda is), and acrobats defying gravity like it's their side hustle.

And let's not forget the pièce de résistance: the cruise director's comedy routine. Talk about laughing till your sides ache! I swear, if this ship ever sinks, we'll be saved by the sheer buoyancy of our collective chuckles.

But hey, all good things must come to an end, right? Whether it's the fatigue from a day packed with adventure or the questionable number of beers I've knocked back, it's high time I bid adieu to consciousness and returned to the land of Nod. May my dreams be as wild as the high seas we sail upon!

Day 2 - Warnemunde Germany

Ah, the best-laid plans of mice and cruisers often go awry! Determined to catch the grand spectacle of our majestic vessel gliding into the Port of Warnemunde, I set my trusty alarm for the ungodly hour of 05:00. With a quick shower to shake off the cobwebs, I eagerly make my way to deck 13, ready to witness maritime magic in action. Or so I thought.

As I stand there, bleary-eyed and brimming with anticipation, it slowly dawns on me: I may have jumped the gun a tad. Turns out, I'm fashionably early to the party, about as fashionably as socks with sandals.

But fear not, for I refuse to let this minor hiccup dampen my spirits. What better time than the crack of dawn to squeeze in a spot of exercise? So off I trot for a few laps around the ship, much to the confusion of the seagulls eyeing me from above.

After working up a sweat that could rival a sauna, it's off to breakfast; I go! Kudos to the ship's culinary wizards for not only keeping our bellies happy but also providing some top-notch entertainment. Bacon or pork scratchings, you ask? Ah, the age-old question, one that could stump even the wisest of philosophers.

But the real highlight of the morning? The showdown of the century: chef vs. chef in a battle of tray arrangement prowess. Protective gloves or bare hands? It's a culinary cage match for the ages!

With breakfast conquered and my appetite for food and drama sated, it's finally time to witness the ship's triumphant arrival in port. Hats off to the crew and the captain for navigating this floating behemoth into such a tight spot, especially with the Holland America ship playing chicken up ahead. It's a sight to behold, and armed with my camera and a gleeful grin, I am ready to capture the moment for posterity. Ah, the joys of cruising!

Ah, the call of adventure beckons, and I, ever the intrepid explorer, heed its siren song. But before I set foot in the wilds of Warnemunde, I wisely opted to let the organised tours take the lead. After all, why blend in with the flock when you can strut your stuff solo?

Armed with only my wits and a trusty jacket (because apparently, Warnemunde's weather has a penchant for mischief), I prepare to face the elements. It's like a hurricane out there, but with a side of sunshine, because why make weather predictable when you can keep everyone guessing?

Peering out the window, I spy the entry point into the terminal building, where the dreaded pack hunters lie in wait. But wait—what's this? A stroke of luck! No photographers in sight! Or so I foolishly think.

Little did I know, they had cunningly disguised themselves as locals, blending seamlessly into the crowd like chameleons at a rainbow convention. Before I can say "smile for the camera," I find myself standing shoulder to shoulder with Herman from down the hall, flashbulbs blazing like fireworks on the Fourth of July.

Ah, the joys of being a tourist! You never know when you'll become an unwitting star in someone else's vacation album. But hey, at least it's a memory to cherish, right? Or a cautionary tale to share with future generations of intrepid travellers.

Ah, Germany, the land of efficiency and order! Armed with my trusty passport, I strutted up to the border like a pro, ready to face the scrutinising gaze of customs officials. But to my surprise, they couldn't be bothered to give it so much as a second glance. Apparently, my face is just that unforgettable.

With entry secured faster than you can say "schnitzel," I embark on a stroll towards the quayside. Ah, the glamorous life of a tourist! My destination? The perfect photo op: the rear of our majestic vessel. But alas, what do my eyes behold? A sight that strikes fear into the heart of every captain: a fender bender! I can already envision the ship's crew scrambling for the duct tape and filler like DIY enthusiasts on a mission.

I can't help but chuckle at the thought of our esteemed bridge crew, praised just moments ago for their navigational prowess, now faced with the prospect of explaining this little mishap. "Oops, sorry about that iceberg-shaped dent, folks! Must've taken a wrong turn at Albuquerque."

But fear not, dear shipmates! If there's one thing I've learned from years of watching DIY disaster shows, it's that duct tape fixes everything. And if not, well, at least we'll have a hilarious story to tell at the next port of call.

A lovely fishing port, a pleasant walk partook along the quayside, lined with a domestic market and local fishermen selling freshly prepared fish and cooked. I would like to add that I am not a fan of eating fish that would try to find the family in a far-off land!

Ah, the siren song of the high seas! While the allure of a round-trip boat adventure tempted me like a siren luring sailors to their doom, I decided to resist its call and dive headfirst into the heart of Warnemunde instead. After all, who needs a boat when you can navigate the treacherous waters of the local town?

As I meandered through the charming streets, I couldn't help but notice the shops bustling with activity, eagerly awaiting the arrival of their newly imported cargo: us cruise passengers. It's like Black Friday but with more sunscreen and fewer stampedes.

And oh, what luck! Warnemunde just so happens to boast a coastline, complete with a promenade lined with market stalls. And what do my wandering eyes behold? A veritable treasure trove of German liquid gold: beer! It would have been downright rude not to indulge in a sampling spree, especially considering the stalls seemed to have sprung up just for my amusement. Or perhaps it's just a happy coincidence that it's Warnemunde week celebrations. Who can say?

But wait, there's more! The local radio station NDR has set up shop, belting out tunes and hosting live bands like it's Woodstock on water. Well, dam it, it looks like I'll just have to stick around and soak in the festivities, armed with nothing but another cold Rostocker Beer and a smile as wide as the river Spree. Cheers to unexpected adventures and impromptu parties!

With visions of a sumptuous shipboard lunch dancing in my head, I saunter back to the vessel, only to find myself caught in a maritime version of "Goldilocks and the Three Ships."

But wait, what's this? A siren song calls out to me from amidst the towering behemoths of the sea: a quaint little ferry offering jaunts to Rostock for a mere 15 Euro. With the promise of adventure and the allure of unlimited photo ops, I throw caution to the wind and leap aboard, staking my claim at the front like a seafaring pioneer.

Oh, how naive I was! Little did I realise that my prime perch would become a frosty prison under the merciless assault of the wind. As I emerge from the hour-long ordeal, I swear I could pass for an iceberg impersonator, all stiff limbs and chattering teeth.

Note to self: next time, opt for a seat behind the safety of the glass panel, where the elements dare not intrude. After all, it's there for a reason, right? But hey, at least the captain's running commentary provided a riveting narrative of the journey's highlights... all in German. Ah, the joys of being linguistically challenged on the high seas! But fear not, dear reader, for I may not speak German, but I'm fluent in the universal language of confused nodding and polite smiles.

Ah, the joys of shore excursions! As I trekked from the dock to the town centre, I couldn't help but marvel at the plethora of shopping opportunities for the devoted shopaholics among us. But fear not, fellow non-shoppers, for amidst the sea of retail therapy lies a treasure trove of historical buildings, just waiting to be admired by those who prefer sightseeing to spending.

And oh, the bars! Like oases in a desert of consumerism, they beckon weary travellers with promises of liquid refreshment and respite from the onslaught of souvenir shops.

But ah, dear reader, beware of the pitfalls of tourist traps! As I soon discovered, not all is as it seems in the land of exclusive deals and tempting offers. Take, for example, the misleading signage promising 'P' Frei. Little did I know that 'P' Frei actually means' Free parking' in German, a revelation that nearly left me in a tight spot, quite literally, as I was chased down the street by a determined restroom attendant wielding a toilet brush.

Ah, dear reader, let us divert our attention from the perilous world of bodily functions and venture into the realm of strategic decision-making. With the astuteness of a seasoned sailor navigating treacherous waters, I meticulously examined the sailing schedule for the boat back to Warnemunde.

Like a savvy gambler at the cruise ship casino, I weighed the odds and swiftly concluded that catching the last boat would be akin to playing a game of cruise ship roulette. With three ships in port and a swarm of eager excursionists clamouring for a spot, I wisely chose to steer clear of the chaos and potential paddle-less predicaments. After all, who needs the stress when you can sip a cocktail and watch the drama unfold from the safety of dry land?

Returning to the sanctuary of the ship around 15:00, I embarked on a noble quest for physical exertion at the poolside bar. But alas, my intentions were quickly thwarted by the allure of relaxation and refreshment. The pool beckoned invitingly, but I opted instead for the ultimate forms of exercise:

lifting burgers to my mouth and hoisting pints of beer in a jubilant celebration of my newfound laziness. Who needs swimming when you can indulge in the joys of gluttony and sloth?

I was only sitting down for a few minutes when NCL service excellence kicked into gear. The crew asked about my day and if I had a great time. Of course, I would like a drink. Silly question; I'll have two. Several beers later, it was off to the cabin for a shower and change of attire for the evening activities.

Ah, the best-laid plans of cruisers and men often go awry, especially when those plans involve beer, dinner, and a show. But fear not, dear reader, for my misadventures aboard the Norwegian Star were nothing short of comedic gold.

With the Ship's daily news in hand, I concocted a foolproof scheme: first, a rendezvous with my beloved brews, then a sumptuous dinner at the Kitchen Garden restaurant, where the food flows like a river of culinary delight. But alas, fate had other ideas.

As I lounged in Gatsby's bar, nursing a cold one or two (who's counting?), I soon realised that time aboard the Norwegian Star is a fickle mistress. With clocks that seemed to be in cahoots with the Bermuda Triangle, I found myself lost in a temporal whirlwind. One moment, I'm at the pointy end of the ship, eagerly awaiting the show's commencement; the next, I'm somehow teleported to the blunt end (aka the rear), scratching my head in bewilderment.

But wait, there's more! As I ventured to Cagney's in search of solace (and another cold beer), I was met with disapproving glances from fellow passengers who had managed to keep track of time better than I had. Another missed show? Well, I'll drink to that!

But fear not, for my evening was far from ruined. With the determination of a parched pirate on the hunt for buried treasure, I embarked on a quest to find the elusive Red Lion and its mysterious Star Bar. Hours passed as I navigated the labyrinthine corridors, stopping at every watering hole along the way, all in the name of camaraderie and liquid courage.

And so, dear reader, as I bid farewell to yet another day aboard the Norwegian Star, I can't help but wonder: what delightful chaos awaits me tomorrow? Only time (or lack thereof) will tell!

Day 3 - Day at Sea

Ah, the best-laid plans cruisers often go astray, especially when faced with the song of a soft, warm quilt and the gentle sway of the high seas. Set the alarm for 05:00, they said. Daily exercise and a brisk walk around the ship, they said. But alas, the sea air whispered sweet nothings into my slumbering ears, and before I knew it, the alarm was silenced, and I was wrapped back under the covers for a few more hours of blissful sleep.

Eventually roused from my cosy cocoon, it was time to face the day, armed with the promise of breakfast and the hope of a stroll along deck 13 to assess the weather. But oh, the cruel hand of fate! Instead of sunshine and gentle breezes, I was greeted with high winds and ominous clouds, effectively squashing any hopes of a leisurely promenade.

But fear not, for NCL, in their infinite wisdom, prioritises passenger safety above all else. With the open decks closed and the ship's state-of-the-art stabilisers working their magic, I found solace in the fact that while the waves may be breaking outside, inside the ship, it's smooth sailing... or swimming, if the fish I swear I saw outside my window is any indication.

And speaking of breakfast, the mystery of bacon versus pork scratchings rages on. But fear not, dear reader, for I am on the case, diligently studying the chefs' choice of protective gloves and deducing that the crispy, crunchy texture can mean only one thing: pork scratchings for the win!

As the open decks remained elusive, I embarked on an indoor adventure, working off my breakfast with a brisk walk around the ship's interior. Ah, the joys of cruising: where even the best-laid exercise plans are no match for the irresistible allure of a buffet spread fit for a king. But hey, who needs restraint when you can have seconds... and thirds... and fourths?

The thrilling life of a cruise-goer! A morning filled with the riveting task of writing this report and attending a lecture on acupuncture has left me yearning for the soothing embrace of a local Chinese medical shop back home. But first things first: time for a beer, because nothing says "stress relief" quite like a cold brewski, am I right?

But wait, there's more! Two more lectures await my eager intellect: one on gemstones and another on art. So here I am, one day at sea, and suddenly,

I'm a connoisseur of fine art and a gemstone aficionado. Who knew a cruise could turn me into a walking encyclopedia of random knowledge? But fear not, dear reader, for should the stress of newfound expertise become too much to bear, I can always rely on the ancient wisdom of acupuncture to restore balance to my overly stimulated mind.

And let's not forget the allure of Bingo! The promise of a $6000 prize beckoned me, only to leave me empty-handed and filled with regret. But hey, it's not about the destination but the journey, right? And what a journey it was, spent in my new favourite haunt, the Red Lion. With each sip from my beverage package, I honed my skills as a seasoned people-watcher, marvelling at fellow cruisers' fascinating quirks and idiosyncrasies. It's amazing what a few beers can do for your ability to spot nationalities based on their antics alone. Cheers to cultural enlightenment, one pint at a time!

With the precision of a well-oiled machine, I managed to snag a reservation at the illustrious Versailles restaurant for 17:30, only to arrive and find myself in a scene straight out of a time-traveling escapade. Tables filled, diners feasting, and the clock teasingly stuck at 17:29. Curse you, mystical elevator of temporal confusion!

But fear not, for I was eventually ushered to my table by the window, armed with a menu bursting with tantalising choices. After much deliberation (and perhaps a coin toss or two), I settled on the soup, followed by a delectable lamb dish, and rounded off with the pièce de résistance: bread and butter pudding. The culinary journey was swift and satisfying, clocking in at a speedy 18:00.

Ah, but the trials of dining aboard a cruise ship! As I began to savour each mouthful, I found myself interrupted at every turn by eager waitstaff inquiring about my satisfaction. Note to self: next time, bring a sign proclaiming, "All is well; let me eat in peace!"

With my belly pleasantly bloated from the feast, I embarked on a quest to work off the excess calories with several laps around the ship. But lo and behold, my efforts were thwarted by the call of the theatre, where a magnificent show awaited courtesy of the ship's entertainment crew.

As I settled into my seat, I couldn't help but notice the curious phenomenon of the audience clustering on the right side of the stage, threatening to tip the ship off-kilter. Ah, the wonders of cruise ship dynamics! But fear not, dear reader, for I had the foresight to arrive 15 minutes early, securing the best seat in the house and avoiding a potential capsize.

Time to finish off the evening with a few drinks in one of the many bars, plus a chat with some of the fellow passengers. I met some friendly Americans and German guests and had a pleasant evening, allowing me to practice more German.

Day 4 -Tallinn Estonia

The comedy of errors continues aboard the excellent ship Norwegian Star! Last night, in a moment of misguided genius, I decided to tinker with time itself, obediently setting the clocks forward one hour as instructed by the daily news. Why? Because apparently, I'm a rule-follower to a fault, no questions asked!

So there I am, bright-eyed and bushy-tailed at the ungodly hour of 06:00, ready to seize the day with a hearty breakfast. Imagine my confusion when I discover that not a single restaurant is open for business. Cue the inevitable facepalm moment as I realise, with a sinking heart, that I've jumped the gun by a solid half-hour. Time to perform the humble act of clock-reversal, courtesy of yours truly, the resident idiot.

With time appropriately adjusted (and my dignity slightly bruised), I embark on a leisurely morning stroll around the eerily deserted decks. Ah, the serenity of being alone with one's thoughts, accompanied only by the gentle hum of the ship's engines and the faint glow of dawn's early light.

Feeling fancy, I opt for a posh breakfast at the Blue Lagoon restaurant, where refinement reigns supreme. Led to my table by a helpful waiter who's already got me chuckling with his early morning banter, I dive headfirst into the Full House breakfast, accompanied by a barrage of twenty questions about my egg preferences, bread choices, and juice selections. Ah, the joys of customisation, courtesy of NCL's breakfast buffet extravaganza!

And let's not forget the eternal breakfast conundrum: bacon or pork scratchings? The same quiz that has plagued me since the Market Garden makes a triumphant return, adding a sprinkle of culinary intrigue to an already delightful morning feast. Truly, breakfast has never been so entertaining—or so confusing!

Ah, the thrilling adventure of joining a pre-arranged excursion: "The Best of Medieval Tallinn." As I arrived at the designated meeting spot, I settled in for a wait, eagerly anticipating the journey ahead. A helpful crew member regaled me with tales of tour logistics, providing valuable insights into the mysterious workings of tour organisation. How enlightening!

Finally, the moment arrived, and I was called to join the throngs of eager cruisers, ticket in hand and proudly sporting a fetching red number three pinned to my shirt. Ah, reminiscent of school days, where names are replaced with numbers and the joys of being herded like cattle abound. As the famous film once proclaimed: "You are a number." How delightfully ominous!

Or perhaps it's a clever ploy to identify us unsuspecting tourists as prime targets for the relentless assault of guidebook peddlers and beverage hawkers. With my number prominently displayed, I braved the onslaught and cunningly slipped past the dreaded pack hounds—the photographers—lying in wait like wolves in sheep's clothing. But alas, their tactics were not so easily thwarted, as a second ambush awaited unsuspecting escapees halfway down the pier. A diabolical double whammy, indeed!

Undeterred, I secured my spot at the front of the bus, ready to embark on a grand adventure through the medieval marvels of Tallinn. Little did I know, the true challenge lay not in the cobblestone streets but in the form of an enormous American tourist struggling to catch his breath after a short stroll. Oxygen on standby, indeed! Ah, the joys of travel—where every step brings a new and unexpected twist to the tale.

The joys of guided tours—a perfect blend of historical enlightenment and slapstick comedy! Our esteemed guide for the day, Teet, greeted us with a name that sparked more curiosity than a cat in a curiosity factory. But fear not, dear travellers, for Teet quickly clarified that his moniker held a different meaning than its English counterpart. Ah, the mysteries of language!

Teet, bless his heart, proved to be a veritable fountain of knowledge on all things Tallinn and Estonia, regaling us with tales of history, occupation, and the occasional jab at Russian liberation—or lack thereof, as he so humorously put it. All hail Teet, the unsung hero of guided tours, keeping our motley crew entertained with a delightful mix of facts and jokes.

Our adventure began with a whirlwind tour of the town, punctuated by stops at palaces and government buildings of architectural splendour—or so we thought. Imagine our dismay as we laid eyes on our first destination, a palace shrouded in scaffolding and swathed in plastic like a giant pink mummy. But fear not, for the gardens provided a picturesque backdrop, complete with the unexpected thrill of surprise sprinkler attacks!

Lesson learned: when in doubt, stand behind the nearest American tourist for protection against rogue sprinklers and overzealous politicians. With soggy shoes and a newfound appreciation for human shields, we pressed on to the next government building, only to be greeted by yet another pink behemoth disguised as a construction site. Ah, the joys of bureaucracy—apparently, politicians are in a hurry no matter where you go!

As Teet-tastic adventure continues, our fearless leader guides us through Tallinn's whimsical wonders! With a wave of his wand—err, guiding stick—Teet regales us with tales of the city's split personality: upper town, lower town, and a whole lot of history in between. Behold, impressive buildings! Marvel at majestic churches! But wait, there's more: a crash course in historical gossip for each landmark, because who doesn't love a juicy backstory?

And then, a stroke of genius: a pit stop at a local gift shop, where we're set free to roam for a grand total of 30 minutes. A brilliant plan, indeed, except for one tiny detail: the looming threat of getting lost in the labyrinthine streets of Tallinn and missing the boat—literally. But hey, nothing says adventure like a mild panic attack, am I right?

Back on the tour bus, our intrepid leader announces the next stop: yet another government building. But fear not, dear comrades, for this one stands proudly without a scaffold in sight, although it does boast a fetching shade of pink. Because apparently, in Tallinn, pink is the new black.

But hold onto your hats, folks, because the real pièce de résistance awaits: a medieval music concert in a church-cum-music venue straight out of a fairy tale. The tunes were so enchanting, I couldn't resist purchasing the CD—perfect for serenading my unsuspecting offspring with centuries-old melodies on the ride home. Take that, modern music!

But wait, there's more! A delightful three-course lunch awaits at a local establishment, defying all scepticism with its culinary prowess. Who knew medieval streets and a medieval feast could be so delightful?

And just like that, our whirlwind adventure draws to a close as we bid farewell to the cobblestone streets and medieval charm, retreating back to the safety of our tour bus for the short journey back to the ship. Because let's face it, folks: who needs to walk when you can cruise?

Tallinn—a quaint little town brimming with history and charm, but don't hold your breath for a bustling local scene. No, my friends, in the summer months, this place transforms into a veritable circus of cruise ship chaos, with throngs of tourists swarming the streets like ants at a picnic. Forget about snapping those postcard-perfect photos; you're more likely to capture a sea of selfie sticks and tour group banners blocking your view.

After a marathon of sightseeing, I decided it was high time to reward myself with a well-deserved beer—or several, who's counting? Off to the Beer Garden on Deck 13, I trotted, where the bartenders possess memory skills that would make Sherlock Holmes green with envy. Without fail, they greeted me by name and had my preferred brew ready before I could even utter a word. It's like magic but with hops and barley!

Basking in the glorious weather, I found myself engaged in lively conversations with fellow passengers, the beer flowing as freely as the laughter. Alas, time slipped away, and before I knew it, I was fashionably late for dinner. A quick pit stop at the poolside grill for a snack—because who needs a full meal when you've got beer?—before scurrying back to the cabin to primp and prep for tonight's entertainment.

The show, alas, was not quite my cup of tea, but hey, you can't win 'em all. So, back to the Beer Garden, I sauntered, where the night stretched out before me like a canvas waiting to be painted with laughter and good times. After all, what's a cruise without a little liquid courage and a lot of camaraderie? Cheers to that!

Day 5 - St Petersburg Russia

The morning after the great clock fiasco—the day I finally got my act together, thanks to the sage wisdom of my ever-attentive Cabin Steward, who kindly left a note reminding me to adjust the clocks for tonight's time warp extravaganza. How did he know I was a walking disaster zone? It's like he's got psychic powers or something!

Feeling like a seasoned breakfast connoisseur after yesterday's culinary triumph at the Blue Lagoon, I decided to stick with what works and head there again. Full House breakfast, here I come! But wait, what's this? The eternal mystery of bacon versus pork scratchings has been solved, but alas, not by me. Oh well, there's always tomorrow's quiz to reclaim my glory. Bring it on!

Consulting my tour ticket for today's adventure, I couldn't help but feel a twinge of disappointment at the vague instructions: "Meet at 12:45 outside immigration." Really? Could they be any more cryptic? It's like they're playing a game of hide-and-seek with us passengers, leaving us to fend for ourselves in the wilds of Russian immigration. How charming.

As I pondered the logistics of navigating the murky waters of immigration, fate intervened in the form of the ever-friendly Archie, our trusty Cruise Director. With a twinkle in his eye and a spring in his step, he graciously took time out of his busy schedule to sit down for a chat and shed some light on the intricacies of Russian immigration. Who needs a guidebook when you've got Archie, the unofficial master of all things bureaucratic?

Ah, the great Russian immigration adventure—the stuff of nightmares for seasoned cruisers and rookie travellers alike. But fear not, dear reader, for I had a cunning plan to outwit the pack hounds, those relentless photographers hell-bent on capturing every awkward moment of our disembarkation. And lo and behold, my strategy paid off! The photographers were nowhere to be seen, vanquished by my stealthy manoeuvres.

As I braved the labyrinthine corridors of Russian immigration, I was pleasantly surprised to find that it wasn't the chaotic nightmare I had envisioned. Well, not until they opened two more booths, and chaos descended faster than you can say "borscht." It was every person for themself as the stampede to the open booths resembled a scene from a Wild West showdown, minus the tumbleweeds.

With immigration conquered and a newfound sense of freedom, I found myself wandering through the charming gift shops outside the terminal, tantalisingly close to the treasures of downtown. But alas, duty called, and I had a tour to catch: "Through the Russian Eyes." The only problem? There were no signs, no helpful staff—just me, a lost soul in a sea of confusion.

But fear not, for I am not one to be deterred by a little thing like getting lost in a foreign country. With the clock ticking and panic setting in, I embarked on a mad dash around the terminal, my eyes scanning the horizon for any sign of salvation. And just when all hope seemed lost, there it was: the tour bus, waiting patiently for stragglers like me. Talk about cutting it close!

Our journey began with a bang as we boarded the tour bus, a relic from a bygone era that had more creaks and groans than a geriatric yoga class. And let's not forget our lovable guide, the diminutive Russian lady whose voice could barely reach the front row, let alone the back. But hey, who needs to hear the tour when you've got the universal language of confusion and laughter?

As we rattled through the ancient streets of St. Petersburg, it quickly became apparent that this wasn't your average sightseeing tour. Oh no, this was the authentic local experience, complete with crumbling facades and pothole-ridden roads that could give the moon's surface a run for its money.

Our first pitstop: the Metro station. A marvel of Soviet engineering and a labyrinth of confusion for unsuspecting tourists. With signs that might as well have been in hieroglyphics, we clung to our guide like shipwreck survivors clinging to driftwood. And let me tell you, that escalator ride down to the platform felt like a descent into the underworld itself. I half expected to encounter Cerberus guarding the gates of Hades at the bottom!

But fear not, for our trials were far from over. Next on the itinerary is the local market. Now, I don't know about you, but when I hear "market," I envision stalls overflowing with trinkets and treasures. Instead, we were treated to a cornucopia of culinary delights, leaving us scratching our heads and playing a rousing game of "Where's Waldo?" with our elusive tour guide.

But wait, there's more! Our adventure continued with a jaunt to the upmarket department store, where we were set loose like a pack of wild animals in a shopping frenzy. And just when we thought we had it all figured out, our guide vanished into thin air, leaving us to wander the aisles in search of her elusive presence. Ah, the joys of guided tours—where getting lost is half the fun!

Ah, the continuing saga of our whimsical wanderings through the streets of St. Petersburg! Our intrepid guide led us on a merry dance through the back alleys and hidden gems of this historic city, regaling us with tales of local lore and, oddly enough, pointing out a shoe shop along the way. Because nothing says "authentic Russian experience" like a good pair of kicks, am I right?

But the real adventure began when our trusty tour bus decided to test the limits of its geriatric engine on a treacherous hill. With the sound of sputtering engines and the collective gasp of tourists holding their breath, our driver stalled the beast, nearly sending us all on an unexpected hiking expedition back to civilisation.

Thankfully, salvation came in the form of our next stop—a cosy cellar bar where we were promised a taste of authentic Russian culture. Little did we know that culture came in the form of vodka shots and mystery meat snacks. Who needs culinary etiquette when you've got a buzz to chase?

As we sampled our way through an assortment of spirits, I couldn't help but notice a familiar scent wafting through the air. It took me a moment to place it, but once I did, there was no mistaking it—the unmistakable aroma of our dear old tour bus, distilled into liquid form. Ah, the sweet smell of adventure!

But all good things must come to an end, and soon, it was time to bid farewell to our guide's favourite gift shop and make our way back to the ship. And let me tell you, nothing brings people together quite like a few drinks and some questionable souvenir shopping. Who says you can't make friends on a solo cruise?

Day 6 - St Petersburg Day Two

The joys of early morning serenity shattered by the cacophony of coffee-clutching cruisers clamoring for a slice of serenity on the deck! My grand plans for a peaceful sunrise were dashed quicker than you can say "caffeine chaos," so I did what any self-respecting adventurer would do—I headed straight for breakfast. And yes, I shamelessly indulged in the bounty of the Market Garden, much to the dismay of my inner Piggy.

But fear not, for the trials and tribulations of yesterday's tour mishaps were but a distant memory as I embarked on today's adventure. Armed with a shiny new sticker bearing the illustrious number 31, I joined the ranks of eager explorers ready to conquer the streets of St. Petersburg.

And oh, what a difference a day makes! No customs chaos, no landing cards, just smooth sailing through passport control (well, except for that poor soul who forgot his excursion ticket and had to face the wrath of Russian bureaucracy). But once on the gleaming, new tour bus, equipped with state-of-the-art earpieces and guided by the dynamic duo of tour guides, it was smooth sailing through the streets of this historic city.

Welcome to the delightful deception of St. Petersburg's canals! Who knew this city was playing hide-and-seek with its islands? As we cruised along, our guide regaled us with tales of landmarks that seemed to have undergone a magical transformation overnight. But fear not, for I chose to put my faith in today's guide duo, who had each other's backs like a pair of mismatched socks.

Once we boarded the boat, it was like entering a palace... well, a floating one, at least. We sailed past what looked like ordinary houses but were, apparently, the grand palaces of yesteryear. Who knew that behind those nondescript facades lay a wealth of regal history?

And speaking of surprises, let's talk about those bridges! Just when I thought I could stand tall for the perfect snapshot, I found myself in a perilous game of limbo with bridges that seemed determined to test the height of my cranium. Note to self: next time, keep thy seat and thy head attached.

Rasputin and the Romanovs! A tale of intrigue, poison, and... palace bouncers? Yes, you heard that right. For the low, low price of 200 Russian Rubles, I bought myself a sticker granting me the divine right to snap photos inside the palace. It was like paying the paparazzi to follow me around, but hey, memories are priceless, right? Or at least 200 Rubles' worth.

Our guide led us through the halls with all the flair of a Russian drama queen, regaling us with tales of Rasputin's untimely demise and the palace's scandalous secrets. But beware the palace bouncers, ever vigilant in their quest to shoo away any lingering tourists like pesky flies at a picnic.

Despite the absence of furniture and knick-knacks (thanks a lot, Hermitage Museum), the palace still had its charm, especially the theatre. I mean, who wouldn't want a mini-theatre in their own home? Just imagine the dramatic reenactments of everyday life. Truly, it's a must-see... or at least worth a few hundred Rubles and a flurry of photos.

Ah, lunchtime a time for feasting and forging friendships! The restaurant was bustling with activity, with tables adorned with numbers like contestants in a culinary lottery. Lucky me, my table sported the same number as my trusty tour sticker, a match made in mealtime heaven.

And what a meal it was! Three courses of culinary delight accompanied by complimentary wine, courtesy of NCL's generosity. It's like they're bribing us with food and booze to keep us coming back for more tours. Well played, NCL, well played.

In between bites of deliciousness, I struck up a conversation with a charming lady on the hunt for a Russian Fairy Tale book. Little did she know, our next stop just happened to be a gift shop. It's like fate but with more souvenirs.

But alas, our gift shop extravaganza caused a minor delay, much to the chagrin of our punctuality-obsessed guide. We hustled our way to the 'Church of Spilled Blood,' where history and tragedy collide in a whirlwind of mosaics and religious relics. It was like speed dating with religious iconography, in and out before you know it.

With time ticking away like a bomb on a movie set, we made a hasty retreat back to the boat, dodging queue-jumpers like seasoned pros. Another day, another adventure, and hopefully, another round of free wine tomorrow. Cheers to cruising life!

Back aboard the Norwegian Star, dodging Russian customs like a pro, it was time for a quick costume change and a mad dash to the Beer Garden. But first, duty calls – gotta jot down today's antics before they slip away into the abyss of my memory.

Dinner at the Blue Lagoon was a taste of home with some good ol' fish and chips, followed by a sinful slice of cheesecake. As for the $49-a-day Unlimited Beverage Package, well, let's just say it's turning out to be more trouble than it's worth. Who knew becoming a boozy sailor could be so expensive?

Mid-meal, a charming lady officer graced my table with her presence and even treated me to a drink on the house. Bless her heart. I'll have to make sure to thank her properly next time our paths cross.

The evening's entertainment was a smorgasbord of shows scattered across the ship. Ah, the luxury of choice! I sampled a bit of everything, from Broadway-style productions to amateur karaoke sessions that sounded suspiciously like a feline choir in distress.

As the night wore on, I indulged in a light snack and a leisurely stroll on deck, watching the sun stubbornly refuse to call it a day until well past bedtime. Oh, the joys of cruising – where even the sun marches to its own beat!

Day 7 - Helsinki Finland

The morning kicked off with a bang – or more like a groggy stumble – as I rose at the ungodly hour of 5:00. After a quick shower to jolt my senses awake, I embarked on a quest for caffeine and stumbled upon yet another hidden gem: a clandestine coffee nook serving up piping hot brews and pastries galore. Seven days on this floating paradise, and I'm still uncovering new caffeine sanctuaries.

With my coffee fix sorted, it was time for breakfast at the elusive Blue Lagoon – a haven of peace amidst the chaos of the Market Garden. Shh, let's keep this tranquil oasis between us, shall we? No need to spill the beans and create a breakfast stampede!

After fueling up, I ventured out to witness our grand arrival in Helsinki, only to find myself ambushed by a crew member wielding a jet wash. Talk about a surprise washy, washy moment! After a quick change into dry clothes, I resumed my deckside stroll, encountering a wheelchair-bound damsel in distress who seemed perplexed by the "walking only" sign. Ah, the joys of cruise ship navigation!

With ample time to spare before my tour, I indulged in a leisurely snack and another round of coffee, soaking in the lazy European morning vibes. No immigration hassle here – just a cosy bus parked conveniently by the quayside, ready to whisk us away on our Helsinki adventure. And as for those pesky pack hounds disguised as Vikings? Let's just say I turned the tables on them with a cheeky snapshot. Nothing throws off a Viking like being caught on film!

Gathered at the bus, we were greeted by our trusty local guide and driver, ready for our grand adventure to the Suomenlinna island fortress. But, lo and behold, we found ourselves with some unexpected time to kill – cue the impromptu Helsinki sightseeing tour!

Arriving at the ferry terminal, our local guide took charge, wrangling tickets while we twiddled our thumbs in anticipation of our island escapade. But alas, our new guide was nowhere to be found. Sensing an opportunity for nautical mischief, I proposed we board the ferry and await her arrival on the fortress island.

As luck would have it, our missing guide magically materialised upon our island arrival – talk about cutting it close! With her at the helm, we embarked on a whirlwind tour of the fortress's six islands (well, five accessible by bridge, anyway). Our guide regaled us with tales of yore, painting vivid pictures of the island's storied past.

However, our merry jaunt was not without its challenges. Amidst the sunshine and history lessons, we found ourselves contending with an unexpected cacophony – courtesy of our erstwhile first guide turned chatty Cathy. Her newfound companions proved a tad too chatty, drowning out our guide's informative spiel.

I jestingly suggested tossing her overboard once back on the ferry for some peace and quiet, but alas, my maritime humour fell flat. Oh well, a comedic opportunity missed!

After our island adventure, we were set loose to roam like seafaring explorers on a quest for buried treasures (or at least some cool island sights). I stumbled upon a submarine-turned-museum, ready to dive into some underwater history. But hold onto your snorkels, folks, because this museum was more of a "blink and you'll miss it" affair. For the princely sum of 5 euros, I zipped through that sub faster than a torpedo through water – not exactly a deep-sea dive into excitement.

But fear not, landlubbers, for the real treasure, lay within the fortress walls. With time ticking like a time bomb, we gathered at the ferry terminal, torn between seizing the moment or waiting for our MIA guide. In the end, we took matters into our own hands, boarding that ferry like swashbuckling pirates on a plundering spree.

Back on solid ground, it was a mad dash through the Finland Market, like a pack of bargain-hungry bandits looting the town. With the clock ticking louder than Big Ben on a caffeine binge, I grabbed a plate of reindeer meatballs, channelling my inner Nordic warrior (apologies to Bambi and all his woodland pals).

So there you have it, folks – a whirlwind tour of island antics and market mayhem. Who needs a guide when you've got a spirit of adventure and a hankering for local delicacies? Ahoy, mateys, until our next escapade on the high seas!

Back on the bus, back to the floating fortress, ready for an afternoon of leisure and luxury. The sun is shining, the breeze is blowing, and I've got my sunscreen at the ready – or so I thought! Just as I'm about to unleash my inner sunbather, the wind picks up, dashing my hopes faster than a seagull snatching a sandwich. Guess I'll have to settle for indoor activities, much to the relief of any passing whales and the disappointment of Greenpeace.

But hold onto your captain's hats, folks, because we've got a Code Red onboard – the Beer Garden is closed! I repeat, the Beer Garden is closed! This is not a drill, people. Someone alert the authorities; this is a national crisis!

In a valiant effort to salvage the evening, I bravely venture into the unknown territory of an art auction. Picture this: me, surrounded by priceless works of art, my wallet trembling in fear at the sight of the price tags. Alas, my dreams of becoming an art connoisseur are dashed when I realise I'm a few dollars short of a masterpiece. Maybe next time, Picasso.

But fear not, dear readers, for the night is young, and the show must go on! I settle into my seat for an evening of high-flying entertainment with 'Due Acrobatique.' The performance kicks off with some elegant ballet – cue my internal panic as I contemplate an escape route. But lo and behold, the acrobatics swoop in to save the day, leaving me spellbound and thoroughly entertained. Well, except for that awkward moment when the whistling began – let's just say it was a snooze-inducing interlude.

In a whirlwind of culture and cocktails, I find myself drawn to the art gallery once more, my newfound sophistication at odds with my uncultured beer cravings. But fear not, for I restore balance to the universe with a pint at the Red Lion before diving headfirst into the adult fun at the Spinnaker Lounge. Ah, the joys of cruising – where every day is a new adventure, and every night is a party waiting to happen!

Day 8 - Stockholm Sweden

Ah, the crack of dawn – the perfect time to rise, shine, and stumble bleary-eyed to the nearest coffee pot. As I sipped my morning brew and surveyed the weather from the lofty heights of deck 13, I couldn't help but feel a twinge of disappointment. It seems the daily bulletin forgot to mention the spectacular show outside – you know, the one where the Ship gracefully glides past a parade of picturesque islands, each one boasting more houses than a real estate agent's dream.

For a solid three hours, I was treated to a scenic spectacle as we cruised into the Port of Stockholm. I snapped at least fifty photos (for the album, of course) before my stomach reminded me it was time for breakfast—and perhaps a bit of post-dinner workout to make room for more indulgence.

Today's itinerary promised a trifecta of adventure: the Vasa Museum, Old Town exploration, and the pièce de résistance – the Ice Bar. Now, I'm not saying the allure of free vodka had anything to do with its popularity, but hey, who can resist a bit of icy refreshment?

With the clock ticking towards tour time, I made my way to the Stardust Theatre, ready to embark on the day's escapades. As the tour was called and the stampede for the exit began, I couldn't help but chuckle at the sight of eager cruisers sprinting towards the promise of adventure. Ah, the thrill of the chase!

On the bus, we were greeted by yet another font of knowledge – our trusty tour guide for the day. Our first stop? The Vasa Museum, of course! But not before a scenic tour of the town, complete with insightful commentary that had us all feeling like locals in no time. Time to dive into history – and maybe a shot of vodka or two – let the adventure begin!

Ah, the museum – a treasure trove of history and a magnet for cruise ship crowds. As I stepped inside, I couldn't help but marvel at the medieval ship on display, painstakingly restored to 98% of its original glory. But alas, the museum's popularity meant it was more crowded than a clown car at a circus.

I counted not one, not two, but six different cruise ships represented by tour guide banners, each one unloading a horde of eager tourists ready to explore. And let's not forget the poor souls on the Hop-on, hop-off tours, stuck in a never-ending queue just to catch a glimpse of the ship.

Inside wasn't much better – navigating through the throngs of people was like trying to swim upstream in a river of selfie sticks. And forget about getting a clear shot of the ship – it was obscured by a sea of heads and outstretched arms wielding cameras.

But fear not, for the real adventure awaited at the Ice Bar! As the bus pulled up outside, there was a stampede to get inside, leaving the poor Hop on Hop off tourists out in the cold – literally.

Once inside, we were handed what can only be described as a glorified poncho with gloves, reminiscent of the ones your mum made you wear on a winter's day. As we waited for the door to open, the excitement in the air was evident – though some folks seemed to think -5 degrees was the Arctic tundra.

But as we stepped inside, all thoughts of cold vanished as we were greeted by walls of ice and frozen statues. The vodka served in ice glasses was a welcome treat, though it did melt rather quickly in the warmth of our hands.

Overall, the Ice Bar was a chilly delight – a novelty not to be missed unless you prefer your drinks without a side of frostbite!

The Old Town – a treasure trove of history and souvenir shops galore! But just as we were getting into the groove of things, we hit a roadblock – literally. The Swedish army, or so we thought, decided to march down the road, complete with a marching band blaring away. Turns out, they were just the palace guard doing their thing, and we were mere spectators in their royal parade.

Once the commotion died down and our trusty bus rolled to a stop, our guide sprang into action; it was time for some serious souvenir shopping. Leading us on a whirlwind walking tour through cobblestone streets and past centuries-old buildings.

I made a beeline for the Viking hat section because, let's face it, who doesn't need a horned helmet in their life? As for the other trinkets, well, let's just say my kids will have plenty of Swedish knick-knacks to clutter up their rooms.

But alas, all good things must come to an end, and before I knew it, it was time to rendezvous back at the bus. But wait, there's more! Our savvy guide had a surprise up her sleeve – an unplanned pit stop at yet another local attraction. Talk about going above and beyond!

As we boarded the bus, I couldn't help but marvel at the day's adventures. Who knew souvenir shopping could be so exhilarating? And as we drove off into the sunset, I couldn't help but wonder what other unexpected delights awaited us on this cruise of comedic proportions.

Ah, the chaos of cruise life! Today's mission: don't miss the boat, literally. After hearing horror stories of stranded passengers resorting to DIY ferry rides, I vowed to be back on board by 15:30 or risk becoming the star of my very own maritime misadventure.

But first, a pit stop at the Market Garden to refuel. Five hours without food? That's practically a hunger emergency! I could already hear the faint sirens of the food police closing in, ready to pounce on any malnourished stragglers.

With my belly full and spirits high, it was time for some liquid nourishment – in the form of a nice, cold beer at the Beer Garden. Who cares if there's no actual garden? The beer is what matters, right?

But wait – the Norwegian Star was hosting a 'White Hot Party,' and I was determined to join in the snowy shenanigans. Off to my cabin, I dashed, white jumper in hand, ready to paint the town white. But alas, a caffeine catastrophe struck en route, leaving my pristine jumper with an unsightly coffee stain.

Back to square one, I changed into my backup outfit, silently mourning the loss of my chance to rename the party 'White & Slight Brown Hot Party.' Oh, well – a missed opportunity for comedy gold.

Finally, party time! The auditorium buzzed with excitement as I mingled with newfound friends and danced the night away. But alas, all good things must come to an end, and as the clock struck bedtime, I bid adieu to the Red Lion, my trusty companion in all things alcohol-related, and surrendered to the sweet embrace of sleep. Until tomorrow, cruise life – until tomorrow.

Day 9 - Day at Sea

Ah, the grand finale of cruise life – the last hurrah at sea! But today, my friends, was no ordinary day of gluttony and showbiz. No, today was a whirlwind of surprises and cultural awakenings, all served with a side of morning coffee.

As per my daily ritual, I embarked on the quest for caffeine, only to stumble upon not one but two new java joints on this floating paradise. Who knew this Ship was a treasure trove of caffeinated delights?

With my coffee fix in hand, it was off to the Blue Lagoon for a breakfast fit for a king – or, in American terms, a 'Full House.' Because why settle for a Full English when you can go all-in?

The morning unfolded with a touch of sophistication as I found myself in Gatsby's, reflecting on yesterday's escapades and attending a lecture on emeralds and gems. Yes, you heard that right – me, the epitome of cultured charm, discussing precious stones like a seasoned gemologist. And hey, I even snagged a tiny emerald sample. Watch out, world!

But wait, there's more – I found myself mingling with the art auction team, inquiring about the whereabouts of some beloved pieces from a previous auction. Cue my second-ever auction experience with a charming young lady named Lauren by my side.

As the bidding began, my heart raced faster than a cheetah in sneakers. The auctioneer announced a starting bid of $1200, sending a momentary panic through my veins. But fear not, dear reader, for the universe smiled upon me, and the price magically adjusted to my liking. With a triumphant shout of 'Yep,' the hammer fell, and the ladies – my treasured artworks – were mine!

For those still sceptical of the auction scene, fear not – it's a delightful romp guided by friendly staff and the promise of a worthwhile investment. So bid boldly, my friends, for in the realm of cruise auctions, even a novice can emerge victorious.

After all that adrenaline, my body was screaming for one thing – beer, glorious beer! Off I trotted to the holy land of deck 13, also known as the Beer Garden. 'Several' beers later (which turned out to be at least six, but who's counting?), my stomach rumbled with hunger, signalling it was time for lunch.

For my final night feast, I opted for the same restaurant as before, hoping for a repeat of the culinary delight. Alas, the universe had other plans, and my dining experience took a nosedive faster than a bird with clipped wings.

The waitress, bless her heart, had the charm of a grumpy cat and the grace of a bull in a China shop. Despite my valiant efforts to assert my rightful place as the first in line, she waltzed past me like I was yesterday's news, attending to tables that arrived fashionably late. I mean, seriously, who does she think she is? The Queen of Sheba?

After what felt like an eternity, my food finally arrived – just in time for the second coming of Noah's Ark, it seemed. And don't even get me started on the raffle shenanigans! People had more tickets than a toddler has tantrums, yet here I was, with my measly two tickets, dreaming of emerald glory.

But alas, my dreams were dashed faster than a speeding bullet when my number didn't come up. Ten calls, ten absentees – talk about a missed opportunity! But hey, who needs a fancy emerald when you've got the priceless memories of dodging rude waiters and surviving raffle disappointments? Cheers to that!

Ah, the dreaded packing ritual awaited us like a hungry sea monster lurking in the depths of our cabin. We gathered our clothes, clean and not-so-clean alike, and stuffed them into the same suitcase, creating a smorgasbord of surprises for any customs officer brave enough to open it. Farewell, dear suitcase, until we meet again at the airport tomorrow – may the odds be ever in your favour!

With packing conquered (or at least attempted), it was time to bid adieu to our trusty crewmates – the bartenders, the waiters, the unsung heroes of our cruise adventure. Off we trotted for one last hurrah, determined to leave no cocktail untouched and no beverage card unscathed.

As the final curtain call beckoned, we shuffled our way to the Stardust Theatre for the pièce de résistance – the Elements show. And let me tell you, folks, it was nothing short of spectacular! Dance, acrobatics, magic – you name it, they had it, all seamlessly woven together like a majestic tapestry of entertainment. The crowd roared with delight, leaping to their feet in a chorus of applause that could rival thunder itself.

But let's not forget the real heroes of the night – the tireless crew members who made it all possible. Led by the incomparable Archie (aka Cruise Director Extraordinaire), they, too, received their moment in the spotlight, showered with well-deserved praise and admiration.

And oh, the artificial snow – a blizzard of chaos for the poor souls tasked with cleaning up the aftermath. Armed with nothing but long-handled brooms, they faced a battle of epic proportions against the snowy onslaught. But fear not, dear readers, for as we bid farewell to the theatre and returned to our cabins; we drifted off to sleep with visions of laughter and merriment dancing in our heads. Ah, the joys of cruising – until we meet again, sweet dreams!

Day 10 - Disembarkation Day In Copenhagen

Ah, the sweet serenade of stress-free mornings aboard the NCL ship – where the only worry is whether you'll have enough room for that last-minute souvenir or if you'll need to sit on your suitcase to close it. But fear not, dear travellers, for NCL has bestowed upon us a gift from the heavens – the colour-coded baggage system, a beacon of hope in the chaotic sea of disembarkation.

So, with a skip in our step and a song in our hearts, we gallivanted around the ship like merry pirates on a treasure hunt, waiting for our designated hue to be called. And when the time came, we dashed off the ship faster than you can say "ahoy matey," leaping onto the waiting bus like eager adventurers on a quest for the holy grail (or, in this case, the airport).

But lo and behold, even the airport gods smiled upon us as we arrived, greeted by NCL-clad angels ready to whisk us away to baggage bliss. Armed with our trusty key cards – the golden tickets to luggage paradise – we breezed through security like seasoned spies on a top-secret mission, navigating our way to the promised land of check-in and bid adieu to our burdensome bags with a heartfelt farewell.

And so, dear readers, as we waved goodbye to our floating home and set sail for the skies, we couldn't help but marvel at the seamless symphony orchestrated by NCL – a grand finale to our comedic cruise adventure. Smooth sailing, my friends, until we meet again on the shores of laughter and merriment!

Observation

Ah, the mysteries of cruise ship life – where the rules are as puzzling as a Rubik's Cube, and the logic is as elusive as the fountain of youth! Let's dive headfirst into this comedic conundrum, shall we?

First up, we have the enigmatic Blue Lagoon Restaurant – perpetually open yet mysteriously closed. It's like a game of hide and seek with your stomach, where the rules keep changing, and your hunger is left scratching its head in confusion.

Next, we encounter the disembarkation day dilemma – calling all easy walk-off passengers, but what about us easy wobble-off passengers? Do we still make the cut, or are we doomed to be left behind in a sea of confusion?

Ah, and who can forget the infamous Deck 7 debacle – walking only, please. Does that mean if you come rolling in with a wheelchair, you're out of luck? It's like trying to solve a riddle wrapped in a mystery inside an enigma – with a side of nonsensical signage.

But wait, there's more! Behold the walking track on Deck 7, longer than the running track on Deck 13 – a true feat of engineering or just another head-scratching cruise ship quirk? It's a race against logic, folks, and the finish line is nowhere in sight!

And let's not overlook the emergency drill – because when the ship's tied up at the dock, you never know when disaster might strike! It's like practising your fire drill in a swimming pool – just in case the flames decide to take a dip.

But perhaps the most perplexing puzzle of all – why open the toilet door with a paper towel but not any other door? Is there some secret bathroom code we're not privy to, or is it just another quirky quirk of cruise ship culture?

And don't even get me started on the poolside paradox – no glass or plastic allowed, yet severed beer bottles abound! It's like trying to solve a Sudoku puzzle with only half the numbers – utterly baffling.

But fear not, dear cruisers, for amidst the chaos and confusion, there's one thing we can always count on – the inexplicable charm of cruise ship life.

So, grab your paper towels, dodge the floating beer bottles, and let's set sail into the wacky world of cruising!

Med Cruise On Norwegian Epic

37

Day 1 - Home to Board Epic

Ah, the joys of embarking on a new adventure – where the journey begins with the ungodly hour of 02:00 and a face full of water to slap the sleep out of your eyes. But fear not, for I, the intrepid traveller, am ready to conquer the day – or so I thought!

Decision time: Coffee or the allure of the Business lounge? I chose the latter, a choice I would soon come to regret. As it turns out, Heathrow Airport hasn't gotten the memo about joining the 24-hour society. So much for my dreams of a pre-flight caffeine fix!

After bidding adieu to my trusty hire car, I arrived at Terminal 5, only to find a ghost town. Check-in desks? Closed. Bag drop? Nowhere to be seen. But fear not, dear reader, for the board promised that salvation would come at 04:30 – a mere 30 minutes away. Little did I know, this was just the beginning of the airport shenanigans!

As the clock struck 05:00, the Bag drop remained elusive, leaving me to ponder whether it was a typo or British Airways' diabolical plan to keep us all on our toes – or rather, on our feet! With gates opening at 06:00, it was a race against time to check-in, clear security, and make a mad dash to 'B' gate, all in pursuit of that elusive dead pig sandwich.

But alas, my dreams of bacon bliss were shattered by a young lady guarding the gates to the Business lounge, informing me that it wouldn't open until 05:30. Oh, the agony of anticipation – the tantalising aroma of bacon teasing me from beyond the door, just out of reach!

And so, dear reader, I stand here at 'B' gate, coffee-less and sandwich-less, pondering the cruel twists and turns of airport life. But fear not, for the adventure has only just begun – and who knows what other delights await me on this comedic crusade through the skies!

Time for stage two of the airport odyssey: the showdown with the stubbornly locked door. But fear not, for where there's a will, there's a way – and in this case, it came in the form of a sneaky lift on the other side of the door. Victory was mine as I emerged triumphant, clutching my prized dead pig sandwich and not one but two piping hot coffees. Take that, healthy intentions!

With breakfast swiftly devoured, it was time to board the plane and bid adieu to the land of bacon bliss. But not before indulging in a full English breakfast on board – much to the chagrin of British Airways, who clearly underestimated my commitment to culinary delights at 30,000 feet.

The journey to Barcelona was but a short hop of one hour and 50 minutes, made all the more enjoyable by the splurge on Business class. Ah, the perks of premium travel – impeccable service and blissful comfort, even if the seats were just like the ones in the back, but with a fancy label slapped on them.

And though the lack of an entertainment system left me twiddling my thumbs, it did afford me the opportunity to kick back, relax, and pen down these hilarious escapades. Who needs in-flight movies when you've got a laptop and a penchant for comedic storytelling?

Ah, the joys of touchdown in Barcelona – where the sun shines, the sangria flows, and the passport control lines are surprisingly speedy. With immigration conquered in record time, I was primed and ready for my maiden voyage shenanigans. But first, the quest for my trusty chauffeur awaited.

According to the grand plan, my driver was to be stationed outside immigration, a beacon of transportation glory in hand, ready to whisk me away to the port. However, as I surveyed the sea of impeccably dressed chauffeurs, I couldn't help but notice a rogue figure amidst the crowd – a Spanish hooligan in shorts and a tee, looking more like he'd just stepped off a soccer pitch than out of a luxury vehicle.

But in the spirit of adventure, I decided to throw caution to the wind and strike up a conversation with this unlikely chauffeur. After all, a second-class ride is still better than a first-class stroll, right? As we chatted away, I casually inquired about the journey time to the port, expecting a leisurely response. Little did I know, I was in for a wild ride.

With a mischievous grin, my newfound driver revealed that the journey would be a mere thirty minutes. What he failed to mention, however, was that this estimation was contingent on one crucial detail – his absence from the driver's seat!

As we careened through the streets of Barcelona at speeds that would make a Formula 1 driver blush, I couldn't help but wonder if we were in a race against time or simply against every other vehicle on the road. But lo and behold, we arrived at the port in record time – a testament to the unparalleled efficiency of Spanish hooligan chauffeurs everywhere.

The grand embarkation, where dreams of sun-soaked days and bottomless beverages come to fruition! With the Norwegian Epic as my vessel of choice, it was time to dive headfirst into the sea of excitement.

Check-in was a breeze, courtesy of NCL's efficiency – within an hour, I was officially onboard and ready to party like a sailor on shore leave. And lucky me, I snagged a cabin pronto, sparing myself the agony of lugging my bag around like a landlubber lost at sea.

Bag stowed, it was time to rekindle my romance with the Norwegian Epic – and what better way to celebrate than with the sacred vow of the Beverage Package? Cue the heavenly chorus of angels as I embarked on a sacred quest for the perfect pint.

But alas, my merriment was momentarily stalled by a perplexing sign looming over the bar, warning that those over 18 required parental permission for libations. A moment of panic ensued – what if one's parental unit had set sail to the great beyond? Would I be doomed to a fate of eternal sobriety, relegated to the realm of soft drinks and lemonade? Oh, the horror!

Nevertheless, fueled by the promise of adventure and the lingering taste of hops on my tongue, I pressed on, indulging in a merry dance of brews and bites at the ship's myriad food outlets. Ah, who needs a diet when you're cruising the high seas?

Ah, the delicate dance of indulgence and restraint on the high seas – a journey fraught with perilous temptations and unexpected twists.

Feeling like a buoyant balloon after an afternoon of imbibing and nibbling, I decided it was high time to restore some semblance of equilibrium and retreat to the sanctuary of the Solo Lounge. The Solo Lounge – purportedly a haven for lone travellers seeking companionship, but in reality, more akin to a raucous youth club where parents offload their offspring for a brief respite.

Yet, amidst the chaos and cacophony, one glimmering beacon of hope emerged – the promise of complimentary coffee, a precious elixir to soothe the soul and invigorate the senses. Why pay upstairs when you can sip in solitude for free? The logic was as clear as the foam atop my latte.

But lo and behold, as I settled into my caffeinated cocoon, a siren call beckoned from behind the bar – the unmistakable cry of a chilled brew, whispering sweet nothings in my ear. It would be uncouth to resist such a seductive invitation, wouldn't it? After all, the beer knew my name, and it would be rude to ignore a personal plea from a libation.

With libations duly indulged and spirits suitably lifted, it was time to face the inevitable – the compulsory lifeboat drill. Oh, the joys of maritime safety protocols! As the crew dutifully instructed us on the finer points of donning life jackets and boarding lifeboats, I couldn't help but wonder – would they ever address the pressing concern of dockside disasters?

But fear not, for NCL had bestowed upon us a glimmer of hope in the form of a bar within the hallowed halls of the lifeboat station. Alas, it remained shuttered during the drill, but that didn't deter me from harbouring fantasies of post-exercise refreshments.

And so, with glasses of orange juice spiked with a generous splash of Southern Comfort, I bid adieu to the trials and tribulations of safety drills and embarked on a culinary adventure to the Garden Cafe, where a Spanish-themed feast awaited. After all, when in Spain, one mustn't shy away from a gastronomic fiesta – even if it does resemble a bustling cattle market.

Navigating the Spanish-themed buffet proved to be a culinary odyssey of epic proportions. Amidst the sea of paella, I found myself lamenting the absence of plump prawns and other savoury treasures, seemingly plucked from the depths of the dish by discerning diners. Fear not, dear Chef, for I shall embark upon a quest to uncover the mysteries of crispy pig skin, known to some as Pork Scratching and to others, as the elusive morning delicacy known as bacon. The investigation shall commence at dawn, fueled by caffeine and curiosity.

As the evening approached, it was time to indulge in some early entertainment before venturing to the Spiegel Tent for a premier dining experience. But first, a visit to the Adults-only bar, H2O – a sanctuary of sophistication and refinement. Or so I thought until I encountered the invisible barrier that mysteriously transformed adults into wide-eyed children. Bravo, NCL, for your innovative approach to age regression.

Eager to partake in the circus spectacle and satisfy my rumbling stomach, I ascended to the Premier Dining area, a realm reserved for the discerning palate and the adventurous spirit. The $20 surcharge was but a trifle, considering it was included in my dining package – a small price to pay for culinary enlightenment.

Opting for a bird's-eye view of the performance, I settled into my seat with anticipation, ready to witness feats of daring and culinary prowess. Yet, as the show unfolded below, I couldn't help but ponder the peculiar seating arrangement – both standard and premier diners intermingling at the same table, rendering the extra cost a curious conundrum indeed.

But fear not, for the Spiegel Tent proved to be a veritable melting pot of camaraderie, where solo travellers found solace in shared conversations and newfound friendships blossomed amidst the spectacle. Ah, the joys of cruising – where every meal is an adventure, and every show a spectacle to behold.

Ah, the spectacle! The show was an extravaganza of talent, a dazzling display of comedy, acrobatics, and magic woven together in a tapestry of entertainment. These performers were like wizards of the stage, conjuring laughter and awe with every flip and flourish.

But alas, my enjoyment was marred by the sight of fellow cruisers stuffing their faces with delicacies while the performers worked their magic. Oh, the injustice! Such a stellar show deserved undivided attention, not distracted munching and crunching.

Undeterred by the culinary cacophony, I ventured to the nightclub for a bit of post-show revelry. Hours slipped by in a blur of music and merriment, fueled by a steady stream of libations from my Beverage Package.

As I swayed to the rhythm of the music, a thought crossed my mind – was the ship gently rocking beneath my feet, or was it merely my own unsteady equilibrium? Blame it on the drinks, I decided, and bid farewell to the night, drifting off to the land of Nod with a contented grin on my face. Ah, the joys of cruising – where every night is a party, and every show a spectacle to remember.

Day 2: A Day at Sea.

Ah, the best-laid plans of mice and men – or, in this case, cruisers! The noble intention of catching the sunrise and embarking on a brisk morning walk dashed by the siren song of a cosy bed. Who can resist the allure of a comfortable mattress and snug quilt, especially at the crack of dawn?

Finally emerging from the depths of slumber around 7 a.m., I embarked on a mission to conquer breakfast. But alas, my hopes were nearly dashed at the prospect of a continental feast – a terrifying vision of cold meats and rabbit food danced in my head. However, salvation came in the form of a menu offering a country platter, a beacon of hope in a sea of culinary uncertainty. Crisis averted, I happily tucked into a hearty English breakfast, bidding adieu to any lingering breakfast-related nightmares.

With sustenance secured, I set forth on a leisurely stroll around the ship, marvelling at the early morning peacefulness. Yet, amidst the calm, I couldn't help but notice the telltale signs of a battle for prime sunbathing real estate. Ah, the elusive towel pixies – mythical creatures tasked with the sacred duty of reserving sun loungers in the dead of night. Though some may doubt their existence, I can assure you, dear reader, that they are as real as the policies they enforce. After all, what's a cruise without a little dash of mystery and intrigue, right?

Time for intellectual pursuits and culinary adventures! After a leisurely stint on a sumptuously comfy sofa, observing the world with the keen eye of a seasoned traveller, it was time to exercise the old noggin. First up, a series of lectures promising enlightenment on both the wonders of cruise destinations and the intricacies of art collecting.

Now, the first lecture was a breeze, filling my brain with visions of exotic locales and enticing adventures. But then came the art lecture – a perilous journey into the realm of temptation. You see, dear reader, the moment my eyes fell upon a masterpiece by the illustrious Linda Le Kniff, I knew I was doomed. For lurking in the shadows of that canvas was the siren call of the art auction, beckoning me with promises of exquisite acquisitions and financial recklessness.

But first, a civilised lunch at the Taste restaurant, where refinement reigned supreme. In the spirit of adventure, I dared to sample scallops followed by Atlantic salmon – a veritable symphony of flavours that danced upon my palate.

With my belly satisfied and my wallet bracing for impact, it was time to face the art auction. Little did I know, my arrival had been foretold – a mysterious informant had tipped off the auctioneers, and Linda Le Kniff's creations awaited my eager gaze. As the bidding commenced, I found myself locked in a fierce battle for artistic supremacy, defending my prized 'Ladies' against rival bidders with a ferocity akin to a Viking warrior.

In the end, victory was mine, though not without a few harrowing moments of suspense. Now, as my 'Ladies' embark on their journey to join me in England (thanks a lot, VAT man), I can rest assured that my cruise has been adorned with a touch of artistic flair – and perhaps a dash of financial folly. Ah, the joys of cruising!

Ah, the spoils of victory! With a triumphant $100 voucher in hand, I'm on a mission to adorn the walls of my loved ones with fine art. My son Hadley shall soon be the proud owner of a masterpiece, while my darling granddaughters Aimee-Leigh and Lola-Mae will each receive a treasure of their own. After all, it's never too early to cultivate an appreciation for the finer things in life!

But enough about art – it's time to quench my thirst with a round of drinky poos! Off to the bar, I trot, ready to indulge in a libation or two. As the beverages flowed as freely as the banter among shipmates, a sudden realisation struck me like a bolt of lightning: I had a reservation at one of the speciality restaurants, but the details had slipped my mind faster than an NCL waiter swooping into refill an empty glass.

With determination in my step and a hint of panic in my heart, I set out to track down the elusive restaurant booking desk. Of course, my luck being what it is, the desk just happened to be stationed amidst a tantalising display of Linda's creations. But fear not, dear reader – armed with steely resolve and pockets firmly clamped shut, I navigated the sea of artistic temptation and zeroed in on the helpful attendant, extracting valuable intel on dining arrangements for not only tonight but the entire week ahead.

With the crucial information secured, it was a mad dash to the cabin for a swift wardrobe change, with only an hour to spare before my scheduled culinary escapade. Ah, the trials and tribulations of a cruise connoisseur!

The infamous Maderno restaurant – a place where culinary dreams collide with gastrointestinal reality! If you dare to venture into this gastronomic battleground, prepare yourself for a feast of epic proportions. Consider this your official warning: don't even think about entering unless you've undergone a rigorous fasting regimen of at least a week. You've been forewarned, my fellow cruisers!

Upon arrival, you'll be escorted to your table by a seemingly friendly waiter whose sole mission is to lull you into a false sense of security. But don't be fooled – behind that welcoming smile lies a cunning plan to lead you straight into the clutches of culinary chaos. Take your seat and behold the ritual of dining in Maderno: first, the drinks flow freely, and the intricacies of the self-service salad buffet are laid bare before you.

But beware the innocuous-looking card on your table, for it holds the key to your gastronomic destiny. One side, innocently green, signals to the staff that you're ready for the main course onslaught. Brace yourself, for the onslaught shall commence forthwith!

Behold as waiters descend upon your table bearing pans of side dishes so vast they could rival a buffet line at a Vegas casino. Mash potatoes, black bean salad, fried bananas – you name it, they've got it. And just when you think you've reached the pinnacle of food-induced euphoria, another waiter arrives brandishing a skewer laden with meats of every variety imaginable. The procession continues until either your stomach protests in agony or you remember the crucial red side of the card, the beacon of salvation in this sea of culinary chaos.

Once the card flips to red, signalling surrender, the onslaught mercifully ceases. And despite the perilous journey through the valley of gluttony, I must admit, it was one of the finest meals I've ever had at sea – and I've had my fair share, let me tell you!

With dinner conquered and dignity (somewhat) intact, it's off to the nearest watering hole for some much-needed post-meal recovery. Here's to surviving another culinary adventure on the high seas!

Day 3 – Naples

Ah, the joys of waking up to the dulcet tones of an alarm summoning me from the cosy embrace of my bed to face the day ahead. With a groan and a grumble, I dragged myself upright, showered off the remnants of sleep, and mustered the courage to confront the world – or at least deck 15 of the ship.

But alas, my plans for a picturesque morning were dashed quicker than you can say, "Iceberg ahead!" The weather, in its infinite wisdom, had decided to throw a temper tantrum, unleashing a torrential downpour accompanied by the dramatic spectacle of thunder and lightning. Boo indeed! But fear not, for I, intrepid photographer extraordinaire, was undeterred in my quest for the perfect snapshot of our majestic vessel pulling into port.

Little did I know, NCL had resurrected the ghost of the Titanic, complete with its own brand of classism. Only those lucky souls in the deluxe cabins of the Haven complex were granted the privilege of gazing over the ship's bow. Outrageous! I braved the elements, teetering perilously over the edge, determined to capture the shot of a lifetime – even if it meant sacrificing my dry clothes to the sea gods.

After a hasty retreat to the sanctuary of my cabin for a costume change, I resumed my morning constitutional around the ship. Note to self: attempting a stair-climbing marathon from deck 5 to deck 15 may seem like a stellar idea at the outset, but trust me, it's a one-way ticket to humiliation city. Lesson learned: save the cardio for after breakfast.

Speaking of which, it was time to refuel at O'Sheehan's Bar and Cafe, where I encountered the age-old debate of egg preparation – sunny side up or down? Who cares! Just give me a plate piled high with bacon and assorted breakfast goodies, and we'll call it a day. But lo and behold, there's always one in every crowd – some nitwit had the audacity to request crispy bacon. Sacrilege! Needless to say, they were promptly escorted off the plank – I mean, politely declined.

Ah, the adventures of breakfast on the high seas – never a dull moment, my friends!

Delightful anticipation of embarking on a grand adventure – or, in my case, a tour of Mount Vesuvius and Pompeii. With time to spare before my escapade, I entertained myself with a game of tour-tastic guessing, sizing up my fellow passengers and wagering on which excursions they'd chosen. Let me tell you, I was on fire with my predictions – until reality hit, and I realised some folks had signed up for walking tours without so much as glancing at the fine print. Classic rookie mistake!

As the clock ticked closer to tour time, a few... shall we say, generously proportioned individuals struggled to their feet, one poor soul relying on a walking stick for support. Methinks she may have overlooked the whole "walking tour" memo, given that our itinerary involved scaling Mount Vesuvius and traipsing around Pompeii. Oh, the irony!

But fear not, for we were all outfitted with snazzy numbered badges, allegedly for easy identification and bus boarding purposes. Call me cynical, but doesn't that also scream, "Hey, look at me, I'm a tourist – pickpocket me!"? Nevertheless, I proudly sported my badge, like a badge of honour, and dutifully followed the herd off the ship and onto the awaiting bus.

Off we jolly well went, singing our hearts out – just kidding, no impromptu musical numbers here. Instead, our first stop turned out to be a not-so-charming little shop peddling shell-based trinkets. I'll admit, I zoned out during the lightning-fast spiel about their wares but couldn't miss the eager salespeople lurking behind every corner, ready to pounce on unsuspecting cruisers like a pack of seagulls eyeing a picnic spread. Ah, the joys of tourist traps – nothing quite like being herded like sheep towards overpriced souvenirs!

Ah, blessed brevity! Our brief sojourn at the tourist trap of trinkets ended after a merciful 15 minutes, and we were finally on our way to the grand Mount Vesuvius. Let me tell you, my heartiest applause goes to our driver, who navigated those treacherous, serpentine mountain roads like a maestro conducting a high-wire symphony.

The real fun began when we reached what I affectionately dubbed the "Torture Trail," or as the brochure euphemistically called it, the "trekking path to the crater." If you envisioned a gentle, tourist-friendly slope, think again. The masterminds behind this trail clearly consulted with Nepalese sherpas – each incline steeper and more treacherous than the last, with the only respite coming in the form of hairpin turns leading to yet another gruelling ascent.

At the outset, they kindly offered us walking sticks. That should have been my first clue. But no, I scoffed at the notion and valiantly set off on my climb. Halfway up, I was forced to swallow my pride and take a "photo break," pretending to capture the stunning views while covertly catching my breath.

Ah, the humiliation of watching a sprightly octogenarian saunter past you. Not one to be outdone, I shoved my camera back in my bag and charged ahead, determined to reach the summit first.

When I finally reached what I believed to be the pinnacle, I was greeted not by the awe-inspiring crater but by a gift shop. The local guides were there, too, hawking souvenirs and bottles of water. "Where's the oxygen?" I gasped. The friendly guide chuckled and pointed up. "Just a bit further," he said, "but hurry, there's a storm coming."

A storm? After all that effort? Not a chance I was missing the crater. I snapped a few triumphant photos, even getting one with me in it for proof of my epic achievement. Then, it was a mad dash down the mountain, racing against the impending storm.

All in all, it was an adventure filled with sweat, pride-swallowing, and a touch of peril. But hey, what's a cruise without a little high-altitude drama?

Coming down Mount Vesuvius was like sliding down a greasy pole compared to the torturous ascent. I even took a moment to shrink the volcano by a couple of centimetres – hey, every little bit helps! Along the way, I snagged two pieces of authentic volcanic rock as souvenirs for my son and granddaughter. They'll love it, even if it's just glorified gravel.

The good news: I made it down before the rain. The bad news: the storm hit with the fury of a vengeful god. Picture seven or eight coachloads of drenched tourists trying to huddle under a gift shop lean-to designed for ten people. We would have been drier if we'd gone for a swim in the Mediterranean. But, hey, I'm on vacation, right?

After standing in the rain for what felt like an eternity, our coach finally showed up. Due to limited space, it couldn't park nearby. I did feel a pang of pity for anyone arriving during the storm because they were barred from climbing up to the crater – safety first, and all that jazz.

With all that rain, nature called, so I made a dash for the Porta Toilets. I didn't see any signs about having to pay to use them, but as I left, I swear

I heard someone shouting at me. Sometimes, being a bit hard of hearing is a blessing. Now, I feel like an international outlaw. Imagine getting home to see my name and photo splashed worldwide: "This man left Mount Vesuvius without paying to use a Porta Loo."

Who knew my Mediterranean cruise would turn me into a criminal mastermind?

Once everyone was herded back onto the bus, we set off for Pompeii. Now, Pompeii is one of those places that makes you feel like Indiana Jones, minus the fedora and whip. Our guide was a fountain of knowledge, spilling facts and tales about every nook and cranny. Unfortunately, Pompeii is too colossal to cover in a short tour. You'd need at least a day to really soak in its ancient grandeur.

The only downside to Pompeii? It's a magnet for tourists, especially when all the cruise ships are in port. It's like trying to navigate a battlefield while dodging selfie sticks and photobombers. A pro tip: hang back at the end of your group. If you're lucky and another group isn't breathing down your neck, you might just snag that perfect, unobstructed shot.

Back on the ship, and I guess Interpol hasn't been alerted about my Porta Loo escapade. Time for a few drinky poos before dinner and tonight's entertainment.

Craving something exotic, I set my sights on the Shangri Chinese restaurant for dinner. The place was swanky, and the waitress seated me at a nice table before handing me a menu. Thank goodness she explained it to me, or I would've just ended up with fried rice and a bowl of soup.

Feeling adventurous, I decided to embrace the cultural experience and use the chopsticks neatly placed on the table. It turns out my technique of stabbing food didn't quite cut it with rice. After what felt like an eternity, I sheepishly asked the waitress for a chopstick tutorial. To my shock and horror, she didn't know how to use them either! Lesson learned: never judge someone's chopstick prowess by their appearance.

Despite my chopstick failure, the food was phenomenal, and I savoured every bite. Definitely worth a visit if you're on board. And next time, I might just stick to the fork.

Food demolished, I headed to the theatre for the Legends in Concert show. This is a top-tier, sell-out-every-time spectacle, so book early. Kudos to

NCL; in one night, I got to see Shakira, Diana Ross, Prince, and The Beatles. Sure, they were impersonators, but they were phenomenal, and I didn't even have to switch ships. I even snagged a photo with "Shakira." Better hit up Photoshop before she buys it herself, thrilled to be next to such a famous personality like me! Well, at least in my world.

To cap off the night, I made my way to deck 15 and the H2O bar. The rain had finally stopped, revealing a beautiful evening. Feeling sophisticated, I downed a couple of glasses of wine. But then I got a hankering for a hot chocolate before bed, so I made a beeline for the Solo Lounge. At least, that was the plan.

The beauty of the Solo Lounge is the charming folks you meet. What was meant to be a quick hot chocolate turned into an hour of delightful conversation with two lovely single American ladies. They probably didn't even mind my wine-fueled storytelling. All in all, a perfect end to a day of cruise ship shenanigans.

Day 4 – Civitavecchia

Once again, the alarm screamed at 05:00, and once again, it was promptly silenced. Another ten minutes in bed sounded like a brilliant idea. Eventually, I dragged myself out, took a quick shower, and completed my morning routine before setting off for a stroll around the ship, fueled by several cups of coffee. As I reached deck 15, I was greeted by a gorgeous day—no sign of yesterday's rain.

I made my maiden voyage to the Garden Cafe for breakfast. Sometimes, it resembles a feeding frenzy, like wildebeest crossing an African river, but the variety is worth it. I started with a bowl of cereal, trying to be healthy, but that didn't last long. I quickly moved on to a hearty-cooked breakfast. To my delight, they had proper bacon, not yesterday's pork scratchings (aka rock-hard bacon). I sat down to enjoy my meal, watching the world—and my fellow passengers—whiz by at lightning speed, presumably afraid they'd miss something crucial.

My tour today, "Hilltops and Country," wasn't meeting until 08:30, so I spent some time wandering the ship. The meeting spot was the Manhattan Room, one of the inclusive restaurants by night, which isn't the best place for my new favourite game of guessing the tour. But I gave it a shot anyway, sitting at the back and observing.

As it turned out, only 20 people were left in the room, which was convenient because we were all on the same tour! Following the usual routine, we were called up, collected our prison numbers—sorry, tour identification numbers—and boarded the coach. With only 20 people on a 56-seater bus, there was plenty of room to stretch out and relax.

This excursion turned out to be one of the best I've ever been on. Our guide, Sabina, was fantastic, balancing perfectly between guiding us and giving us space to explore on our own. The first hour and a half was spent on the bus, heading to a quaint little town in the countryside, with Sabina providing a lively commentary on the local area and sprinkling in some Roman history for good measure.

We arrived at the town, and the first thing that struck me was the absence of any other coaches from competing cruise lines. Imagine that—an unspoiled spot without the usual overcrowding. Well done, NCL, for finding this gem! It felt like we had the place to ourselves, with only a few locals and our group wandering the charming, old, walled town. Plenty of time to take photos without jostling for position and really soak in the beauty of the place.

After a leisurely hour exploring, it was time for a drive through the countryside to the medieval city of Civita di Bagnoregio, built in 800 BC on top of a mountain. Now, the coach couldn't take us all the way to Civita, so we stopped in a nearby village and waited for a shuttle bus. No problem there—plenty of time to browse the gift shop, which was surprisingly reasonably priced, given its off-the-beaten-path location.

When the shuttle bus finally arrived, we played a game of sardines, packing ourselves tightly inside. But once we reached Civita, the journey was absolutely worth it. The town is perched on a mountaintop, looking like something out of a fairy tale, though apparently, it gets smaller as bits fall off. To enter, we had to cross a steep bridge, the only access point, which was just wide enough for pedestrians, mopeds, and the occasional small 4x4 buggy.

To reach the bridge, we first had to descend 82 steps—I counted them, knowing I'd have to climb them later. After the steps, there was a relatively steep slope and then, of course, a kiosk to pay for entry to the town. Fortunately, since I was on a tour, my ticket was already covered. As I stared at the very steep incline of the bridge, memories of the Mount Vesuvius climb came flooding back. But this time, I was determined—no granny was going to humiliate me by zooming past. With teeth gritted, I started the ascent, ready for whatever Civita had in store.

Mission accomplished! I was the first to conquer the top, triumphantly entering the town, and immediately hit by the glorious sight: no crowds. We were the only tour group there. Well played, NCL, for keeping this treasure hidden from the other cruise lines.

The town itself was a picturesque gem, with its tiny streets and complete lack of vehicles—save for the occasional moped, which was like spotting a unicorn. Plenty of small bars and restaurants lined the streets, and because this place is off the major tourist radar, the prices were delightfully reasonable.

I stumbled upon a tiny museum housed in an ancient building dedicated to olive oil production. It cost just one euro to enter, and to my amazement, it turned out to be the House of Geppetto, Pinocchio's dad. They even filmed the latest Pinocchio movie here last year. I half-expected my nose to grow when I told everyone about it later.

With two hours of free time, we had plenty of opportunity to explore and enjoy lunch. Our small group quickly developed a camaraderie, including Paco from the NCL Shore Excursion team, who had tagged along, presumably to ensure we didn't get lost or buy the town.

After a fantastic time, it was soon time to leave. The descent down the bridge was much easier than the climb up, but, as they say, what goes down often needs a drink. Luckily, at the top of the stairs, there was a bar. We all gathered there, and liquid oxygen was provided—okay, it was a large beer, but it did the trick.

All back on the bus, we headed back to the ship, still buzzing from our day of epic adventures. This excursion was perfect for anyone wanting to escape the usual cruise crowds. But remember, it's a secret, so keep your lips sealed! If large groups start flocking here, it wouldn't be the same.

Back on the ship, I decided to maximise my dining package benefits. My reservation at Cagney's Steakhouse was fast approaching, so I took a quick shower, changed into something more fitting for a steak feast, and headed off to see what culinary delights awaited me.

Seated next to the window, I perused the menu, which was filled with mouth-watering options. Naturally, I opted for one item from each section because why not? For the main course, I chose a rather large bison steak, cooked to perfection—not burnt, not still mooing, but just right. I enjoyed a leisurely dinner, savouring each bite. NCL doesn't rush you through like cattle; you can take your time and really enjoy the meal.

After dinner, it was time to sample the entertainment offerings on board. I started with the Manhattan Showband in the auditorium. What a great band! The singer had a voice that could melt butter; definitely worth stopping by for a listen.

Once that was over, I embarked on a tour to see what else was on offer. Nearly made a grave error when I walked into the Bliss Bar and was greeted by a horrible screeching sound. Karaoke! I fled the scene faster than a cat with its tail on fire. Instead, I retreated to the H2O bar and spent the rest of the evening grooving to the smooth sounds of the '70s.

As the night wore on, I decided to cap it off with a coffee in the Solo Lounge. Upon entering, I was hit by a scene that made me double-check the door: three families, ranging from ages 10 to 80, were all playing games together. It looked more like a family reunion than a lounge for solo travellers. NCL might want to reconsider the use of that room.

All in all, another day of cruising well spent, filled with laughter, good food, and a few surprises. Until tomorrow's adventure!

Day 5 - Livorno–Florence & Pisa

Ah, a new day in a new city! Time to roll out of bed and go through the usual morning ritual of dressing and showering—although not necessarily in that order. Then it's off to stretch the legs and make my grand entrance at the port. But first, a crucial pit stop: breakfast at the Garden Cafe. Today, I decided to be a beacon of health and only went back for seconds of cereal. Moderation, they say, is key.

Today's tour promised the wonders of Florence & Pisa on your own, with a meeting time of 08:00. So, with an hour to kill, I indulged in several cups of coffee. If you know where to look, you can find plenty of spots around the ship to fuel up on your morning java fix.

Finally, the appointed time arrived, and I made my way to the Manhattan Dining Room as per the tour ticket's instructions. As I sat there eagerly awaiting the day's adventures and my designated number, it hit me like a ton of bricks—I'd been hoodwinked! Bamboozled! The ticket clearly stated "Florence & Pisa on my own," but here I was, surrounded by about a hundred fellow "on my own" adventurers. Talk about false advertising!

But alas, there was no time to dwell on my misfortune. Before long, all us solo explorers were herded off the ship and onto several buses. I must hand it to NCL—they sure know how to make mass organisations look like a piece of cake.

Our first stop: Pisa and its famous leaning tower. The bus dropped us off at a vast coach stop about 15 minutes away from the tower and church. And let me tell you, it was a stark contrast from yesterday's peaceful excursion. Before we even set foot off the bus, hawkers descended upon us like seagulls on a bag of chips. Umbrellas, anyone? I'm not saying it was raining, but you'd need water wings to navigate through the crowd. As we made our way—er, swam our way—to the Plaza, we were bombarded by hawkers at every turn. One even had the audacity to try and sell me sunglasses! I mean, come on—can't they see the sun shining?

Ah, the Plaza—a bustling hub of touristy excitement and hawkers peddling everything from umbrellas to ponchos, all at bargain-basement prices! Well, at least that's what they claim. As the rain poured down like a biblical flood, people huddled in doorways, desperately seeking refuge from the downpour. And there I was, steadfast in my refusal to surrender to the temptation of an overpriced umbrella. After all, who needs shelter when you have the indomitable spirit of optimism, right?

I must admit, though, I did entertain the notion of engaging in some creative bartering. When one particularly persistent hawker tried to sell me yet another umbrella, I kindly offered him a punch in the face as a fair trade. Shockingly, he declined my generous proposal and scurried off into the rain-soaked abyss. Oh well, can't blame a guy for trying!

With an hour of free time on my hands and a complimentary bottle of water from the tour guide (thanks, but I'll pass), I embarked on a mission to explore the Plaza and capture some iconic photos—rain-soaked selfies included, of course. As I merrily strolled around, belting out tunes and giggling to myself like a deranged Disney character, I couldn't help but marvel at the absurdity of it all.

After a brief shopping spree at the market stalls—where haggling is not just encouraged but practically mandatory—I rejoined the group at the pre-appointed meeting point. Well, almost everyone. There's always that one family who operates on their own time, oblivious to the fact that the world doesn't revolve around them. Classic!

Ah, Florence—a city steeped in history, culture, and the occasional rain shower. As we disembarked the bus on the outskirts of this pedestrian paradise, I couldn't help but feel like a modern-day explorer about to conquer uncharted territory. Armed with nothing but a trusty bottle of water and a sense of adventure, we dove headfirst into the maze of streets, ready to uncover Florence's hidden gems.

With the rain finally taking a break and the sun peeking out from behind the clouds, the city came alive with a newfound energy. And let me tell you, nothing says "Italian fashion icon" quite like a hastily purchased hat from one of Florence's finest hawkers. As the sun beamed down, I strutted through the streets, channelling my inner fashionista and belting out tunes about the sun having his hat on. Classic.

As the day drew to a close, we regrouped as planned, including the perpetually tardy family who managed to make it on time this go-around. Back on the bus, we braced ourselves for the uncomfortable journey back to the ship—a delightful hour and a half spent squished against the window by a couple who clearly believed in the concept of personal space as a myth.

Arriving back onboard a tad fashionably late, I barely had time to change out of my exploratory attire before making my way to La Cucina Italian Restaurant. With expectations as high as the Leaning Tower of Pisa, I eagerly awaited to see what culinary delights awaited me. And let me tell you, dear reader, the food and service did not disappoint. It was a culinary experience fit for a king—or at least for a slightly soggy adventurer returning from a day in Florence's labyrinthine streets.

It was a night of aquatic delights! First up, we had the soup with shrimps—a culinary masterpiece served with flair by the folks at NCL. Picture this: a bowl filled with dry ingredients awaiting the grand finale of a liquid pour-over. It was like watching a shrimp symphony unfold before my very eyes.

Next on the menu: Lobster with a side of pasta, or should I say pasta with a cameo appearance by four tiny lobster pieces? Either way, it was a tantalising treat for my taste buds. And because I had been a paragon of fitness with all that walking, I indulged in a decadent Chocolate tart, washed down with a glass of wine fit for a connoisseur. Ah, the joys of cruising cuisine!

With the evening still young and the weather balmy, I decided to take in a movie under the stars at H2O. And what luck! The screening turned out to be the latest Hobbit flick. Imagine watching Bilbo Baggins embark on his epic journey while sipping on a cold brew and basking in the warm breeze. It's like cinema heaven, minus the sticky floors and overpriced snacks. Bonus: the ever-attentive NCL staff were on hand to keep the refreshments flowing. Talk about service with a smile!

But beware of the perils of movie snacks—they're as tempting as the One Ring itself! Before I knew it, I was munching away like a hungry Hobbit, courtesy of the friendly waiter who kept plying me with treats. By the time the credits rolled, I was ready to waddle my way to the next entertainment hotspot: the comedy club.

Ah, the comedy club—a beacon of laughter in the night. I dashed in faster than a Pisa Plaza hawker chasing after unsuspecting tourists. The show, aptly named Dual Pianos, had me in stitches from start to finish. The only downside? The booking process, which requires the strategic planning skills of a military tactician. Note to self: book shows early, or risk missing out on all the fun.

And with that, dear reader, it was off to the land of Nod, where dreams of shrimp symphonies and hobbit-sized feasts awaited. Until tomorrow, when the adventures of cruising life continue!

Day 6 – Cannes

Ah, the crack of dawn—a time when most sensible folks are snug in their beds, dreaming of sugar-plum fairies or, in my case, a buffet breakfast bonanza. But not me! No, sir, I was up at the ungodly hour of 5:30 a.m. Why? Because I'm a rebel, that's why. Plus, who needs sleep when there's a whole day of holiday shenanigans ahead?

After the obligatory morning rituals (you know, brushing teeth, cursing at the alarm clock, the usual), I made my way to deck 15 for my daily dose of liquid sanity: a gallon of coffee. Ah, the elixir of life! As I sipped my java and basked in the glorious sunshine, I couldn't help but notice the telltale signs of the towel pixies at work. Yes, they strike again, claiming prime sunbathing real estate with their mystical towel magic. But hey, who am I to judge? If you can't beat 'em, join 'em!

Breakfast was a feast fit for a king—or at least a hungry holidaymaker like myself. Full English breakfast? Check. Cereals? Check. Pastries? Double check. Because, let's face it, I'll need all the fuel I can get for a day of epic adventures on dry land.

Speaking of adventures, it was time for a new experience: tendering ashore. Like a wide-eyed schoolboy on a field trip, I eagerly awaited my turn to hop aboard the tender/lifeboat combo. But wait, what's this? One of the seats clearly marked "For Emergency Use Only"? I mean, aren't they all supposed to be for emergencies? Note to self: don't sit in the emergency seats unless absolutely necessary. Got it.

The journey to shore was brief but exhilarating, with 200 of my fellow cruisers packed into the tender like sardines in a can. Once ashore, good old NCL was there to lend a helping hand, along with the local tourist board, because, let's face it, even seasoned adventurers like myself could use a little guidance now and then.

Armed with a map and a sense of adventure, I set off to explore the old town. Or so I thought. It turns out that my navigational skills were about as reliable as those of a chocolate teapot. Left instead of right, old town instead of new—oops! But hey, getting lost is all part of the adventure, right? At least, that's what I'll tell myself as I embark on my unintentional scenic route. Onward, brave explorer!

The perfect opportunity for my brain to take an unauthorised vacation! After a leisurely stroll along the beachfront that would make Forrest Gump proud, I decided it was high time to consult the local oracle—a kiosk proprietor who I hoped could rescue me from my cartographic calamity.

But alas, it seems my brain had pulled a Houdini and disappeared without a trace. The helpful gent pointed to a spot about six feet to the left of the map and declared, "You are here!" Well, technically, he wasn't wrong. Turns out, I had embarked on a scenic detour that would make even Magellan scratch his head in confusion.

With my tail tucked firmly between my legs (metaphorically speaking, of course), I embarked on the Walk of Shame back to square one. Who knew reading a map could be so darn tricky? But fear not, for I was determined to conquer this city—or at least find my way to the old town without further incident.

After some more misguided meandering, I finally stumbled upon the crown jewel of my expedition: the castle, towering majestically over the city like a slightly less intimidating version of Hogwarts. And let me tell you, the views from up there were worth every wrong turn and lost brain cells.

With sightseeing checked off the list (and still no gift for my son in sight), it was time to bid adieu to Cannes and head back to the ship. But wait, what's this? A miniature train offering tours around the town? Where was this little locomotive when I needed it most? Oh well, better late than never, I suppose.

As I made my way back to the port, I couldn't help but notice the tour buses and friendly shore excursion staff greeting me like a long-lost friend. "Enjoy your visit to Cannes?" they chirped, unaware of the epic saga that had unfolded in my quest for direction.

And just when I thought my misadventures were over, I was greeted by a not-so-friendly surprise on the other side of the check-in desk: several busloads of happy cruisers awaiting their tender boats. Talk about impeccable timing! Looks like my brain and I were in for a serious heart-to-heart once we were reunited. But hey, at least I hadn't missed the boat—literally!

Ah, back on the good ship Lollipop, where the Pepsi flows like water and the salads are so good, they'll make you question your life choices. But fear not, dear reader, for I've mastered the art of balance—two Pepsis to wash down my leafy greens because hydration is key, right?

After a leisurely lunch that would make a rabbit proud, it was time to unwind before the evening's culinary showdown at Maderno. But first, a curious announcement over the ship's intercom: "For Spanish speakers, grassy arse." Now, call me intrigued, but I scoured every nook and cranny of the ship, only to find disappointment. No grass on anyone's derrière, folks. False advertising at its finest.

And speaking of elusive treasures, where on earth was this mythical cake shop they boasted about on the Ship's TV? Perhaps it required a secret decoder ring or a treasure map. Ah, the mysteries of the high seas!

But I digress. The hour had come to face the ultimate gastronomic challenge: Maderno. With a few stretching exercises (and maybe a victory lap or two around the ship), I donned my finest attire and mentally prepared for battle. Upon arrival, I was greeted like a returning hero by the ship's head waiter, who knew my name before I even flashed my room key. Talk about service!

Seated at my table, I eyed the buffet like a seasoned strategist, sticking to my game plan amidst the tempting array of choices. Then, with a dramatic flourish, I flipped my card from red to green, signalling the start of the meat marathon. Waiters descended upon me like vultures, skewers of meat in hand, ready to test my mettle.

But fear not, for I emerged victorious from this meaty melee, dessert in hand and a triumphant grin on my face. They say laughter is the best medicine, but I'd argue that a hearty meal at Maderno comes in at a close second. So, if you ever find yourself aboard this floating feast of delights, do yourself a favour and take on the Maderno challenge. Your taste buds will thank you!

With my belly full enough to rival a Thanksgiving turkey, I embarked on a noble quest to wobble off the excess calories. Ah, the joys of post-feast exercise—a delicate dance between fitness and food comas.

But lo and behold, an invitation awaited me at the Art Gallery, reserved exclusively for us art aficionados. I strutted in with all the grace of a connoisseur, ready to mingle with fellow collectors and perhaps snag a masterpiece or two. Imagine my delight when I won a $100 voucher, only to realise that the only pieces within my budget were, well, not exactly masterpieces. Oh, the cruel twists of fate!

For those with a penchant for fine art or simply a desire to rub elbows with the cultured elite, the art auctions are a must-visit. The staff, bless their hearts, are as charming as they come, making even the most clueless bloke feel like a seasoned art connoisseur. And let's not forget the eye candy—those two lovely ladies could charm the paint right off a canvas!

But enough art talk, for it was time to unleash my inner party animal at NCL's legendary White Hot Party. Deck 15 transformed into a sea of white-clad revellers, gyrating to the beat like there was no tomorrow. I joined in the festivities, shaking my groove thing until the wee hours of the morning before bidding farewell to the night and diving headfirst into the land of nod. Ah, the glamorous life of a cruiser!

Day 7 – Palma

The ship leisurely strolls into Palma at a leisurely 13:00, as if the captain decided to take a scenic route through the seven seas, stopping to smell the ocean breeze and, of course, squeeze in one last round of onboard sales because nothing says "vacation" like a relentless assault on your wallet.

But hey, before you start grumbling about the late arrival, remember—it's all part of the freestyle cruise experience! You can spend as much or as little as you like, no strings attached. So what if they try to tempt you with duty-free goodies and spa treatments? Just smile and wave, folks, smile and wave.

As for me, I decided to indulge in some extra beauty sleep because, let's face it, sleeping is a sport, and I'm going for gold. After a caffeine-fueled morning and a quick scan of the daily log (spoiler alert: more sales!), I sauntered over to the final Art Auction, hoping to strike gold. Alas, all I got was another $100 bid credit. Not exactly a masterpiece, but hey, it's the thought that counts, right?

With only an hour until departure on tour, I dashed to the Garden Café for a pre-adventure feast. Little did I know, the tour had a few surprises in store for us. First up, a detour to a pearl gift shop—because nothing says "cave exploration" like a guilt trip into buying overpriced pearls, am I right?

And speaking of caves, our much-anticipated visit turned out to be a bit of a disappointment. No photos allowed inside? Cue the collective gasps of horror from the entire coach. But fear not, dear passengers, for our guide had a brilliant solution: forced photoshoots with a cave photographer. Because who wouldn't want a candid shot of themselves looking bewildered in a cave?

Needless to say, I politely declined the offer, but not before experiencing the full force of the photographer's enthusiasm. Flash! Bang! And just like that, another hilarious adventure in the world of cruising. Who needs souvenirs when you have memories like these, right?

Ah, the cave adventure—a journey into the depths of... well, not very far. After patiently waiting for the group ahead to inch their way through the caverns, we finally entered, only to realise that the promise of unlimited cave time was just a cruel joke. Instead of leisurely exploring, we were herded along like reluctant sheep by guides stationed at every twist and turn. Note to self: next time, bring a shepherd's crook.

Emerging from the caves, we were whisked away to Porto Cristo, a quaint little village by the sea. Picture-perfect if you're into crowded beaches and overpriced trinkets. With a whopping two hours of free time, I quickly discovered that there's only so much one can do in a village the size of a postage stamp. Cue the yawns of boredom and the longing for the open sea.

Back on the ship just in time for my reservation at Cagney's Steakhouse, I made a dramatic entrance, camera and bag in hand, ready to feast like there's no tomorrow. And feast I did, indulging in a veritable meat extravaganza of shrimp, soup, and a steak the size of a small country. Hey, it's the last night—might as well go out with a bang!

As for the great bag disappearance saga, let's just say that NCL's trust in its passengers may be slightly... misplaced. A mysterious $3.65 charge for a "housekeeping item" appeared on my bill, leaving me scratching my head and wondering if I accidentally packed a mini vacuum cleaner. Note to self: check luggage for rogue vacuum cleaners.

But hey, who needs to dwell on petty charges when there's a bottomless drink package to conquer? So off to the bar I went, where I spent the evening chatting up some lovely ladies named Jane, Beverly, and... well, a few whose names escaped me faster than a runaway lifeboat. Ah, the joys of cruising—where the drinks flow freely, the conversations are entertaining, and the only worry is whether you'll remember to wake up in time for disembarkation. Cheers to that!

Day 8 - Barcelona & Disembark

Dawn—a time when even the sun is hitting the snooze button. Up bright and early at 04:45, I embarked on the ritual of showering, scrubbing, and bidding farewell to my cosy cabin for the week. But horror of horrors, when I reached deck 15 for my morning coffee fix, there wasn't a cup or glass in sight! Come on, NCL, don't play hide-and-seek with the caffeine vessels.

In a stroke of genius—or so I thought—I assumed the Garden Café would be open at 05:00, considering the early exodus of passengers starting at 07:00. But alas, I was met with locked doors and hungry stomachs. Finally, at the stroke of 05:30, I indulged in what I aptly dubbed my "last supper" on the ship.

Today's grand finale was a tour that conveniently ended at the airport—a stroke of scheduling brilliance, or so I thought. Little did I know that the advertised flight-friendly tour would dump me at the airport a whopping 10 hours before my flight instead of the promised five. Thanks for the unexpected bonus time, NCL. Airport adventures, here I come!

Now, onto the grand finale: disembarkation. Gathered in the epic Theatre at a reasonable 07:30, we were assigned our bus numbers and set off to reclaim our bags, which, by the sound of it, weren't too pleased about their extended vacation on the baggage carousel. With suitcases in hand and grumbling luggage in tow, we boarded the bus bound for today's adventure: Montserrat Monastery. From cinema check-in to bus boarding, the whole ordeal took a swift 45 minutes, leaving me feeling like a seasoned pro in the art of cruise disembarkation.

Ah, the scenic tour of Barcelona—a crash course in local lore and expert navigation, courtesy of our guide. Seriously, this guy knew more about Barcelona than the pigeons in Plaza Catalunya. Maybe he should moonlight as a Palm Springs tour guide and show them how it's done!

But enough about the cityscape—it was time to ascend to new heights, quite literally, as we embarked on the treacherous journey to Montserrat Monastery. Now, there were plenty of ways to reach the summit: cable cars for the faint-hearted, trains for the leisurely, and for the truly bonkers; there were cyclists huffing and puffing their way up, not to mention a lone lunatic attempting to outrun gravity itself.

As we wound our way up the mountain, the views were nothing short of spectacular, prompting a photo frenzy among the passengers. But if you were expecting a quaint little chapel at the peak, think again! Montserrat Monastery sprawls across the landscape like a religious theme park, complete with its own mountain train that defies all laws of physics.

With a mere hour and a half to explore this sprawling wonderland, I decided to hike up to St. Michael's Cross for the promised panoramic views. Little did I know that the "gentle slope" would morph into a vertical climb that would make even Spider-Man break a sweat. But after a gruelling ascent, I reached the summit and was rewarded with vistas that made my knees weak and my camera happy.

Back at the monastery, I attempted to sneak into the Basilica for a peek, but alas, a service was in progress. Undeterred, I dipped my hand into the holy water font—half expecting to burst into flames—and, much to my surprise, emerged unscathed. Feeling downright saintly, I said a quick prayer for the family and even threw in one for myself because why not?

As our time at Montserrat came to a close, I reluctantly made my way back to the bus, already plotting my return to this mountaintop marvel. Barcelona, you may have stolen my heart, but Montserrat, you've earned yourself a spot on my cruise bucket list.

Ah, the joys of airport purgatory—a thrilling saga of charging ports and desperate searches for outlets. Here I am, stranded in Barcelona airport, with only 10 hours to kill. But fear not, fellow travellers, for I come bearing wisdom gleaned from the trenches of cruise life.

Let me drop a nugget of wisdom on you: in this brave new world of airline regulations, where your gadgets must prove their worthiness or face banishment, it's essential to juice up your electronics before hitting the skies. Because let me tell you, finding a power outlet in this airport is like trying to find a needle in a haystack. After scouring every nook and cranny for hours, the only sockets I stumbled upon were nestled in a dingy eatery tucked away in the darkest depths of the departure hall. Talk about a hidden treasure!

But enough about my electrifying adventures—let's talk highlights. From Beverly to Jane, Lauren to Emily, and let's not forget good ol' Paco from the Shore Excursion department, I've met more characters than a Shakespearean comedy. And let's give a round of applause to the art auction team and the unsung heroes of the Norwegian Epic crew, without whom this epic adventure would have been about as exciting as watching paint dry on the poop deck.

Ah, my cruising compendium of delights! Let's delve into the treasure trove of my favourites, where libations flow like the mighty rivers and dining is an art form unto itself.

Top Bars:

1. Solo Lounge: Where the drinks flow freely and the conversations are as smooth as a freshly waxed dance floor.

2. Malting's: The hustle and bustle here ensures you'll get your booze fix in record time—ain't nobody got time to wait!

3. H2O: A serene oasis for film buffs and beer aficionados alike, where relaxation reigns supreme.

Eating Extravaganzas:

1. Maderno: Prepare thy stomach for the culinary gauntlet and feast upon delights fit for a king—but beware fasting may be required to conquer this culinary Everest.

2. Cagney's: A meat lover's paradise where succulence knows no bounds.

3. Shangi's: For a taste of the Orient that'll have you bowing in gratitude to the culinary gods.

Tour Treasures:

1. Hilltop Towns and Countryside: Shh, it's a secret! But trust me, the views are worth the clandestine adventure.

2. Montserrat Monastery: Prepare to be awestruck by vistas so breathtaking that they'll make your selfie stick quiver with anticipation.

3. Mount Vesuvius: A volcano with a view where you can both marvel at nature's fury and burn off those excess calories from the buffet.

Ship Hangouts:

1. Art Gallery: Where brushstrokes meet bargains, and every purchase feels like an investment in your cultured future.

2. Solo Lounge: From dawn till dusk, it's the sanctuary of solitude where introverts reign supreme.

3. Malting's: Escape the crowds and find solace amidst the barley and hops—it's a beautiful thing.

Best Shows:

1. Circus Spiegel Tent: Prepare to be dazzled by death-defying feats and acrobatic wonders that'll leave you questioning your own physical prowess.

2. Legends: Three performers, three legends, and one heck of a good time.

3. Duelling Pianos: Tickling the ivories and tickling your funny bone, with a side of audience participation for good measure.

And there you have it, folks—the pinnacle of cruise life, as decreed by yours truly. Now go forth and cruise with gusto!

14-Day Iberian Peninsula & Western Mediterranean Solo Adventure

Well folks, gather 'round for the tale of my upcoming solo escapade aboard the illustrious Norwegian Epic. Now, I may have sailed on this vessel a couple of times before, but fear not because, apparently, she's had a makeover! Yep, Norwegian Cruise Line is treating us to the thrill of a "new" ship after her refit. And let me tell you, the excitement is palpable!

You see, NCL has decided to kick off the party early. None of this waiting until we're on board nonsense. Oh no, they've gone ahead and started the fun months in advance! Picture this: a lineup of tantalising games to get us in the cruising spirit. We've got classics like "Guess Which Day We Actually Set Sail," "Is It a 13 or 14-Day Cruise?," and, of course, the pièce de résistance: "How Many Days Will You Spend in the Departure Port?"

And let me tell you, there are no cheat codes here, folks. NCL isn't dropping any hints, like a sneaky email or a carrier pigeon with a message strapped to its leg. Oh, no. If you want to crack this code, you'll need the skills of Sherlock Holmes himself. You might even find yourself diving deep into the abyss of MY.NCL.com, scouring for clues like a cruise-themed Nancy Drew.

So, as I prepare for this whirlwind adventure, I raise a toast to the memory of Smudge Cat, my faithful feline companion of two decades. Here's to you, old friend, and here's to the hilarity that awaits me aboard the Norwegian Epic! Let the games begin!

Day 1 - Start of Cruise

Ah, the delicate dance of not saying too much about the taxi driver, who may potentially be my only ride back from this cruising adventure. Can't risk offending her, especially since she's one of the daughters of the house, and trust me, getting a whack around the head is not on my to-do list today. Self-preservation, my friends, self-preservation.

So, after what felt like an eternity but was actually just a measly 20 minutes of traffic-induced torture, I finally arrived at the port. Ah, the luxury of not having to drag myself out of bed at the crack of dawn to endure the chaos of the airport. Home port departures, my darlings, they're the real MVP.

Once safely deposited at the harbor, bags handed over to the porters (who I suspect have a secret society dedicated to the art of luggage juggling), it was time to dive headfirst into the terminal madness. The check-in process, a tried and tested routine of sheep-like behaviour, with yours truly following blindly behind the person in front, navigating through the maze of ropes like a contestant on a game show.

Ah, security, the great equaliser of airport antics. Watching unsuspecting souls do the mini striptease of shame as they unload every last gadget from their pockets, hoping to avoid the dreaded beep of judgment. It's like a comedic ballet, I tell you.

But the real entertainment begins in the waiting hall. Behold the frenzy of free magazines! Suddenly, everyone morphs into hoarders, grabbing every glossy publication in sight like they're going out of style. I half expect someone to whip out a suitcase just to accommodate their newfound literary treasures.

Despite the chaos, the ship filled up faster than a balloon at a birthday party. And there I was, at the back of the ship, beer in hand, gazing wistfully at my home port and my son's humble abode.

But fear not, my thirsty friends, for Norwegian Cruise Line, has bestowed upon us a gift of pure genius: the all-powerful room key, now equipped with the holy grail of beverages and dining. No more scavenger hunts for the elusive Beverage Package benefactor. They've even strategically placed the restaurant reservation desk in front of a painting by Lina Kniff because nothing says "bon appétit" like a dash of conspiracy.

And so, with a drink in hand and a twinkle in my eye, I embarked on this floating adventure, ready to embrace the absurdity that awaits. Cheers to cruising, where the only thing more plentiful than the buffet is the laughter!

The sweet nectar of victory! Or, in my case, the sweet nectar of several beers down the hatch. With my thirst quenched, and my spirits lifted, it was time to embark on a journey of discovery aboard the newly refurbished Norwegian Epic. Now, finding my way around the ship was a bit like navigating a maze blindfolded, but eventually, I stumbled upon the Bliss lounge, looking spiffier than ever. As for the old Jazz Club, now transformed into the Cavern, it still had that cosy cave-like vibe, though I couldn't help but notice the severe lack of seating. Mental note: check the photos from the last cruise for evidence of overcrowding.

But what really caught my eye was the peculiar sight outside the Cavern Club's door: a statue of a dog mid-poop. Now, call me crazy, but I couldn't shake the feeling that there was a deeper message here. Is it a commentary on the state of the club's facilities, or perhaps a subtle warning about what awaits inside? The mysteries of cruise ship artistry, my friends, they never cease to amaze.

After my stroll around the ship and a quick pit stop at my old haunt, the Maltings, I decided it was time to rehydrate. And what better way to do so than with a refreshing glass of orange juice... spiked with Southern Comfort? Ah, the joys of sailing the high seas, where even the innocent act of drinking juice comes with a side of rebellion. And don't get me started on the parental permission sign. I mean, I practically went on a quest worthy of Frodo Baggins himself to secure written consent, but alas, the angelic messenger never arrived in time. So here I am, breaking the rules and raising a glass to my newfound freedom. Cheers to living on the edge!

Now, with the ship freshly out of dry dock and my room ready and waiting, it was time to tackle the monumental task of unpacking. But not before admiring the welcoming sight of a sparkling wine bottle calling out to me like a siren song. I resisted its charms for now, though, knowing that the real adventure awaited beyond my suitcase.

And speaking of adventures, it was high time I ventured into the realm of onboard cuisine. Two hours on a cruise ship without a single bite to eat? The food police would surely be on high alert, ready to launch a search party at any moment. So, with a growling stomach and a sense of culinary anticipation, I set forth to conquer the buffet and satisfy my cravings. After all, on a cruise ship, calories don't count... right?

Ah, the joyous pursuit of gluttony at sea! With a stomach rumbling louder than the ship's foghorn, I embarked on a culinary odyssey through the Garden Cafe and various other gastronomic hotspots onboard. Hey, it's vacation time, people! Let me indulge in my food fantasies now and deal with the consequences later. Who needs a beach body when you can have a buffet body? Am I right?

Now, with my belly full to bursting, it was time to waddle off the calories with a leisurely stroll around deck 15. And lo and behold, a miraculous sight greeted me: not a single towel left abandoned on a sunbed! It's a true testament to human ingenuity, folks. Either the Towel Pixies have met their demise (cue dramatic music), or Mother Nature herself decided to intervene with her charming British weather, a delightful mix of 10 degrees and wind. Oh, the whims of fate!

But it seems I've left my mark on this ship, as evidenced by the flurry of crew members eager to greet me like a long-lost friend. Either I made quite the impression on my last voyage, or they're just really good at faking enthusiasm. Let's hope it's the former!

Ah, but then came the dreaded Obligatory Emergency Drills. Gone are the days of lounging next to a bar during muster station duties; this time, I found myself corralled into the theatre like a reluctant sheep. But fear not, dear readers, for I sat with bated breath, eagerly awaiting new insights into emergency procedures. Alas, it was not to be. The only change? A competition to see which muster station can bellow the loudest and a crash course in life jacket fashion. Forget about finding the lifeboats or, you know, surviving an actual emergency. Who needs practicality when you have the power of vocal projection and fashion finesse? Ah, cruising, where safety takes a backseat to spectacle!

The delightful pastime of mingling with fellow cruisers and crew, accompanied by the noble quest to single-handedly tackle the beverage package. Ah, the joys of people-watching, where today's entertainment included a man bemoaning the audacity of the pool deck music for daring to disturb his peace. Clearly, he missed the memo about signing up for the QM2's library tours instead. Bless his cotton socks.

But enough frivolity, it was time to embark on a gastronomic adventure at my first booked speciality restaurant: Cagney's Steak House. Guided by a kind waiter to a table with promises of sweeping sea views and live entertainment, I couldn't help but chuckle as I realised it was as dark as a conspiracy theorist's basement outside, with a couple strategically blocking any chance of ocean glimpses. Well played, universe, well played.

Now, onto the culinary delights! A classic Shrimp Cocktail for starters, which, let's be honest, is just a fancy rebranding of the beloved prawn cocktail from yesteryear. But fear not, dear readers, for it was a delightful trip down memory lane.

Ah, the pièce de résistance: the 16oz Ribeye steak. A tantalising temptation on the menu that proved to be more than I bargained for. Who knew a steak could be the size of a small child? Lesson learned, folks: when faced with a mountain of meat, tread carefully and maybe skip the white wine unless you're prepared for a bout of food-induced hibernation.

Now, onto the steak itself. Despite a slight misunderstanding in the kitchen, resulting in a steak that could have doubled as a vocal warm-up exercise for a choir, it was still a culinary triumph. I mean, who doesn't love a steak with a side of unexpected moo?

And so, the evening drew to a close, with a merry jaunt to various watering holes around the ship before bidding adieu to consciousness for the night. Ah, the land of nod, where dreams are as wild as the open sea, and the only waves are the gentle lullabies of the ship's rocking motion. Until tomorrow, my dear shipmates, until tomorrow.

Day 2 - Day at Sea

Cruise ship mornings, where the alarm clock becomes your mortal enemy, and your body and brain engage in a battle of wills worthy of an epic showdown. Set for 05:00, the alarm blared its obnoxious tune, only to be met with the resounding chorus of "five more minutes" from my brain. But before we could say "snooze," my body had pulled a fast one, leaping out of bed, showering, shaving, and marching up to deck 15 in search of the elixir of life: coffee.

And thus, the day began! After guzzling down enough java to fuel a small army and completing several laps around the ship (because why not start the day with a brisk stroll at sea?), it was time to tackle the most important meal of the day: breakfast. Remembering the glorious feasts of past cruises, I ventured into O'Sheehan's, only to be met with a breakfast that could only be described as a chef's hat gone rogue. Methinks a new breakfast joint is in order for tomorrow's culinary escapades.

With breakfast bravely consumed (or endured, depending on your perspective), it was time to consult the Freestyle daily and dive headfirst into the ocean of onboard activities. And let me tell you, folks, NCL does not mess around when it comes to keeping you entertained. From hidden games to interactive adventures, boredom is a word banished from the lexicon of the high seas.

First up: Hunt the Mini Golf, a thrilling scavenger hunt proudly advertised in the Freestyle Daily. Spoiler alert: the mini golf remains as elusive as a mythical sea creature. But fear not, for I embarked on a noble quest to uncover its hiding place, armed with determination and a 'Been There, Done That' booklet (free to anyone brave enough to venture forth). Seven bars crossed off the list later; it was time for round two: Spot the Difference, a game of wits involving interactive notice boards and sharp observation skills.

But the pièce de résistance? Bowling in the Bliss Lounge. Or so the Freestyle Daily would have you believe. Alas, I found no lanes, only perplexed cleaners and a sense of bewilderment. Perhaps O'Sheehan's holds the key to this maritime mystery, its arcade game a beacon of hope in a sea of confusion. Oh, NCL, the joys of a ship fresh out of refit, where even basic amenities become a game of hide and seek. Ah, cruising, where every day is an adventure, whether you like it or not!

Lunchtime, the sacred hour of gastronomic exploration! With a plethora of dining options at my disposal, I faced the daunting task of choosing just one. But why settle for one when you can conquer three? Yes, call me a culinary daredevil, but my 'Been There Done That' booklet demanded it, and who am I to argue with a list?

The afternoon unfolded in the delightful realm of the Art Auction, where Linda Le Kniff's masterpieces beckoned like sirens on a rocky shore. Determined to resist the siren call of art acquisition, I navigated the treacherous waters of temptation, dodging eager staff and sidestepping towards the exit like a seasoned art connoisseur. No, Stephen, resist the urge! But oh, the allure of a canvas whispering sweet promises of aesthetic delight.

Having narrowly escaped the clutches of art-induced bankruptcy, I embarked on the noble quest of relaxation and, ahem, further exploration of the ship's beverage offerings. The Garden Cafe beckoned with its song of culinary delights, and I must say, it did not disappoint. A feast fit for a seafaring king enjoyed amidst the company of fellow pub-crawling enthusiasts.

But the real highlight of the evening? The grand opening premier performance of Priscilla Queen of the Desert in the theatre. A bold move by NCL met with mixed reactions from the audience. Some walked out in a huff, but oh, what fools they were! The show was a triumph of talent and flamboyance, leaving me eager to experience its splendour once more.

As the evening waned and the promise of laughter loomed on the horizon, I found myself in the cosy confines of the Cavern Club, where seating was as scarce as pirate treasure. But fear not, for the Towel Pixies had evolved; their nefarious deeds now focused on drink placement and seat-saving. A formidable force to reckon with, indeed, as even the waiters dared not cross them.

And so, with tears of laughter streaming down my face courtesy of the Comedy Magician, I bid adieu to the night and surrendered myself to the embrace of the land of Nod. Ah, cruising, where every moment is an adventure, and every laugh is a treasure worth seeking. Until tomorrow, dear shipmates, until tomorrow.

Day 3 – Vigo

Ah, the delightful dance of the morning routine, where the promise of life-revitalizing coffee is abruptly dashed by the cruel absence of cups. Deck 15, the promised land of caffeinated salvation, lay barren, cupless, like a deserted island in a sea of disappointment. Down to deck 6, I trudge to O'Sheehan's, the beacon of morning caffeine, where the java flows like a river of hope.

As the ship nears the port of Vigo, it's a race against time to guzzle down a gallon of coffee and devour the daily log, all in the name of shipboard efficiency. And then, a miracle of sorts occurs: a healthy breakfast is on the horizon! Cereal, the breakfast of champions (or so I tell myself), followed by a hearty Full English because balance is key, my friends. And let's not forget the two glasses of orange juice, because health.

With breakfast bravely conquered, it was time for the morning's main event: the theatre meeting for my first tour of the cruise, ominously titled 'Spirit of Galistiter.' Ah, but the true challenge lay in the art of Guess the Tour, a game made even more thrilling by the unfamiliarity of the excursions on offer.

Observing the flurry of activity as fellow cruisers prepared for their walking tours, it became clear that the prospect of excessive walking had sparked a primal instinct in us all: the closer to the departure point, the better. Like eager penguins huddling together for warmth, we crowded around the designated meeting spot, determined to minimise any unnecessary steps.

As the first tour group was called, I breathed a sigh of relief, thankful to have dodged the mass exodus. But alas, my own tour beckoned, and with it came the sobering realisation that my day would be spent traversing kilometres of uneven ground and cobblestones. And just when I thought things couldn't get any more surreal, a man on a mobility scooter zoomed past, eager to join the walking tour. Ah, the spirit of adventure knows no bounds, my friends, not even the constraints of mobility.

The thrilling saga of the bus tour, where the promise of enlightening commentary is drowned out by the roar of the engine and the collective snores of half-awake passengers. As we rumbled out of the port, our tour guide, perched at the front like a seafaring oracle, attempted to regale us with tales of Vigo's wonders. Alas, his words were lost in the wind, leaving me with only fleeting snippets of wisdom. But fear not, dear reader, for by journey's end, I had amassed a treasure trove of knowledge about Vigo's prime parking spots. A true win-win situation, if you ask me.

Our first stop: an ancient fort boasting views so breathtaking, they could make a sea captain weep tears of joy. And thanks to NCL's commendable crowd control efforts (or perhaps just sheer luck), we were spared the horror of overcrowding. Kudos, NCL, kudos indeed. Our guide led us through the fort's labyrinthine corridors, each corner revealing a new vista ripe for the snapping of Instagram-worthy photos. Bravo, good sir, bravo.

But lo and behold, our journey took an unexpected turn as we stumbled upon a wine and food-tasting extravaganza nestled within the fort's walls. And in a moment of sheer audacity (or perhaps just sheer thirst), I boldly led the charge, seizing the opportunity to sample the offerings with gusto. After all, someone had to ensure the quality of the wine, and who better than yours truly?

With glasses drained and stomachs sated, we embarked on our next adventure: an ancient Roman-style site boasting views fit for a postcard. But alas, our tour was not without its share of villains: the dreaded Photo Bores, those insatiable shutterbugs who stop at nothing to capture the perfect shot, heedless of the havoc they wreak upon their fellow travellers. It is my humble suggestion that these offenders be banished to the depths of the cargo hold, where their antics can trouble us no more.

One final stop afforded us a glimpse of the Norwegian Epic in all her glory, a fitting end to our jaunt through the streets of Vigo. As we bid farewell to the port and boarded our ship once more, I couldn't help but reflect on the absurdity of it all. Ah, cruising, where every tour is an adventure, and every adventure is a tale worth telling. Until next time, Vigo, until next time.

Ah, the timeless struggle of cruise time, where minutes feel like hours and hours feel like eternity. With a thirst that could rival a desert wanderer's, I made a beeline for H2O, the holy grail of adult beverages, at the back of the ship. But lo and behold, a miracle of sorts occurred: the kids vacated their table like seagulls scattering before the arrival of a feast. And so, with a sigh of relief, I settled in for a few well-deserved cold ones because hydration is key, my friends.

Ah, the joys of cruising solo, where solitude is but a fleeting illusion shattered by chance encounters with fellow adventurers. Enter Ray and Aszu, the dynamic duo from Hazelmere, whose company proved to be as delightful as a summer breeze on the high seas. Hours flew by in a whirlwind of laughter and banter, interrupted only by NCL's feeble attempt to explain our hour-long circle dance around the ocean. Setting the magnetic compass, they claimed. But let's be real, we all know the real culprit: Ray and his cocktail-shaking antics. Stop the stirring, stop the spinning—it's maritime physics 101, folks.

But as the clock ticked on and the hunger pangs grew louder, it was time to refuel at the Garden Cafe, where culinary delights awaited like buried treasure. The freedom to feast or famine, to indulge or abstain, to be as lazy as a sloth or as active as a caffeinated squirrel. And so, with a belly full of food and a heart full of contentment, I retreated to my stateroom, where sleep claimed me like a siren's song. Ah, the joys of cruise life, where every day is an adventure and every night is a comedy of errors. Until tomorrow, dear shipmates, until tomorrow.

Day 4 – Lisbon

The delightful consequences of an early night: a 3 AM rendezvous with the wide-eyed wonder of insomnia. But fear not, for in the wee hours of the morning, the Norwegian Epic beckoned like a siren in the night, promising 24-hour delights of epic proportions. And lo and behold, O'Sheehan's, that beacon of caffeine-fueled salvation, welcomed me with open arms and steaming cups of coffee. Ah, the joys of cruising, where even sleepless nights come with a side of java.

But as the darkness of night gave way to the faint glimmer of dawn, I embarked on a quest for the elusive NCL secret game of the day. An art show in Fat Cats, they said. But alas, Fat Cats proved as elusive as a mermaid in a desert, leaving me to ponder the mysteries of time and space aboard the Norwegian Epic. Perhaps NCL's secret game involves a dash of time travel? Who knows.

But the true highlight of the morning came in the form of a surprise obstacle course on Deck 15, courtesy of the conveniently placed sun lounger. A perfect opportunity for a morning limping session, courtesy of my newfound sprained ankle. Ah, the lack of risk assessment by the HSE Officer, a fellow connoisseur of shipboard mishaps.

But fear not, for breakfast awaited in the Garden Cafe, where healthy intentions were swiftly abandoned in favour of a hearty feast of dead pig and assorted goodies. Because let's be real, who can resist the siren song of bacon?

With breakfast conquered and my ankle suitably sprained, I embarked on a leisurely stroll around the ship, capturing stunning photos of our arrival in Lisbon. And then, it was time for the pièce de résistance: the Sintra 4x4 adventure. But not before a thrilling game of guess the tour, where half the group unwittingly departed for destinations unknown, leaving me to revel in the glory of a tour still intact. And so, with prison number in hand and adventure on the horizon, I boarded my 4x4 chariot, ready to conquer the wilds of Sintra. Cruising, where every day brings a new adventure and every mishap is just another story to tell. Onward to glory!

Ah, the wild ride of adventure! Buckle up, folks, because we're off to Sintra, the picturesque town nestled in the mountains, and yours truly scored the coveted front seat in the lead vehicle. No views of rear ends in my photos, thank you very much!

Joining me on this escapade were a colorful cast of characters, including the Captain's son from the UK (not the ship's captain, mind you), a delightful couple from the US, and the self-proclaimed Captain himself—a Scottish man living in Spain who insisted on being called Captain. Ah, cruising, where even the land excursions come with their own cast of characters.

Our journey was not just a drive; it was an educational experience led by our driver, who served up a delightful mix of standard tour info and off-the-wall tidbits about Portugal, Lisbon, and Sintra. It's not every day you get a history lesson with a side of laughs!

Upon arriving in Sintra, we were set loose to explore the charming town for 45 glorious minutes. Tiny back streets, historic palaces—there was no shortage of sights to behold. And let's not forget the off-road adventure that followed, courtesy of Extremo Ambiente. When they say off-road, they mean it, folks! Dirt tracks, forest trails, and expert driving skills that would make even James Bond blush.

But the real highlight? The wine tour, of course! Forget yesterday's wine tour; this one was a grape-stomping good time. The owner regaled us with tales of Portugal's finest wines and then taught us the delicate art of wine tasting. Several glasses of both white and red later, I found myself in a spirited conversation with two lovely ladies from another vehicle. And when we spotted another tour bottling their own wine, well, let's just say my charm went into overdrive.

With a dash of wit and a sprinkle of persuasion, we managed to finagle our way into the wine bottling action, complete with personalised labels proclaiming us as the master vintners. Sure, our bottle may be missing a cork, but who needs it when the wine tastes this good? The sweet taste of victory—or should I say the smooth, full-bodied taste of a perfectly crafted red. Cheers to adventure, my friends!

Stop soon over and back on the vehicles with looks of envy from the others who had not pushed their luck at the winery.

Our rollercoaster ride of adventure continues! After some hair-raising driving down tiny tracks, we hit the coast for some evening scenic views and photo ops. And let me tell you, folks; I nailed the perfect selfie with a breathtaking backdrop—yours truly with a view fit for a postcard!

But wait, there's more! We made one last pit stop at the most westerly point in Europe before heading back to the ship. Talk about going out with a bang!

The tour wrapped up around 3:00 PM, and let me tell you, it was the second-best tour I've ever been on (and I've been on a few). Hats off to NCL for putting together such a stellar experience, and a big shoutout to Extremo Ambiente for making it all happen. From the heart-pounding driving to the wine-tasting extravaganza, it was a journey to remember.

Now, let's talk about the heartbreak of bidding adieu to my beloved bottle of red wine before boarding the ship. NCL's policy, you see. But hey, I'm all for supporting the cause of keeping cruise prices down (and maybe indulging in a few of their drinks along the way).

Back on the ship, it was a quick change of attire before hitting up H2O for some pre-dinner drinks. Then it was off to the Maderno restaurant for a feast fit for a king—well, more like a feast fit for someone who's already eaten too much but can't resist the temptation of delicious food.

And just when I thought the evening couldn't get any better, NCL pulled out all the stops with a surprise dolphin show right near the ship. Dolphins, folks! How they orchestrated this aquatic spectacle, I'll never know, but let's keep it our little secret, shall we?

The night wrapped up with some onboard entertainment, including a violin duo with skills so sharp they could cut through the seas. With that, it was time to bid adieu to another day of cruising and wait with bated breath to see what tomorrow has in store. Ah, the joys of life on the high seas!

Day 5 - Another Day at Sea

The joys of vacation lie in the art of the leisurely lie-in. My ambitious plans to rise with the sun were quickly dashed by the call of the oh-so-comfy bed, which seemed to have developed a magnetic pull overnight. But hey, who can blame a tired traveller for seeking refuge in the embrace of slumber?

Eventually, I roused myself from the depths of dreamland and shuffled up on deck, only to be greeted by gale-force winds and temperatures cold enough to freeze the feathers off a penguin. Lovely weather for a cruise, isn't it?

In a bold move, I opted for breakfast at the Taste restaurant, breaking from my usual routine. And let me tell you, folks, it was a game-changer! The presentation was top-notch, the food quality was sky-high, and I found myself wondering why I hadn't dined there sooner. Although, I must confess, deciphering the menu felt like solving a Rubik's Cube blindfolded. Thank goodness for the helpful waiter who guided me through the culinary maze.

With breakfast conquered, it was time for my daily hobble around the ship to burn off those extra calories. Ah, the joys of exercise!

But hold the phone, folks! The real excitement unfolded in O'Sheehan's, where I found myself glued to a seat for three hours, catching up on reports and eavesdropping on the Atrium's bustling activities. Who needs cable TV when you've got front-row seats to the drama of ship life?

Now, brace yourselves for the plot twist—I somehow managed to catch a cold onboard. Blame it on a rogue germ or a sneaky passenger who didn't disclose their sniffles on the health declaration form. Regardless, I spent the day lounging, sipping drinks, and contemplating the mysteries of life.

As we sailed through the picturesque straits of Gibraltar, I couldn't help but marvel at the stunning views of Europe and North Africa. Shame about Gibraltar being camera-shy, though. Note to self: next time, book a seat on the mainland side.

And then came lunch at O'Sheehan's—round two. Spoiler alert: it was a disaster. The fish and chips arrived in a sad excuse for a tray; the mushy peas were more liquid than solid, and the tartar sauce... well, let's just say it was more white than green. When I questioned the waitress about the pea situation, her response was a classic: "The peas must have melted." Right.

On a brighter note, the bar was conveniently nearby to drown my culinary sorrows. Cheers to that!

Dinner at the Garden Cafe proved to be a delightful affair, made even more memorable by the company of two world-famous violin players. Bravo, NCL, for sprinkling a bit of stardust on an otherwise ordinary evening.

Feeling under the weather, I bid adieu to the day's adventures and retired early for some much-needed shut-eye. Ah, the sweet embrace of sleep awaits!

Day 6 – Cartagena

Ah, the consequences of an early night have come knocking, and here I am, wide awake at the ungodly hour of 3 a.m., parked on deck 7 for some prime people-watching entertainment. And let me tell you, folks, the show is on! Watching the party animals stumble out of the Bliss Lounge is like witnessing a comedy sketch come to life. They're swaying like seaweed in a storm, but hey, who am I to judge? It's definitely them, not the ship, doing the tango.

With an early start in Cartagena looming on the horizon, I opted for a quick breakfast at the Garden Café. After all, I didn't want to miss out on the walking tour extravaganza. Who needs sleep when there's adventure afoot?

Settling into my seat at the Epic Theatre, I eagerly awaited the Cartagena walking tour—a fitting end to a week of indulgence. Lucky for me, I've got another week of shenanigans ahead in Barcelona. Bring it on!

As the tour game reached expert level, I effortlessly identified my fellow adventurers, especially the ones who were wider than they were tall. Ah, the joys of leisurely strolls with like-minded companions.

But hold onto your hats, folks, because this walking tour comes with a twist! Instead of hitting the pavement right away, we were herded onto a bus. A walking tour that starts on wheels? Only on the good ol' Epic, folks!

Once we arrived in Cartagena, it was snap-happy time as we captured all the sights before the tourist hordes descended. Kudos to the Excursions department for the early bird special!

Our tour guide, bless her heart, was a font of knowledge and banter, keeping us engaged and entertained as we traipsed around town. With each historical tidbit and scenic viewpoint, she had us hanging on her every word—and snapping away like paparazzi at a red carpet event.

And that's the beauty of NCL-organized tours, folks! No aimless wandering or getting lost in the shuffle—just curated experiences that hit all the high notes.

With an hour of free time to explore on our own, I opted to skip the souvenir shops and soak in the sights one last time. Because when it comes to cruising adventures, every moment counts!

Back on board just in time for the lunchtime shenanigans! Off I went to the Garden Café, embracing my inner health guru with a salad. Yes, you heard that right, folks—a salad! Don't worry, I promise no more shocking revelations. You can pick yourselves up off the floor now. Just watch out for any rogue croutons on your way up!

After my brief dalliance with greens, it was straight to the H2O bar for some much-needed hydration. And by hydration, I mean several cold beers. Because, let's face it, nothing says "refreshing" like a chilled brew while watching the world sail by. Cheers to that!

Dinner plans were set in stone: Shanghai Chinese restaurant it was. A quick pit stop back at the stateroom for a spruce-up, and I was ready to rock the chopsticks. And let me tell you, the service at this joint was top-notch, full of banter and flair that made the meal an absolute delight.

I opted for three courses, and even when the main course took its sweet time, I didn't mind one bit. The playful banter continued, with the waitress plying me with an unexpected second starter. Now, that's what I call service with a side of sass!

With the evening still young, it was time for a few more rounds before diving into the onboard entertainment. But hold onto your drinks, folks, because I stumbled upon a curious phenomenon: the ever-changing prices of my beloved Southern Comfort and Orange Juice concoction.

In the Shanghai Restaurant, it's $10.33, but wait, head over to Maltings Bar, and suddenly it's $11.21! What's the deal with that? I did a double-take and went back to Maltings later, only to find the price magically reverted to $10.33. Talk about a barroom mystery!

As the ship swayed gently under the night sky, I bid adieu to another day of high-seas hilarity, eagerly awaiting the adventures that tomorrow will bring. Ahoy, land of Nod, here I come! Until next time, folks, may your voyages be as entertaining as mine. Cheers to a cruise well-sailed!

Day 7 – Barcelona

Rise and shine at the crack of dawn, or as I like to call it, the ungodly hour of 4 a.m.! Off I trotted to O'Sheehan's, where my caffeine addiction was met with open arms by Jessy and the gang. It's like Cheers but with coffee instead of beer and a lot less Norm. Nothing like a steaming cup of joe to kickstart the day, especially when accompanied by the comforting familiarity of my regular brew.

After an hour of pounding away at my keyboard and drowning in Java, it was time to tackle the day. Back to Taste restaurant for breakfast, where I was greeted by a waiter who seemed to have misplaced his happy pill. Maybe he needs a vacation, or perhaps he's auditioning for the role of Grumpy in the next Snow White reboot.

Being a back-to-back cruiser newbie, I was in uncharted waters. Do I pack my bags? Do I need to rebook everything? Cue the existential crisis. But fear not, for NCL had it all sorted, complete with a Paddington Bear-sized label and a handy-dandy letter explaining the drill.

With no tour to rush off to, I strolled leisurely into Barcelona's city centre, burning off last night's indulgences one step at a time. Thirty minutes on foot turned into an expedition worthy of Bear Grylls, but hey, at least I earned my gluttony privileges for the day.

Barcelona, with its maze of narrow streets and hidden gems, was a feast for the senses. Literally, if you count the temptation of street food. I stumbled upon a human pyramid contest, a sight that made me question my existence and marvel at human ingenuity all at once. Take that, main tourist drag!

Back on board, the Paddington Bear sticker saga continued, with me fumbling my way through embarkation like a lost soul in a sea of seasoned cruisers. But eventually, I found my way to H2O, where a cold Stella and a burger awaited me, the perfect reward for a day of urban exploration.

The saga of the elusive emergency drill continues! Once again, I found myself on the outside looking in, denied the chance to boogie down with the life jackets. But fear not, for the Solo Lounge beckoned, offering solace in the form of caffeine and consolation cookies. Because when life hands you a snub, munch on a cookie and pretend it's a gold medal. Cheers to making the best of a safety drill snub!

Tonight's culinary adventure led me to Teppanyaki, where the chef doubles as a culinary wizard and stand-up comedian. Picture this: a chef juggling spatulas while flipping shrimp into his hat. It's dinner and a show, folks! And let me tell you, the food was fresher than a cucumber in a snowstorm. Just be sure to bring your patience because dinner at Teppanyaki is a marathon, not a sprint. Strap in and prepare for a two-hour gastronomic journey!

While wandering the ship, I stumbled upon the Park West lady, who lured me into an art raffle with promises of grandeur. Spoiler alert: I didn't win squat. But wait, there's more! Suddenly, I found myself in a bidding war over a Linda Le Kniff masterpiece. I tried to resist, but my hand had a mind of its own, stubbornly refusing to back down until I was the proud owner of a painting. The best part? The auctioneer declared me the winner at the low, low price of zero dollars! Who says you can't win big on a cruise?

Flush with victory, I sauntered over to O'Sheehan's for a victory beer or two, basking in the glow of my newfound artistic acquisition. But the night was young, and as luck would have it, the duelling pianos show was in full swing at Headliners. Thanks to NCL's open show policy, I waltzed right in and found myself swept away by the music and merriment. Audience participation, sing-alongs, and laughter filled the air, proving once again that the best memories are made when you least expect them. Cheers to spontaneous fun and unexpected wins!

Day 8 - Another Day at Sea

Ah, the joys of the daily grind at sea! Rolled out of bed fashionably late; blame it on the cosy quilt, not my lack of motivation. Who needs an alarm clock when you have a bed that hugs you tighter than a clingy friend?

Now, typically, I'm not one to revel in the leisurely pace of sea days, but today was a whirlwind of activity from dawn till dusk. Breakfast at the Garden Café kickstarted the day, followed by a marathon of shipside strolls on deck 7. Epic, indeed, because trying to navigate this floating behemoth is like trying to find your way out of a maze after a few too many cocktails.

In a moment of spontaneity, I found myself perched at the Atrium bar, ordering a round of Cokes (or was it Pepsi? Who can tell the difference?). Little did I know, I was about to witness the culinary magic of a fruit and veggie wizard. Move over, Gordon Ramsay. There's a new chef in town, and they're turning cucumbers into swans and apples into art.

Lunch beckoned from deck 15, and like a dutiful sailor, I heeded its call. But not before cracking the code of NCL's sneaky mystery game. The elusive mini-golf course revealed itself, cleverly disguised as the Kids Pool. Hats off to NCL for keeping us on our toes!

Feeling emboldened by my recent victory at the art auction, I waltzed back for round two. Little did I know, Park West had deployed their secret weapons: two enchanting ladies who could charm the paint off a canvas. Their tactics were devious yet effective, and before I knew it, I was the proud owner of yet another Linda Le Kniff masterpiece. Note to self: next time, leave the bidding paddle at home or invest in some handcuffs for my wallet.

With my artistic endeavours fulfilled, I ventured to a cruise presentation, only to realise I knew more about NCL than I thought possible. Who needs a tour guide when you've been to more ports than a seasoned sailor? Ah, the joys of cruising, where every day brings a new adventure and a fresh reminder to listen to your own advice, especially when it involves bidding wars and art acquisitions.

Ah, the elusive VIP treatment! Managed to snag an invite to the Captain's shindig up in the swanky Epic Lounge, the pinnacle of posh on this floating fortress. Feeling like a high roller, I strutted in a cool 10 minutes early, ready to bask in the lap of luxury.

But hold onto your life vests, folks, because I was met with a frostier reception than the iceberg that sank the Titanic. One officer, decked out in dazzling white, gave me the stink eye, practically shooing me back downstairs like a stray seagull. Even after I flashed my golden ticket, they still treated me like I was trying to crash a yacht party.

Thank the cruise gods for the cavalry, though! Once the rest of the officers swanned in, the atmosphere warmed up faster than a tropical island sunset. Suddenly, I was rubbing elbows with the ship's elite, feeling more like a VIP than the last jelly bean in the jar. Cheers to NCL for making me feel like royalty, even if it was just for one cocktail-fueled soirée.

With the Captain's bash in the rearview mirror, it was off to round two: the Latitudes Members extravaganza in the Bliss Lounge. Champagne flowed like a river, and wine flowed like... well, a slightly slower river. Suffice it to say, it was a booze-fueled carnival, and I was front and centre for the ride.

As the night wore on, I found myself in H2O, ready to catch a flick under the stars. But hold onto your popcorn, because the movie selection was straight out of the stone age. I'm talking black and white classics, folks, like they raided Granny's VHS collection. Note to NCL: next time, let's stick to movies that haven't been collecting dust since the last ice age.

But hey, with all that complimentary wine sloshing around, who needs a blockbuster? Time to hit the hay and sail off into dreamland, fueled by free-flowing spirits and memories of rubbing shoulders with the ship's upper crust. Ah, the glamorous life of a cruiser!

Day 9 – Naples

Picture this: it's the crack of dawn, the birds are still hitting snooze, and there I am, planted at O'Sheehan's like a loyal coffee-sipping sentinel. Just me, the night crew, and an unexpected guest: Granny. Yep, she plops down right beside me in a move that's more surprising than finding a pirate in the buffet line.

Now, being the epitome of manners (and secretly wondering if I somehow inherited a "Talk to Me" sign), I engage in some polite chit-chat with Sandy. Turns out, she's not just your average early bird; she's a full-on cruise buddy in the making. Who knew the secret to making friends was lurking in the wee hours at O'Sheehan's?

Fast forward to Naples, where the sun's barely peeping over the horizon, and I'm ready for my first shore excursion. Armed with a belly full of breakfast and a dubious talent for guessing tours, I head to the Epic Theatre for the grand reveal. Spoiler alert: my success rate? A solid 50%, which in cruise terms means I'm basically a psychic.

But hold the anchovies! As we board the "Walking through Naples, Secret Tunnels, and Pizza" adventure, I spot a fella who looks like he's been hitting the buffet a bit too hard. Turns out, it's just my own reflection in the window. Classic mix-up, am I right?

Off we go, limping through the streets of Naples like a gang of mismatched pirates, with me nursing a sunburn that rivals a lobster's hue. As if that weren't enough, we're each adorned with a sticky number like some bizarre tourist initiation. Spoiler alert: nobody's fooling anyone with those sneaky attempts to blend in. Nice try, matey.

And just when I thought things couldn't get any weirder, they hand us radios to wear like some kind of tourist walkie-talkie brigade. Because nothing says "blend in" like broadcasting your whereabouts to the entire city. Smooth move, Naples, smooth move.

Naples, where the streets are paved with pizza, and the tour guides are as lively as a caffeinated clown at a birthday party. Our fearless leader for the day? Monica, the queen of Naples, is knowledgeable and the master of keeping us entertained.

As we sauntered through the city streets, Monica's commentary boomed in our earpieces like a hyperactive DJ at a silent disco. Genius, really. No need to strain to hear over the bustling crowds or the occasional scooter symphony. Plus, it gave me the freedom to wander off course and pretend I was on some clandestine mission.

Now, picture this: we stumble upon a bustling square, given 45 minutes of freedom to explore. Sounds like a dream, right? Well, let's just say my dream turned into a race against time when I realised I'd left my watch back on the ship. Cue the frantic glances at imaginary wristwatches and the occasional panicked sprint back to the meeting point.

But fear not, fellow adventurers, for we eventually regrouped, albeit fashionably late for some. Hey, when you're cruising through history and snapping selfies like a paparazzi pro, time tends to slip away faster than an ice cube on a hot deck.

And just when I thought the day couldn't get any more thrilling, Monica unveils the pièce de résistance: the entrance to the Secret Tunnels of Naples. Yep, you heard that right. Hidden tunnels beneath the bustling streets, just waiting to be explored. Thank goodness for organised tours, or I'd probably end up lost in a gelato shop somewhere, blissfully unaware of Naples' hidden treasures.

The tunnels of Naples! Like a hidden treasure chest buried beneath layers of marinara sauce and ancient history. Trust me, folks, these tunnels are the real deal, straight out of an Indiana Jones movie, minus the fedora and whip (although I would've looked pretty snazzy).

Picture this: we descend down a rickety staircase, deeper and deeper into the belly of Naples. I swear, it felt like we were venturing into the realm of pizza legends. And let me tell you, these tunnels have more history than a library on wheels.

We're talking artifacts from World War II, folks. Bombs, bunkers, and maybe even a stray pepperoni or two. It's like stepping back in time, except instead of dinosaurs, we've got pizza-loving soldiers.

But wait, there's more! These tunnels aren't just a relic from the past; they're a journey through time itself. We're talking tunnels from the 1800s, folks. That's right, tunnels are so old that they predate sliced bread. And let me tell you, they go on for miles. I wouldn't be surprised if we stumbled upon Atlantis down there.

And just when you think it couldn't get any better, we emerge near the sea like triumphant pizza pirates, ready to plunder the nearest pizzeria for all its cheesy goodness. And let me tell you, unlimited pizza and wine? It's like winning the lottery but with more carbs.

We settle in at a table with three friendly strangers, united by our love for pizza and our inability to say no to free wine. That's the magic of cruising, folks. No matter where you're from, you're bound to find common ground over a slice of pepperoni.

After several rounds of pizza-induced bliss, it's time to waddle back to the ship, bellies full and heart's content. So here's to you, NCL, for the adventure of a lifetime, and of course, to Monica, our fearless guide through the tunnels of pizza paradise. You rock, Monica!

Back on board at 14:00, which can only mean one thing: it's time to hit up my favourite watering hole, H2O. And who do I find there? None other than the legendary Ida, the waiter with jokes as cold as the Stella he serves. I hand over my Beer Token, a.k.a. the Freestyle card, and before I know it, I'm swimming in a sea of laughter and brewskis.

Hours fly by as I bask in the sunshine, sipping on cold ones and watching life on deck unfold. But eventually, duty calls, and I find myself drawn to the Solo Lounge, where solo travellers unite in a symphony of camaraderie and good times. Sadly, my stint there is short-lived, as I must bid adieu to my newfound friends and make my way to Cagney's for round two of culinary bliss.

This time, I'm feeling adventurous and opt for the 8oz Bison steak, complete with garlic mashed potato and mushrooms. And let me tell you, folks, it's a meal fit for a king or at least a slightly tipsy cruise enthusiast. With a view of the ship leaving port as my backdrop, I dig in with gusto, savouring every juicy bite.

As the night wears on and the possibilities seem endless, I embark on a mission to conquer as many onboard destinations as humanly possible. From the piano bar to the karaoke lounge, I leave no stone unturned in my quest for entertainment. But as the hours tick by, I can't help but wonder: is the boat swaying, or is it just me? Spoiler alert: it's definitely me.

And so, with a contented sigh and a belly full of bison, I bid farewell to the night and surrender to the sweet embrace of sleep. Ah, the life of a cruiser. Never a dull moment, and always a good story to tell.

Day 10 – Civitavecchia

Ah, the joys of waking up at the crack of dawn, or in my case, the crack of "Why am I awake at 03:00?!" But hey, when life gives you an early start, you make the most of it, right? So, I stumble out of bed, hit the shower, and somehow manage to cobble together a semi-coherent review for the day ahead. Then it's off to the Garden Café for a hearty breakfast of dead pig (because why not?) and omelettes, with a side of cereal for good measure. Gotta keep things balanced, you know?

But as luck would have it, the weather gods decide to play a little prank on us, unleashing a torrential downpour upon our ship. No worries, though. Who needs an umbrella when you've got a perfectly waterproof epidermis? Am I right?

Undeterred by the soggy forecast, I set my sights on the hilltop town of Orvieto because why settle for one hill when you can conquer two? After a brief rendezvous in the Headliners lounge (spoiler alert: I didn't win "Guess the Tour"), it's time to board the coach for our two-hour journey to Orvieto.

Now, finding the coach was a bit of an adventure in itself, what with the excursions staff blending in with the crowd like undercover agents trying to dodge the rain. Note to self: suggest NCL invest in some snazzy waterproof jackets for future excursions.

Finally, we arrive at the base of Orvieto, greeted by the charming sight of a funicular railway. And let me tell you, riding a funicular is like being on a rollercoaster without the loops—slightly less thrilling but just as exhilarating.

With each clickety-clack of the ascending railcar, I snap more photos than a paparazzo at a celebrity wedding. And just when I think the fun's over, we hop onto a tiny bus for the final leg of our journey to the town itself.

Our guide is the perfect blend of historical insights and unexpected detours into the world of sausage semantics. Yes, you heard that right. Our guide, bless her heart, decided to delve into the riveting topic of Hog vs. Pork sausages, leaving me more bewildered than a chicken in a grocery store.

But let's not dwell on the sausage saga, shall we? After the tour, we were set loose upon the town like a pack of caffeinated tourists on a mission.

Picture quaint streets, charming squares, and the occasional game of dodge-the-car as we navigated through the labyrinthine alleys.

Now, here's where the real comedy kicks in. Despite being granted a luxurious three hours of free time, the entire group unanimously decided that three hours of aimless wandering was about two hours too long. Even our guide couldn't bear to spend another minute roaming the streets.

Back on the ship, it's every man (or woman) for themselves at the Garden Café, where I promptly assembled a mountain of food fit for a hungry sailor. No reservations? No problem. I found solace in the Solo Lounge, where camaraderie flowed as freely as the beer (which, depending on your perspective, may or may not have been a good thing).

But the real magic happened at O'Sheehan's, where strangers became friends faster than you can say "bottoms up." Just when I thought the night was winding down, a siren's song lured me downstairs to the atrium, where a young songstress and the Manhattan band transformed the atmosphere from sleepy to sensational. Needless to say, I stayed and listened, completely captivated for another glorious hour. Ah, the sweet serenade of cruise ship life.

Day 11 – Livorno

The joys of a leisurely morning, where even the alarm clock struggles to rouse you from your slumber. Dragging myself out of bed at the crack of 04:30, I embarked on the epic quest for caffeine and productivity, armed with nothing but a laptop and a hearty appetite for yesterday's shenanigans.

As I sipped my coffee and typed away, I couldn't help but marvel at the nautical prowess of our captain and crew. Manoeuvring this mammoth vessel into port is no small feat—it's like watching a ballet performed by giants, with the ship gracefully pirouetting into its designated spot. And let's not forget the humble tugboats standing by, just in case the Epic decides to throw a curveball.

Speaking of size, the Norwegian Epic is a beast in its own right. Watching it dock next to smaller ships is like witnessing David vs Goliath if Goliath had a penchant for luxury cruises and oversized tenders. Seriously, the Epic's tenders could probably double as vacation homes for garden gnomes.

Now, when it comes to disembarking in Livorno, it's a choose-your-own-adventure extravaganza. Shuttle bus, taxi, or DIY car rental—take your pick. Personally, I opted for the shuttle bus, which promised a straightforward journey. Spoiler alert: finding the bus stop was a breeze, but locating the elusive ticket seller was like searching for a needle in a haystack. Ah, the joys of cruise ship logistics!

Picture this: a scene straight out of a slapstick comedy. There I was, standing in the pouring rain, scouring the docks like a lost puppy searching for its owner. Turns out, the elusive shuttle bus wasn't hiding in plain sight—it was disguised as a shelter, with the ticket seller playing a game of hide-and-seek behind a veil of rain-soaked passengers.

But wait, it gets better! When the bus finally rolled into view, it looked less like the sleek transport advertised on the big screen and more like a relic from the Jurassic era. I half-expected Fred Flintstone to step out, offering to pedal us to town on foot-powered wheels.

Now, here's the kicker: the price of admission to this soggy adventure? A mere 5 Euros. Bargain, right? Well, hold onto your raincoats because catching the last bus back is like trying to squeeze into skinny jeans after an all-you-can-eat buffet—uncomfortable and downright impossible. Trust me, you don't want to be left stranded on the docks, waving goodbye to your cruise ship like a forlorn castaway.

Livorno, the city that's like Venice's quirky cousin, except instead of gondolas, they've got cars hogging the spotlight. Picture me strolling through streets lined with canals, feeling like I'm in a poor man's version of an Italian fairytale. But hey, who needs water taxis when you've got a Fiat zooming past?

Now, if you're a history buff, Livorno's got you covered with not one but two ancient forts. Well, sort of. One's off-limits, probably guarded by a grumpy ghost or two, while the other's more like a glorified wall with a park in the middle. Not exactly a blockbuster tourist attraction, but hey, it's got character!

And let's not forget the shopping extravaganza awaiting the brave souls willing to tackle Livorno's market building. It's like stepping into a time warp, except instead of Marty McFly, you've got bargain-hunting tourists weaving through aisles of local treasures.

But here's the kicker: getting lost in Livorno is like playing a game of hide-and-seek with Mother Nature herself. Just when you think you've got it all figured out, bam! The skies open up, testing your waterproofing skills. Spoiler alert: my skin passed the test with flying colours, but my clothes? Not so much.

So, for all you lost souls out there, fear not! Just follow these foolproof tips: snap a few pics of your surroundings, befriend a local taxi driver with said pics, and always remember that the sea's never too far away. And if all else fails, just hop on an NCL tour and let someone else do the navigating.

But hey, enough of the public service announcements. Back on the ship, it's time for a wardrobe change, some grub, and, if the stars align, a cold beer in hand. Or, you know, a refreshing Pepsi. Who says you can't have a little fun in the sun, even if it's fashionably late?

Ah, the delightful pastime of lounging around and shooting the breeze with fellow cruisers, swapping tales of adventure and exhaustion. And let me tell you, the ones who've tackled Roma for the day? Well, they've earned themselves a gold medal in the Olympic sport of sightseeing. Seriously, it's like running a marathon in flip-flops.

But hey, enough about the Olympic-level tourism. Let's talk dinner. Tonight's culinary adventure? Italian style, baby! So, I dusted off my finest duds, which, let's be honest, have been chilling in the closet, waiting for their moment to shine.

Now, finding the restaurant was a bit like navigating a maze, especially with the Garden Café tempting me at every turn. But once I made it, oh boy, what a view! Front row seats to the ship's grand exit from the port, with a side of pasta? Sign me up!

But here's the kicker: despite the food being top-notch, the service was playing hard to get. I mean, I practically had to wave semaphore flags to get a drink! At one point, I even dropped a subtle reminder that I had a departure date looming, and voila! Suddenly, food appeared faster than you could say "Bon appétit!"

With dinner conquered, it was off to O'Sheehan's for a nightcap and some tunes courtesy of Summer Breeze. Spoiler alert: they were so good, I ended up staying 'til the cows came home. Or, you know, until my head started spinning like a tilt-a-whirl.

But the real kicker? As I sauntered back to my cabin, a horrifying cacophony assaulted my eardrums. Karaoke. And let me tell you, it sounded like someone was trying to perform a duet with a dying walrus. Note to NCL: a warning sign outside the Bliss lounge might just save some eardrums from certain destruction.

And with that, it was lights out and off to dreamland. Ah, the sweet embrace of sleep awaits.

Day 12 – Cannes

Ah, the eternal struggle with the dawn chorus, also known as the 4 AM wake-up call. But today, I emerged victorious in the battle of the blankets and claimed an extra hour of precious slumber. Take that, morning!

Once I pried myself from the clutches of my cosy cocoon, it was off to my caffeine sanctuary for a dose of liquid motivation. And what do you know, the breakfast brigade greeted me with a cheerful "Fashionably late, I see!" Ah, nothing like a bit of sarcasm to kickstart the day.

Now, onto today's escapade: Cannes! And let me tell you, it's a tale of two ships and a sea of fellow cruisers. But fear not, for we're embarking on a tender adventure! So, take your time with breakfast, or if you're like me and your beauty sleep is non-negotiable, hit that snooze button with gusto.

The tender experience, where you can truly feel like a seafaring explorer. Just wait for your designated time slot, then make your grand descent to Deck 4, aka the loading dock. And here's a pro tip: timing is everything! Aim for the tender's doorway like a boss and avoid an impromptu dip in the ocean. But hey, if you're feeling daring, there's always the option for a salty splash!

Once ashore, the world is your oyster! No need for taxis or buses; we're hoofing it, baby! And what better destination than Palm Beach? Soak in the sights, snap those brag-worthy photos, and burn off yesterday's buffet bonanza in style. Just watch out for those pesky pay-to-pee toilets along the way. Ah, the joys of French hospitality!

A good tip for you on this little walk is to take some change with you as most public toilets in France you have to pay to use at the cost of 50 cents. However, there are a couple of free ones and even a free public WC situated near the Little Train stop halfway along the seafront; I found this one by accident.

Joys of navigating foreign lands in search of basic necessities! Here I am, with a bladder full to bursting, attempting to charm my way into purchasing some sweet relief in the form of ice cream in an attempt to get change. Ah, the things we do for comfort!

But alas, my quest for restroom redemption hit a snag when I stumbled upon an "out of order" sign. Cue the frantic waddle as I hobbled another 20 meters in a desperate bid to find sanctuary. My daughter's disapproving growl echoed in my mind as I finally stumbled upon a free WC. Victory!

As I strolled the streets, hoping to rub elbows with the rich and famous, reality hit me like a soggy baguette to the face. The only celebrity sighting I encountered was my own reflection in a shop window. Ah, the life of a self-proclaimed superstar!

But fear not, fellow travellers, for Cannes has more to offer than just failed star-gazing attempts. Dive into the bustling town centre, where narrow streets weave a tapestry of shopping and dining delights. And if you're lucky, you might stumble upon the local market, where even the octopi are staging daring escapes! Go, Octy, go!

For breathtaking views and Insta-worthy snapshots, make your ascent to the castle on the hill. Trust me, the panoramic vistas of Cannes and its coastline are worth every step. Just be sure to watch out for rogue cephalopods on the loose!

The glamorous Cannes excursion was a whirlwind of splendour, but now it's back to reality aboard the Norwegian Epic. The ship looms majestically on the horizon, beckoning with promises of cold beer and sunshine-soaked decks. But first, a minor obstacle: 192 steps to conquer.

With each step, I ascended closer to beer nirvana, but by the time I reached the summit, I resembled a crazed marathon runner gasping for air. Oxygen supply? Nowhere in sight. But fear not, for where there's a will to drink, there's always a way. Cheers to resourcefulness!

Just as I was about to indulge in my hard-earned brew, fate intervened in the form of a young woman named Love, who, ironically, served wine. A beer conundrum ensued, but in the spirit of adventure (and thirst), rules were bent, and a beer was procured. Thanks, Love, for the liquid rebellion!

After a refreshing salad (and a gentle scolding for past floor lounging antics), it was time to dive back into the ship's bustling activities. With endless entertainment options, there's never a dull moment aboard the Epic. Who knows what hilarity awaits around the next corner? Time to find out!

Ah, the glamorous life of rubbing elbows with ship officers at the Captain's VIP Cocktail party! I fired off questions left and right, like a rapid-fire round of Cruise Trivia, only to be met with promises of replies that floated away like lost balloons at a birthday party. But fear not, for the hero of the hour emerged in the form of the Shore Excursions Manager, Irvine, who swooped in with answers obtained through what can only be described as email acrobatics. Bravo, Irvine, for your epic customer service acrobatics! As for the elusive Food & Beverage Manager, well, the waiting game continues.

After a cheeky power nap to recover from the whirlwind of socialising, it was time for the Solo Gathering, where solo cruisers unite for an hour of camaraderie and laughs. Nothing like a group therapy session for solo travellers to share tales of adventure and mishaps on the high seas.

But enough chit-chat, it was time to indulge in round two at Cagney's. From soup to steak, with a side of kitchen theatrics, the meal was a culinary symphony of flavours and acrobatics. If those chefs moved any faster, they'd leave skid marks on the linoleum!

With a belly full of gastronomic delights, it was off for a leisurely stroll along deck 7, where the gentle rocking of the ship and the twinkling stars above provided the perfect backdrop for post-feast contemplation.

As the night wore on, the party continued with visits to Bliss Lounge and O'Sheehan's, where entertainment flowed like the ship's complimentary cocktails. Ah, the joys of cruising, where every night holds the promise of new adventures and unexpected delights!

Day 13 – Palma

Ah, the joys of a leisurely morning on the high seas, where time moves at a pace slower than a sloth on vacation. Palma can wait, darling! We've got coffees to sip and wallets to empty before we hit shore. But hey, who's complaining? Not me, not when it means I can stretch out the ol' holiday budget a little further.

So, the morning ritual begins with a pilgrimage to O'Sheehan's for the sacred ceremony of morning coffee. And lo and behold, Sandy, the coffee connoisseur from yesterday, joins the party, making it a regular caffeine-fueled rendezvous. Who knew morning coffee could lead to such charming encounters?

But let's not forget the most important meal of the day: breakfast at the Garden Café, where I feast like a king overlooking the vast expanse of the Mediterranean. And amidst the serenity, a flock of birds flies by, squawking their gratitude for the passing cruise ship. "Thank the heavens, we're saved from this exhausting flight!" they seem to cry. Ah, the wonders of avian humour!

But alas, my morning stroll is rudely interrupted by the invasion of Bollywood. H2O, my sanctuary of serenity, is transformed into a chaotic film set, complete with equipment blocking my path like obstacles in a Mario Kart race. And to top it off, a cheeky cameraman has the audacity to aim his lens in my direction. Oh no, my friend, you don't want to capture this face without permission. I'll have you filming from angles you never knew existed!

And just when I thought things couldn't get any more absurd, I stumble upon the mysteries of wheelchair rentals and oxygen leases. I wonder if they return the oxygen at the end of the hire period? Is there a giant vacuum sucking up used oxygen somewhere on the ship? And what's with all the ambulances at every port? Ah, the mysteries of cruise life, where even the mundane becomes a comedy of errors!

The frenzy of disembarkation day in Palma, where everyone's rushing off the ship like it's a Black Friday sale and the cameras are ready to capture every awkward moment. But fear not, my fellow cruisers, for there are plenty of ways to escape the chaos and explore this sunny paradise.

First off, we've got the tried-and-true shore excursions arranged by NCL, complete with guides, security, and the assurance that you won't end up stranded on the dock like a lost seagull. Because let's face it, missing the boat would be a Titanic-sized disaster.

Then there's the option of hopping on the Shuttle bus, where tickets are sold by the friendly faces of NCL—well, maybe not the ones who blocked the rear of the ship, but we'll let that slide. For a mere $15 round trip, you'll be whisked away to Palma in just 10 minutes, leaving you with ample time to frolic in the streets like a carefree tourist.

But for the adventurous souls (or those looking to burn off those buffet-induced calories), there's always the option to walk. Yes, you heard me right—put on those walking shoes and strut your stuff for a leisurely one-hour stroll to Palma Cathedral. Sure, it's a bit of a trek, but think of the photo ops! And hey, you can always justify that extra drink (or two) by reminding yourself that you'll have to walk back. Unless, of course, you're sneaky enough to snag a taxi—but shh, that'll be our little secret.

The age-old dilemma of getting back on board: risk the eternal wait for the lifts or embark on a Mount Everest-esque climb up the 192 steps to food and drink heaven on deck 15. Because let's be real, after being away from the ship for a whopping 4 ½ hours, you're practically on the brink of starvation.

Not one to gamble with my grumbling stomach, I opted for the early bird approach and headed back a good hour and a half before crunch time. But did I take the easy lift route? Oh no, not me. I decided to tackle those 192 steps like a glutton for punishment because, apparently, my idea of a relaxing vacation involves a Stairmaster workout.

Finally reaching the summit, gasping for air like a fish out of water, I made a beeline for the nearest oasis of liquid oxygen—the Wave Bar. But alas, my plans for a refreshing beer were thwarted by the presence of the film crew, still lingering like a bad smell on the last day of the cruise. Talk about a buzzkill.

Refuelling with a small snack at the Garden Café, I couldn't resist the siren call of the Chinese restaurant for one last hurrah. Sure, I may have chickened out of facing the wrath of the Maître D for not returning sooner, but hey, who can resist top-notch food and service? Certainly not this hungry cruiser.

Ah, the best-laid plans of cruisers often go awry, as evidenced by my failed attempt at a simple coffee (fine, beer) outing to the Solo Lounge. But hey, when life gives you unexpected detours, just roll with it, right? So, there I was, stuck in the Solo Lounge for what felt like an eternity, mingling with my fellow solo sailors and inadvertently discovering the joys of impromptu socialising.

Of course, all that chatting worked up an appetite, leading me to yet another gastronomic adventure at the Garden Café. Because why settle for one excellent meal when you can have two. Am I right? Fully satiated, I waddled over to O'Sheehan's for some post-feast entertainment.

Little did I know, I was in for a treat—a show called "Family Feuds" (or as we know it across the pond, "Family Fortunes"). But wait, plot twist! The host had the wrong answer sheet, turning the game into a hilarious game of mismatched responses. It was like watching a comedy of errors unfold right before my eyes.

With my sides thoroughly split from laughter, I decided to cap off the night with a visit to the Headliners Club for some duelling pianos action. Now, don't get me wrong, it's a blast the first couple of times. But after a while, you start to notice the subtle behind-the-scenes antics. Ever catch them sneaking peeks at the song requests and slyly discarding the ones they don't fancy? It's like witnessing a musical magic trick with a side of recycled jokes and tunes. But hey, who am I to rain on their piano parade? It's all in good fun, right?

The final frontier of cruise life: packing up the memories and shoving them back into your suitcase. Why anyone would voluntarily lug their own luggage off the ship is beyond me. I mean, come on, we're on vacation, not auditioning for a strongman competition.

But hey, to each their own. Maybe they enjoy the added challenge of schlepping their bags around like a backpacking champ. Who needs the gym when you can get a full-body workout just trying to manoeuvre through the buffet line with a suitcase in tow?

Now, onto the great luggage label quest. According to the Freestyle Daily, I was supposed to snag some grey tags for my bags. Easy peasy, right?

Wrong. Those elusive tags were nowhere to be found. It was like hunting for buried treasure, except the booty was a set of luggage tags, and the map led straight to confusion.

Off to the Customer Service Desk, I trotted, ready to unleash my best-puzzled passenger routine. Lo and behold, turns out there was a glitch in the matrix. No record of my transfer arrangements? No problem! A quick shuffle of papers and voila, I emerged victorious with tags in hand.

Thus, with bags tagged and ready to roll, I bid adieu to the chaos of packing and embraced the promise of disembarkation day, where adventures awaited—assuming I didn't accidentally cartwheel off the gangway with my overstuffed suitcase in tow.

Day 14 – Barcelona Disembarkation Day

Ah, the grand finale of the cruise, where the body decides it's time to rise and shine at the ungodly hour of 4:00 AM. I swear, if my internal clock had a snooze button, I'd be pounding it like a contestant on a game show.

But hey, what's a cruise without a morning pilgrimage to the sacred coffee shrine at O'Sheehan's? I offered my heartfelt thanks to the coffee gods (a.k.a. the crew) before embarking on a breakfast adventure fit for a swine connoisseur. Yep, today's menu featured a delightful array of bacon-laden delights that would make a cardiologist weep.

Joined by Sandy, my faithful coffee companion, we embarked on the waiting game for our turn to disembark. Ah, the joys of anticipation, where time stretches longer than a marathon runner's leg muscles. But fear not, for NCL had a cunning plan to keep us entertained: intercom announcements! Because nothing says "excitement" like the dulcet tones of a disembodied voice summoning you to freedom.

And let's not forget the thrilling quest to retrieve our stashed wine treasures. Like archaeologists excavating ancient artefacts, we ventured to the towel area in search of our prized bottles. Armed with nothing but a crumpled piece of paper (because losing it would be akin to losing the Holy Grail), we exchanged our token for a glorious bottle of red, sealing the deal with the finesse of a seasoned negotiator.

Thus, with coffee consumed, bacon savoured, and wine secured, we awaited the final chapter of our seafaring saga, ready to bid adieu to the floating paradise and return to the land of alarm clocks and rush-hour traffic. But fear not, for the memories—and perhaps a lingering caffeine buzz—would sustain us until our next nautical escapade.

Ah, the joys of disembarkation day, where the excitement of the journey's end collides head-on with the harsh reality of airport purgatory. My letter, delivered with all the subtlety of a slap in the face, decreed that my grand exit from the ship would occur at the ungodly hour of 8:15 AM. "But why, oh why?" I pondered as I stared mournfully at the digits on my clock, silently mourning the lost hours of precious sleep.

Yes, you heard it right, folks. NCL had a knack for scheduling departures with all the finesse of a blindfolded juggler attempting a three-ring circus act. With my flight back to the UK not scheduled until the distant future of 20:20, I faced the prospect of a ten-hour marathon through the labyrinthine halls of Barcelona airport. Fun times, right?

And don't even get me started on those supposedly convenient airport drop-offs from tours. Sure, they'll whisk you away from the ship with all the efficiency of a getaway car, but what's the trade-off? A leisurely midday arrival at the airport, leaving you with a mere eight hours to twiddle your thumbs and contemplate the meaning of life amidst duty-free perfume samples.

But fear not, dear readers, for I am not one to wallow in airport woes without offering a solution. Behold, my brilliant suggestion: let's ditch the vague departure times and opt for drop-off times instead. Imagine the possibilities! With a clear window of opportunity, passengers can plan their flights with military precision or seize the day with impromptu airport adventures. It's a win-win, folks.

The infamous Barcelona airport is a place where freedom is but a distant dream, and bureaucracy reigns supreme. Once you step through those customs gates, you're entering a realm of rules and regulations that would make even the most seasoned traveller quiver in their flip-flops. It's like being trapped in a high-stakes game of airport limbo: how low can you go before you're stuck in gate purgatory for all eternity?

And let me tell you, dear readers, venturing into the forbidden land of the gate area is not for the faint of heart. Once you cross that threshold, there's no turning back. It's like stepping into a black hole of duty-free temptation, where time stands still, and your flight status becomes a distant memory. Trust me, I speak from experience—three hours of my life disappeared faster than a duty-free bargain on clearance.

But fear not, for every cloud has a silver lining, and mine came in the form of Kathy and Patty, my fellow comrades-in-delay. We bonded over shared tales of touristic adventures gone awry and turned our gate confinement into a makeshift party zone. Who needs in-flight entertainment when you've got witty banter and airport snacks? Am I right?

Eventually, after what felt like an eternity but was probably just a really long layover, I found myself winging my way to London Gatwick. Of course, the journey wasn't without its own set of hurdles—thanks, British weather—but at least the promise of a cosy hotel room at the Hamptons awaited me, conveniently located just a stone's throw (or a tired shuffle) away from the departure lounge. And lo and behold, even in the wee hours of the morning, my room awaited like a beacon of hope in a sea of airport chaos. They say home is where the heart is, but after that ordeal, home was wherever there was a bed and a hot shower.

Conclusion

The highs and lows of cruising—like a rollercoaster ride through a sea of buffet lines and deck chairs. But fear not, dear readers, for I have tales to tell and laughs to share from my recent escapade aboard the good ship Epic.

First off, let's talk ports of call—because who doesn't love a good ol' fashioned shore excursion? Vigo and Lisbon were like hidden gems, shining brightly amidst a sea of overcrowded tourist traps. The tour in Lisbon was so good that it nearly knocked my socks off—the second-best excursion I've ever had with NCL, and that's saying something!

Now, let's raise a glass to the unsung heroes of the high seas—the crew. These folks are like ninjas in crisp white uniforms, silently ensuring our every need is met with a smile. Some of them even remembered me from my last voyage over a year ago! And don't even get me started on the captain's cocktail party—I felt like royalty rubbing elbows with the officers. Next up, I'm gunning for that behind-the-scenes tour—watch out, engine room, here I come!

Ah, dining on the Epic—a culinary adventure fit for a king (or queen, or humble comedian). The dining package is a stroke of genius, offering a different gastronomic delight every night. Sure, I had to cancel a few reservations due to conflicting schedules with my nightly binge-watching of onboard infomercials and talent shows, but hey, that's the price you pay for being a cruise connoisseur.

And let's not forget the watering holes—because what's a cruise without a few cheeky cocktails? Shoutout to Adi, the MVP of the H2O bar, who greets everyone with a warm smile and a memory like a steel trap. I swear, he knew my drink order before I did—now that's service!

Entertainment-wise, the Epic truly lives up to its name. "Priscilla Queen of the Desert" was a spectacle to behold—although I'm pretty sure my rendition of "It's Raining Men" during karaoke night stole the show.

Last but not least, a tip of the hat to Park West—the art gallery onboard where beauty and intelligence collide. The Park West team are like art aficionados with a dash of charm, always ready to chat about brush strokes and colour palettes. And let's not forget the stunning ladies on display—proof that beauty and brains go hand in hand.

Well, folks, that's all from me for now. Until next time, may your seas be calm and your cocktails be bottomless! Cheers to the next adventure!

The Big 45 Day Solo Adventure

Day 1

Ahoy, fellow travellers! The big adventure has commenced—a 44-day cruise from the Caribbean through the Panama Canal all the way to Alaska. It's like an epic quest, but with more sunscreen and fewer dragons. Unlike my last solo escapade, this one involves a mini-Odyssey just to board the ship. Several days of travel to meet the Norwegian Getaway in sunny Miami, which is a bit like Frodo travelling from the Shire to Mordor, but with more sunburn and fewer magical rings.

After waving a teary goodbye to the children and the grandchildren (who seemed a bit too eager to see me off, if you ask me), I took a short drive to Southampton Coach Station. There, I embarked on the thrilling combo of two coach trips, culminating in my arrival at the Sheraton Skyway Hotel at Heathrow Airport for the night.

Now, let's discuss this "impressive" hotel. It boasts a Sky Bar. Naturally, I imagined it perched high atop the building, with sweeping views of the tarmac. Nope! The Sky Bar is actually on the ground floor, right behind reception. The only thing sky-high about it is the misleading name. It's like naming a basement dive bar "Cloud Nine."

The Sky Bar itself features a small swimming pool with a bar plonked in the centre, surrounded by palm trees and comfy seats, all enclosed under a glass roof. It's like a tropical paradise—if tropical paradises came with a front desk and a view of the airport shuttle.

Just as I envisioned myself lounging with a cold drink in hand, I discovered the bar doesn't open until 18:00. Foiled! Instead, I settled for a coffee from the conveniently located Starbucks in the reception area. Nothing screams "exotic vacation" like a lukewarm latte.

Feeling hungry? The hotel offers several restaurants, but if you're anything like me and prefer not to shell out £10 for a burger, rejoice! There's a McDonald's just a five-minute walk away. Yes, folks, when luxury beckons, there's always a Big Mac to answer the call.

And let's talk breakfast. The Full English breakfast is priced at an eye-watering £18.00. Eighteen quid for some beans on toast and a sausage? I think not! Another visit to McDonald's in the morning, methinks. Good news: it's open 24/7. Because when you're setting sail on a 44-day cruise, nothing says "bon voyage" like a McMuffin at sunrise.

The appointed time for the Sky Bar to open had finally graced us with its presence, like the arrival of a long-lost friend who owes you money. It was time for a relaxing drink by the palm trees and pool. I opted for a small bottle of London Pride Bitter, which turned out to be a posh way of saying "expensive thimble of beer." Fifteen minutes of doing absolutely nothing but watching the world spin by followed, which, let's be honest, is the dream.

Now, you'd think that for £5.50 a bottle, they'd throw in a gold-plated coaster or a complimentary yacht ride, but alas, it was just the one bottle for me. Budget blown, I reluctantly pried myself away from my luxurious vantage point and headed for the Sports Bar, which flung open its doors at the gentlemanly hour of 18:00.

The Sports Bar is a delightful spot to sip a drink solo or with friends while basking in the glow of numerous large TV screens. Naturally, they're all playing sports because what else would a sports bar show? The local weather report? Unfortunately, the other end of the bar is reserved for dining only, which is a bit like dangling a giant carrot in front of a rabbit and then saying, "Sorry, this is for the diners only, mate."

In an act of sheer desperation, I asked if a bag of crisps qualified me to sit in the dining area. The answer was a resounding no, crisps being the unworthy peasants in the kingdom of meals. Clearly, the hotel should rebrand this area as a restaurant where you can sip your overpriced drink in a tiny, cramped space while glaring at the empty dining area just out of reach.

The food did look tempting, though slightly overpriced, and I might have considered it if I hadn't witnessed the chef licking his fingers before artfully arranging customer plates. Decidedly, I stuck to my crisps and my principles.

With a long day ahead, I opted for an early night in my exceptionally cosy room. The bed felt like it was crafted by celestial beings out of clouds and angel whispers. I lay down, feeling like a king, or at least like someone who'd successfully navigated the treacherous waters of cruise ship bars without completely bankrupting myself.

Day 2 - Heathrow – Miami Saturday

It was either pure excitement or my body clock still stuck on Home time, but I found myself bright-eyed and bushy-tailed at the ungodly hour of 04:00. Far too early to head to the airport, I decided to take a stroll toward the 24-hour McDonald's. Now, this decision was a no-brainer: shell out £18.00 for a hotel breakfast or snag a dead pig sandwich at McDonald's for £3.49. It's simple math, really.

When the time came to check out of the hotel, the process was blissfully straightforward. You could either drop your room key in a dedicated box or leave it on the reception desk. Naturally, I chose the old-fashioned route, chatting up the receptionist to reclaim my cash deposit. It's nice to see that in this age of plastic, cash still has a role beyond just filling tip jars and Christmas stockings.

Transportation to the airport was courtesy of the Hotel Hopper bus, run by National Express. To keep things easy, the Sheraton has a handy ticket machine right in the reception area, available at any time during your stay. The journey itself was a breezy 15 minutes, and despite my grim expectations of lengthy security queues, I was pleasantly surprised to find myself lounging with a coffee within the hour.

Modern travel has its perks, one of them being the automated check-in kiosks. These beauties print boarding passes and luggage labels faster than you can say, "Why isn't my flight on time?" This marvel of technology leaves you with extra time to explore the airport, which, in my case, means locating the nearest duty-free shop and convincing myself I need another bottle of cologne.

All in all, it's not a bad start to the day for someone who began it contemplating the virtues of a McMuffin at an hour when most sane people are still dreaming about winning the lottery.

Boarding was a swift affair, but British Airways, in their infinite wisdom and concern for your cardiovascular health, decided to place the boarding gate at a distance that made me question if they were secretly training us for a marathon. Bravo, BA! Nothing like a good sprint to get the blood pumping before a nine-hour sit-a-thon.

As a proud member of the BA Executive Club, I was among the first to board despite being relegated to the last row of cattle class. Strangely, the second person to board in cattle class plopped down right next to me. Now, let's talk about Economy class. Unless you've been on a hunger strike for six months or you're a five-year-old child, these seats make you question the concept of personal space.

I have a dream, a simple one: to meet the person who decided on the width of economy seats and deliver a hearty slap on behalf of all air travellers. You just know this genius flies First Class, probably while laughing at our plight.

If you haven't heard, BA now offers pre-booked meals, a service for which you can pay a little extra. Before you roll your eyes and mutter "money-making scheme," let me assure you, it's worth every penny. First, you get served before everyone else, regardless of your seat. No wrestling with plastic trays and cutlery—oh no, we're talking china plates and real cutlery, like you're at a five-star restaurant that happens to be hurtling through the sky at 35,000 feet. They even let you keep the china cup, which is great because I needed another piece of dishware to add to my eclectic collection of stolen hotel shampoos and tiny soaps.

Well, I soon arrived at Miami Airport, ready to face the dreaded US Customs. True to form, British Airways had thoughtfully parked the plane as far away from Passport Control as humanly possible. Just like at Heathrow, this helpful gesture ensured that my blood circulation was in peak condition by the time I got there.

US Passport Control was its usual marathon of patience. After spending an hour zigzagging through what can only be described as sheep-control pens, I couldn't resist the urge to make some "baaar" noises. This earned me a perplexed look from a very important-looking person, but hey, sometimes you have to make your own entertainment.

When I finally reached the CBP Office for processing, it wasn't nearly as bad as those TV shows make it out to be. With that ordeal behind me and my bags in tow, I set off to find the hotel shuttle bus. Here's a pro tip: the signs in Miami Airport will attempt to mislead you to different levels. Ignore them and stay on the level you arrived on unless you fancy a scenic tour involving several escalators. I've fallen for this trick every time I've been here, so trust me on this one.

Another nugget of wisdom: when you exit the building, turn left and walk up the road a bit. Most people cluster near the door, waiting for the same bus, which fills up faster than a sale on Black Friday. By walking a little further, I managed to flag down the bus and secure a spot as the second passenger. Sure enough, when we stopped near the door, the bus filled up, and not everyone could get on. Mission accomplished, I smugly settled in for the ride, feeling like I'd outsmarted the system – or at least avoided another long wait.

The bus rolled up to the Sheraton Miami Airport within 10 minutes, and I was all set to check-in. Bags unloaded, I sauntered to the reception desk, only to be greeted by every traveller's worst nightmare: the hotel couldn't find my booking. Fantastic. Just what I needed after a long day of dodging airport escalators.

Lucky for me, I had all my paperwork. The accommodating young lady behind the desk took one look at it and disappeared into the back. She returned swiftly, problem sorted. Turns out the company that booked my room—no, not my travel company, that would be too simple and not nearly entertaining enough—Mainly Hotel Beds, had cancelled and then rebooked the reservation. Because why not add a little drama to my day?

If you're heading for Miami Port in the morning, here's a hot tip: the hotel offers a shuttle bus that departs several times a day for just $10. Considering a taxi costs around $25, this is a steal. You can book your spot at the Bell service desk in the lobby.

So, with my booking fiasco resolved and my shuttle plans set, I could finally relax. Well, as much as one can relax while navigating the wild world of travel logistics.

Day 3 - Miami – Norwegian Getaway Sunday

Yet again, I found myself up at sparrow's fart—or more accurately, up before any sparrows even considered the idea of getting up and farting. Thanks to the time difference, I was now nine hours behind my usual time. I decided to make the most of it, snapping photos of the hotel and then heading out for a long walk in the crisp morning air.

During my stroll, I stumbled upon a sign at the back of the hotel warning guests to stay away from the rocks along the river due to the presence of poisonous snakes and alligators. Guess who's steering clear of the rocks? That's right, this guy. Alligators, I can handle. But poisonous snakes? Hissing Sid and I are not going to be pals.

With two hours to kill before the bus to the port, I thought I'd brave the All-American Breakfast. It was your standard buffet, except they served pork scratchings instead of bacon. They called it "crispy bacon," but I wasn't fooled for a second.

The menu price was steep but not unexpected for a hotel of this calibre. However, due to the American habit of not including tax in the listed price and the seemingly mandatory tipping for everything, including breathing, the costs quickly added up. For example, breakfast was advertised at $19, but after tax and tips, it totalled $23. Makes you hesitant to hand over your bags to the driver for fear he'll expect a tip for lifting them.

Speaking of tips, I had some time to kill, so I developed a handy guide to tipping. It's free to anyone who wants one, and trust me, it's a game-changer. I'll put it in the back of this book.

Much like the Sheraton at Heathrow, the checkout process here was a breeze. In just a couple of minutes, I was done and my cash deposit was returned with no questions asked. All in all, a successful, if early, start to the day.

All aboard the bus for a short hop to Miami Port to meet our floating home for the next week: the Norwegian Getaway. The NCL check-in system was its usual efficient self, whisking us through security and check-in in a breezy 30 minutes. We then found ourselves seated in the waiting room, twiddling our thumbs and wondering if we'd accidentally signed up for a waiting contest. Must admit, this was a bit longer than usual, probably because the Norwegian Getaway is so enormous it could double as a small country.

After a brief two-hour wait (yes, brief in cruise terms), we finally shuffled up the gangway. The first thing that hits you is the sheer size of this ship. Walking down one side feels like a marathon. Compared to this, the Norwegian Epic looks like a bathtub toy, and trust me, that's saying something—I've sailed on her three times.

Since staterooms weren't ready upon boarding, it was time to explore. Camera in hand, I set off to find my favourite spot on Norwegian ships: the H2O Adults Only Bar, usually located at the rear. This turned into quite the scavenger hunt, as the entrance is hidden through a sliding door at the back of the Flamingo Bar and Grill. After what felt like several laps around the ship, I finally found it.

Now, you'd think a bar advertised as "Adults Only" would, you know, only have adults. But no, it was swarming with more kids than a daycare. Either NCL has installed some kind of age-reversing machine, or they've decided to interpret "Adults Only" as a suggestion rather than a rule. Seriously, NCL, if you're not going to enforce the adults-only rule, are there any other rules we can ignore onboard? Asking for a friend.

After a few beers to dull the frustration, I set off to find the Solo accommodation and lounge. This proved to be another adventure, as the entrance is tucked away down a corridor rather than off the main area. But persistence paid off, and I found my cosy little solo retreat.

The adventure had just begun, and already it was proving to be an entertaining mix of hide-and-seek and survival of the fittest. Here's to a week of cruising, Norwegian style!

Just to check if my stateroom was ready, I tried my card in the door. No dice. The door stayed stubbornly shut, so I decided to continue my exploration.

Speaking of accommodation, one thing I really appreciate about the Getaway is how they've hidden the Haven suites. On the Epic, the Haven sticks out like a sore thumb—like someone built a mansion in the middle of a theme park. Here, it's tucked away, out of sight, and much easier on the eyes. Kudos to NCL for that one.

I took a leisurely stroll around 678 Ocean Place, which lives up to the hype. It's worth wandering through all three decks. The layout of La Bistro is particularly charming—I could almost imagine I was in Paris, minus the constant honking and the risk of stepping into something unpleasant. NCL has also brought back the Waterfront, which I love. It offers a relaxing atmosphere perfect for a quiet walk or a drink while watching the world float by.

If you're like me, you can now enjoy a walk around three-quarters of the ship or just park yourself at one of the many bars along the Waterfront. It's a lovely spot to sip a cocktail and pretend you're the star of a glamorous travel ad.

Of course, being a former safety officer, I couldn't help but notice a few frayed and improperly tied secondary retention ropes on the lifeboats during my wanderings. These wouldn't pass any audit on Lifting & Securing Regulations. Sorry, once a safety officer, always a safety officer. But don't let my nitpicking detract from the fact that this is an awe-inspiring ship.

So, here's to more exploring, more drinks, and hopefully finding my way into my stateroom before the next ice age. Cheers!

I made my way to the Mojito Bar, thinking I'd start slow with an orange juice topped with a splash of Southern Comfort. But the bartender had other ideas. Passionate about his craft, he soon had me sampling a variety of Mojitos. I'm glad he did because I discovered a new favourite drink I'd never have tried on my own. If you're on your first cruise and using the drinks package, throw caution to the wind and experiment. What have you got to lose besides your balance?

Eventually, my bag started giving me the cold shoulder, insisting it was time to find the cabin. Reluctantly, I tore myself away from the bar and headed for my stateroom. Tried the key again—no luck. Just before marching to the Customer Service desk to demand a functional key, I double-checked my paperwork. Good thing I did. Turns out this idiot had been trying to break into the wrong stateroom for the past two hours.

I finally found the right door, tried my key, and voilà, I was in! This is where NCL's extraordinary service shined. Awaiting me were not one, but two bottles of sparkling wine, complete with chocolate-covered strawberries. And wait, there's more! They'd left toiletries usually reserved for Haven guests, plus Haven slippers and a dressing gown. Thanks, NCL, you really know how to make a person feel special.

Having been on the ship for several hours without a bite to eat, I was beginning to feel like I might waste away. Off to the Flamingo Bar and Grill I went. The food there is excellent and worth the visit—not just to satisfy hunger but also to soak up some of the alcohol, which, if you're like me, is flowing more freely than usual.

So, here's to Mojitos, unexpected luxuries, and not starving to death on day one. Cheers!

Time for the compulsory lifeboat drill, so like a good little cruiser, I headed off to the Muster station in the Getaway Theatre. This training is mandatory for everyone on board, even if you're a cruise veteran with hundreds of voyages under your belt. Skipping it is a one-way ticket to being unceremoniously booted off at the next port.

I have to admit; after the lacklustre muster drill on my last cruise aboard the Norwegian Epic, this emergency lifeboat drill was a breath of fresh sea air. The muster station leader did a fantastic job, dispensing a treasure trove of vital information. I now feel well-prepared for any emergency at sea. Kudos to the muster station leader!

That said, I'm still a bit foggy on what to do in case of an emergency while we're in port. Do I casually stroll down the gangway onto the docks, achieving instant safety while I watch everyone else scramble to their muster stations? Or do I hike up several decks only to come back down again because, you know, safety first?

Either way, it's nice to know that if the ship does decide to take an unexpected dive, I'll be well-prepared. For now, I think I'll stick to my own emergency plan: locate the nearest bar, order a drink, and hope for the best. Cheers to safety drills and the mysterious ways of maritime emergency protocols!

Today was a no-plan day, perfect for more exploring aboard the fantastic Getaway. I discovered my new favourite evening spot: the Waterfront. It's the perfect place to sit back, relax, and watch the sunset over the horizon, even better than the Sunset Bar. The only downside? Smokers who think that just because they're outside, they have a free pass to turn the air into their personal ashtray.

After a pleasant evening dodging secondhand smoke, I decided it was time to retire to my stateroom and enter the world of nod. For some reason, I decided to use the Interactive TV in the room. Checking my account, I discovered that despite having a drinks package, there were charges for my drinks. They were small amounts, mostly tax, but still. Customer Service will be hearing from me in the morning.

For anyone on their first NCL cruise or even planning one, let me tell you: the interactive TV in your room is a godsend. It's not just for watching TV; you can do everything from booking excursions and dining reservations to snagging entertainment spots, all from the comfort of your stateroom. So don't follow the herd to the lobby—channel your inner lazy genius and handle your plans with a few clicks.

And with that, it's off to bed. Sweet dreams of sunsets and smoke-free zones.

Day 4 - Great Stirrup Caye

Well, it's started again—the epic showdown between Body and Brain. Picture this: it's 02:00, and the Body decides it's time to haul itself out of bed. Brain, ever the sensible one, is yelling, "Stay in bed for at least another couple of hours, you fool!" But Body, the stubborn mule, is already halfway to the shower before Brain can catch up. Score one for Body. So, I found myself heading to customer services at this ungodly hour to sort out those pesky charges on my account.

The accommodating lady at the desk quickly explained the charges, pointing an accusatory finger at the American Tax Man. Apparently, the U.S. government applies these charges on all purchases until the ship leaves American waters. Here's a tip: don't be tempted to buy anything until you're out in international waters unless you enjoy donating to Uncle Sam.

Another great tip? If you need to talk to someone in Customer Services, get up early. And by early, I mean before 05:00. The desk is staffed 24/7, and I've never encountered a queue at that time. Your questions are answered quickly and professionally without the hassle of waiting in line.

So, there you have it. Body won this morning's battle, but Brain is planning a cunning counterattack involving a nap later. Stay tuned for the next thrilling installment of Body vs. Brain.

Still hours until breakfast, and the ship is a ghost town except for the hard-working cleaning staff who move like silent ninjas with mops. Perfect time to snap those all-important photos of the ship's interior without someone's Uncle Bob photobombing your masterpiece. If all this sneaky photo-taking makes you hungry and thirsty, you're in luck—O'Sheehan's restaurant is open 24/7.

Taking my own advice, I made a pit stop at O'Sheehan's for a cup of coffee. I found a nice server and asked for a cup of joe. Her reply? "The coffee machine is behind the counter; help yourself." Great, a DIY coffee experience. The floor was wet, and I had flashbacks of that time on the Epic when some genius turned off the deck lights, and I twisted my ankle. So, I did my best impersonation of a penguin on ice and carefully shuffled over to the machine.

I considered asking for breakfast but quickly nixed the idea, fearing I'd be handed a chef's hat and pointed to the kitchen. I decided to wait until 06:00 when the Garden Café opens—a safer bet than O'Sheehan's DIY culinary adventure.

Finally, 06:00 rolled around, and it was time for breakfast at the Garden Café. One of the best things about eating here is you can have breakfast just the way you want it, without the risk of having to cook it yourself. No more playing chef at O'Sheehan's; just pure, unadulterated breakfast bliss.

Breakfast consumed, and I had a couple of hours to kill before my first grand adventure of the cruise—a wave runner/Jet Ski tour of Great Stirrup Cay. The ticket stated the meeting point was in the Getaway Theatre at 08:45, but the ship's PA system kept announcing that anyone with an excursion could get off the ship anytime. A bit of a mixed message, right? Personally, I preferred waiting for the tender boats to arrive rather than launching myself overboard.

Great Stirrup Cay, NCL's private island in the Bahamas, requires the ship to anchor offshore and send tender boats to ferry us beach-seeking landlubbers to paradise.

Still baffled by the conflicting instructions—ticket says theatre, PA says go ashore—I decided to embrace my inner explorer and hopped on a tender boat for the short ride to the island. Once I landed on the white sandy shores, the mystery unravelled: the Shore Excursions Desk and the actual meeting point were on the island.

Pro tip: if you have a tour at Great Stirrup Cay, as soon as the ship drops anchor, get off and head to the island pronto. This way, you avoid the long wait for the tender boats later and get more time to soak up the Bahamian sun.

With an hour and a half to kill before the wave runner tour, I had plenty of time to explore the island. This all-inclusive private island concept, pioneered by NCL, is sheer brilliance. Other cruise lines are catching on, like Royal Caribbean with their private island, which is a quarter the size of NCL's. Imagine cramming 4000-plus cruisers onto a tiny island—talk about cosy. But I digress, back to Great Stirrup Cay.

The island is essentially an all-inclusive resort if you have the drinks package. You can do everything from lying on the beach doing absolutely nothing but perfecting your sun-worshipping skills to jet skiing and parasailing for the more adventurous. With lifeguards everywhere, it's a safe spot for the whole family, whether you're swimming or exploring the underwater world with a snorkel.

Finally, the moment arrived for the much-anticipated Wave Runner tour—a first for little old me. After filling out a mountain of waiver forms, we were led to the other side of the island to fill out even more forms. The tour description mentioned that drivers must have a valid license, but nobody ever checked. Paperwork complete and the all-important safety video watched, we were lined up by experience. If you thought this meant anything, you'd be as wrong as I was. Once on the pier and issued our jet skis, all semblance of order flew out the window.

If you expected a gentle ride around the islands, think again. This was a fast, thrill-seeking adventure regardless of your experience level. The guides were fantastic, giving a quick intro to the jet skis before we took off. Each group had several guides, and we followed the leader in a single file. Not to brag, but when I glanced at the speedometer, I was zipping across the open sea at 50 mph. We made a quick stop halfway through to learn about the local area, then it was back to full speed, bouncing over waves and loving every second.

This adventure was definitely not for the faint-hearted, but it was exhilarating. Just remember, if you're signing up for a wave runner tour, leave your gentle expectations on the ship and prepare for a high-speed thrill ride.

This tour is recommended to anyone no matter the level of experience you will have fun; the tour lasts for about 1 ½ hour, so plenty of time to try out other activities on the island later.

What day on the beach would be complete without a BBQ? Or, if you're feeling fancy, a full lunch buffet? No worries—NCL has you covered. They've relocated their chefs to the island for the day, armed with enough food and equipment to satisfy any appetite.

Here's another tip: during lunch hours, the BBQs, buffets, and bars get busier than a beehive in summer. Head to the far end of the island and the lagoon, where the queues are smaller, but the service is just as top-notch. Plus, if you're cruising with small children, the lagoon is a safe place for them to swim and play, complete with its own lifeguard. It's a win-win: peace of mind for you and fun for the kiddos.

As the day wound down, it was time to head back to the ship via tender boat. The weather decided to add a touch of drama, with the sea getting a bit choppy. But don't worry—you're in the capable hands of NCL's skilled seamen. They could navigate these waters with their eyes closed (though I'd prefer they didn't). So, sit back, enjoy the ride, and maybe hold on to your hat.

Once back on board, I sought out some liquid refreshments at my (now ex-) favourite place on Norwegian ships, H2O. For the second cruise in a row, NCL showed its ugly side by closing the bar for a private party, unceremoniously kicking out all the cruisers who were enjoying their evening. Just a thought, NCL: on your next ship or refurbishment, how about installing a dedicated private party area instead of annoying paying guests?

Annoyed but undeterred, I joined other disgruntled cruisers and moved to one of the many other outside bars. A few pleasant hours were spent on the Waterfront with a few drinky poos, chatting with fellow cruisers until hunger struck. It had been ages—well, a few hours—since my last meal, and I needed a snack before the dinner/magic show at 20:45.

Early evening was spent in the Atrium. Some might think this is just where the customer service desks are located, but in reality, it's a lively hub for game shows and demonstrations. Definitely worth spending several hours here if you need a good laugh.

Then, it was time for the much-anticipated illusion magic dinner show. I arrived early to snag a prime seat at the front, along with another eager family. The appointed time came and went, with no sign of the show starting. Finally, I tracked down someone from the Box Office who was as useful as a chocolate teapot. After some prodding, he checked his computer and discovered my booking wasn't there. My paperwork said "confirmed," but apparently, that meant nothing.

Looks like I'm in for another early morning visit to the Customer Service desk. Just another day in the life of a cruiser, right?

Day 5 - A Day at Sea

Today's entry is brought to you by the mysterious void where my memory should be. That's right, folks, I left this day blank. It was a good day, I'm sure of it. But can I remember what happened? Absolutely not. Oops, my bad.

So, let's just imagine it was a day filled with sunshine, laughter, and possibly a few too many margaritas. Hey, if you're going to forget something, it might as well be something fabulous!

Day 6 - Ocho Rios

The body had won the morning battle yet again, dragging me to O'Sheehan's self-service restaurant for my morning coffee. After a cup of cold disappointment, I went in search of hotter caffeine fixes up on deck 15 and to see what weather surprises awaited us happy cruisers.

It was still dark outside, making it hard to judge the weather, but my gut told me I'd need my waterproof jacket today. Naturally, I ignored that gut feeling. Spoiler alert: I regretted it later.

This cruise had turned me into a human garbage disposal, overindulging in all the food and drink. It was time to put a little effort into exercise. The fitness room, or as I like to call it, the torture chamber, was out of the question. Apparently, every ship has one for those who forget they're on vacation and insist on punishing themselves. Personally, I've never seen one.

Good news though: on the NCL Getaway, you can walk around most of deck 15 with a small detour inside past the stairs. After an hour of walking (and dodging other early risers), I was ready for breakfast at the Garden Café.

The ship arrived in Ocho Rios at 07:30, giving me plenty of time to head to the front of the ship and watch us glide into port. One of the Getaway's significant advantages over the Epic is the excellent vantage point for snapping photos of the town of Ocho Rios, Jamaica.

The ship docks near the town, which is only a five-minute walk from the port. If organised tours aren't your thing, there are plenty of activities close by, such as local stalls selling souvenirs and beaches for relaxing under the Caribbean sun, swimming, and, of course, shopping and sightseeing in the local town.

So, as I strolled off the ship, still sans a waterproof jacket, I embraced the adventure, ready to see what Ocho Rios had to offer—whether it be sun, rain, or a perfect mix of both.

NCL organises enough tours to cover everyone's taste, and they offer the added security of knowing you'll be back on the ship before it sails—or it will wait for you. That's not a luxury you have if you go it alone. This is why I always opt for an NCL-organized tour and recommend it to everyone. Today was the day for the second organised tour of the cruise: Jamaican

Bobsleigh & Zipline. My ticket indicated a report time to the Getaway Theatre.

I tried to play my favourite game, "Spot the Tour," but I must be out of practice. I didn't guess a single one correctly—people must have actually started reading the information before booking.

NCL pulled a good one on us today. On all other ships, you enter the theatre from the top, and tours leave from the bottom near the stage. Naturally, everyone piled into the lower part of the theatre near the normal exit. The punchline? Today, we had to exit the way we came in. So, back up, we all went.

My tour was called, so with ticket, room key, and photo ID in hand, I followed the instructions from the Shore Excursions crew. Once unloaded from the ship, I made my way to the building at the Quayside/Dock, where I was given not one but two fancy wristbands before boarding the small buses for the short ride to Mystic Mountain, home of the bobsleigh ride.

At this point, I realised we hadn't been issued the usual prison number tags that we proudly wear all day so everyone knows we're from the ship and can raise their prices accordingly. The wristband is a much better idea since you only have to show it to people who need to see it.

So off we went, feeling slightly less like tagged livestock and more like adventurous tourists ready for a thrill.

Upon arrival at Mystic Mountain, we were given a brief rundown of what to expect before boarding the Sky Explorer ride. A fancy name for a chairlift to the top of the mountain, it offers fantastic views of the island and the ports. It's the perfect opportunity for a photo op of the ship in port. Today, the Getaway was joined by the Norwegian Spirit, the only two ships docked. Well played, NCL, keeping the ports to yourselves.

But I digress, back to the Sky Explorer. The ride takes about 15 minutes, and you better be ready to smile at Tower 10 because there's a camera snapping photos of your journey up. Naturally, you can buy this photo at the top for a small fortune.

Once your ride is over, you're greeted by some lovely young ladies who, depending on your tour/tours and the length of the queues, will direct you accordingly. Be prepared to do the rides in any order.

My first adventure was the Jamaican Bobsleigh ride. For those wondering, "But there's no snow in Jamaica," you're right. The bobsleigh runs down metal tracks to the bottom of the mountain. Inspired by the Jamaican Bobsleigh team and the Disney film *Cool Runnings*, you board your individual bobsleigh, though you can join them together if you prefer not to go solo.

Finally, my turn arrived. I hopped into the bobsleigh, received a quick briefing on controlling the descent (pulling the handles back to slow down), and off I went. The ride is very safe; even if you left the brakes off the whole way, you'd still arrive in one piece, albeit very quickly. You can hear all the so-called brave ones at the top boasting about not using the brakes. Trust me, they all chickened out and used them.

Only three more bobsleighs in front of me when Jamaica decided to remind us why it has a rainforest. The skies opened, and I found myself trapped in a bobsleigh, getting thoroughly soaked. Too late to turn back, I zoomed down the mountain at high speed, twisting and turning through the rain. Before you know it, you're at the bottom, drenched but exhilarated, being pulled back up to the top.

I'm not saying I got wet, but I would have stayed drier if I had jumped into the sea. The fun was highlighted by the woman in the shop who cheerfully remarked, "Welcome to the Jamaican Rain Forest." If you want a photo of your ride, there's a shot taken during your descent that you can purchase in the shop. If only I had listened to my gut earlier, I could have avoided the soaking.

Deciding I couldn't get any wetter, I headed to the Zip Line adventure, which consists of several aerial ropeways coursing down the mountain. Time for round two!

First stop: the staging area, where you are outfitted with safety harnesses and hard hats that make you look like an extra from a low-budget action movie. Two guides led us in small groups to the starting point.

Everything here screams safety—you're secured not with one but two safety devices for each thrilling zip across the wires. One guide clips you in, and the other unclips you at the landing point, which is sometimes high up in the trees, where they secure you to a safety lanyard. If you can keep your camera steady, this is prime time for some epic video footage!

The zip lines themselves weave between trees, some of which seem a bit too close for comfort but add to the thrill. This whole experience is made even more enjoyable by the guides, who not only keep you safe but also inject humour and camaraderie into the group.

Once the ride ends, you meet the Sky Explorer halfway down the mountain. From there, you can either head to the bottom or ride back to the top to enjoy more of the facilities. Just make sure you keep an eye on the clock so you don't miss the ship.

The only minor gripe I had with this tour was the tipping culture at Mystic Mountain. It seemed like everyone, including a guy standing at the bottom doing absolutely nothing, expected a tip. Even he had a bucket out for contributions. I half expected the trees to start asking for tips, too!

As I headed back to the ship, I was directed to the shuttle bus stop conveniently situated next to a cluster of local stalls selling all sorts of touristy trinkets and drinks. The bus trip was mercifully short, and getting back into the port was a breeze—just flash your room key at the security guard, and you're on your way back to the ship. A quick reminder: if you've picked up any local brew, the lovely folks at NCL will keep it safe for you until the end of the cruise. They must think we're a bunch of raging pirates otherwise.

Back on board, freshly showered and sporting dry clothes, I headed down to O'Sheehan's for a little drinky poo or two. I also needed to transfer today's video to my hard drive—preserving evidence of my daring feats and occasional misadventures.

By now, it had been six whole hours since breakfast, and I was convinced I might waste away. So, I decided to order fish and chips. What a revelation compared to the ones I had on the Norwegian Epic last November! Gone were the cheap-looking plastic baskets, replaced by stylish metal trays. The food itself was a masterpiece—crispy, golden fish and perfectly cooked chips. It just goes to show that NCL listens to customer feedback. I will definitely be having this again.

With a satisfied belly and my video safely backed up, I raised my glass to another day of cruising shenanigans. Cheers to NCL and their ever-improving fish and chips!

I stayed for more drinks than planned, which is the cruise code for "I lost count after three." Eventually, I pried myself off the seat and dropped my computer back in the stateroom, then, guided by autopilot, headed up to the Garden Café because, naturally, it was 17:00 and my stomach operates on its own time zone.

Upon arrival, I remembered I had a reservation at Ocean Blue Restaurant at 19:00. "No problem," I thought, "I'll just have a small snack." Yeah, right. Buffets are like a black hole for willpower. Before I knew it, my plate was piled high. It must have been an overzealous buffet fairy because it certainly wasn't me.

Ocean Blue is a seafood specialty restaurant, which means it comes with an extra fee—even if you have the dining package. In this case, it was an additional $17.50. The restaurant also has a fine dress code, a bit like Le Bistro's posh cousin.

Being my first visit and unable to read the dimly lit menu (seriously, who designs these things?), I was at a loss. No worries, though—the accommodating staff were on hand to help. They were so welcoming and helpful; they could've convinced me to order squid on toast, and I probably would have.

The food and service at Ocean Blue were first class. Every staff member made a point of welcoming me, making it feel like the friendliest seafood joint on the high seas. If there were an award for the best department on the ship, Ocean Blue would win hands down.

After a delicious meal, it was time to burn off some calories with a short walk. Then, it was an early night and off to the world of Nod. Just another day in paradise, filled with laughter, food, and the occasional unplanned buffet binge. Cheers!

Day 7 - Grand Cayman

Dragged my sorry butt out of bed at the ungodly hour of 04:00. After the usual morning nonsense was out of the way, I headed to O'Sheehan's for some morning coffee and to catch up on my daily write-up.

I decided to question the staff on why the coffee was cold. They pointed out that they don't start making fresh coffee until 05:30. I mentioned that O'Sheehan's is advertised as being open 24 hours, but apparently, that only applies if you're in the market for a pre-made sandwich and a cold coffee. Oh well, pass the microwave!

The ship was arriving in Grand Cayman at 08:00, so there wasn't a lot of time to spare this morning. I made a quick stop at the Garden Café for my daily dead pig feast (bacon, for the uninitiated).

The meeting point for today's excursion was, as usual, the Getaway Theatre. Cue the first game of the day: guess the tour. I must have my mojo back because I correctly guessed three tours, including one I wasn't on. NCL started the games early with a round of musical chairs without the music, moving us from seat to seat. All part of the fun, right?

Since George Town, Grand Cayman, doesn't have a large dock, everyone was taken ashore by local tender boats. It's a great way to support the local community. The tender trip was short and sweet, taking only five minutes.

For those who've never been to Grand Cayman, it's a British Overseas Territory in the sunny Caribbean. They use Cayman Island Dollars, and, good news for Brits, they drive on the left side of the road, which is, of course, the correct side of the road.

With that, I was off to explore another day in paradise, fueled by my microwave-warmed coffee and ready for whatever adventure lay ahead.

As the tender boats drop you off at the main port, which is charmingly small, you find yourself right in the middle of town. This place is a paradise for shopaholics, with plenty of local restaurants and quirky shops to explore. The town stretches along the seafront, making it the perfect spot for a leisurely walk after your organised tours.

Now, onto my tour of the day: "A Taste of the Caymans." This tour does exactly what it says on the tin. If you're a non-drinker, this might not be your cup of tea—or rum punch, as the case may be. Let me explain.

We were met on shore by the tour company and introduced to our guide, John. One of the great things about NCL tours is they try to keep the group sizes manageable. There were only 16 of us on our bus, which meant no wrestling for the best seats. Another group was doing the same tour, but they were going in reverse order, so we wouldn't be bumping into them all day.

So, there we were, ready to embark on a boozy adventure through the Cayman Islands. If you're looking to sip and savour your way through paradise, this tour is definitely for you. If not, well, there's always the shopping.

The first stop on our adventure was the Tortuga Rum Cake factory, where we had 15 minutes to explore the shop and, more importantly, sample the world-famous rum cake washed down with several samples of the local rum. Oh dear, this was just the beginning.

Back on the bus, minus one woman who thought the schedule was merely a suggestion, we headed to the Cayman Brewery Company for a guided tour. But first, we hit the shop area, which conveniently doubles as a bar. Here, we sampled all six of their beers, plus one to take on the tour. Because clearly, we needed to stay hydrated.

After a tour of the brewery (during which I paid more attention to my beer than the brewing process), we were back in the shop to sample more or buy some to take away. Just remember, any booze you buy will be babysat by NCL until the end of the cruise.

Next stop: the Phathoms Rum Factory. Here, 14 bottles of different types of rum were lined up along the counter. We started at one end, working our way down with a shot from each bottle, accompanied by a detailed description from the brewery staff. They don't skimp on the measures, and if you're feeling bold, you can fill the shot glass to the brim.

With the drinking part temporarily over, we took a tour to see how the rum is made. But no sooner had the tour ended than we were back to sampling. Who needs a drinks package when you've got tours like this?

Wobbling back to the bus, it was clear we were well on our way to a tipsy, fun-filled day. Cheers to more adventures and even more rum!

The tour wrapped up at noon, leaving plenty of time for a stroll along the seafront and some leisurely browsing through the shops—if that's your thing—before re-boarding the tenders back to the ship. Here's a pro tip: don't wait until the last minute to board the tenders. I got back on board a full two hours before the last tender, and when I looked back, the queue stretched from the tender boat right onto the street.

I chatted with one poor soul who said it took him 45 minutes of queuing to get to the tender. Meanwhile, my journey from security to back on board took a mere 10 minutes. Timing is everything, my friends.

With the morning's adventures behind me, it was time for lunch. I headed to the Garden Café for a bite, then planned to hit deck 16 for some panoramic views of Grand Cayman and a few photos. Well, that was the plan anyway.

After lunch, as I strolled past the Vibe Bar on deck 16, the ever-friendly barman Adi called me over. I stopped for a beer, which, predictably, turned into several. What can I say? The best-laid plans of cruisers often go astray, especially when there's a cold drink and good company involved. Cheers to spontaneity!

The afternoon was spent at the bar with a small group of newfound friends, sharing laughs and tales of our cruising misadventures. With 21 bars on the Getaway, there's always a quiet nook to be found if you know where to look.

After the drinking session, it was time to head back to the stateroom and get ready for the evening's entertainment at the Getaway Theatre: the musical *Legally Blonde*. After a quick shower and donning my smartest attire, I made my way to the theatre. Finding a seat proved to be an unexpected challenge, despite plenty of empty seats, thanks to people reserving entire rows for their yet-to-arrive friends. Seriously, folks, why not arrive together and spare us the seat-saving saga? First come, first served should be the golden rule.

The show was fantastic—definitely worth watching. I highly recommend it to everyone.

Tonight was the night of the signature Glow Party at the H2O bar on deck 15, an absolute must for all partygoers. But if neon dance parties aren't your thing, fear not—there's always something happening around the ship.

From live jazz at the Fat Cats club to a charming couple singing and playing the piano in the Mojito Bar, the entertainment options are endless.

With the day winding down, it was the perfect time to retreat to my stateroom and head off to the land of nod, content and eagerly anticipating tomorrow's adventures. Cheers to another fabulous day at sea!

Day 8 - Cozumel / Playa de Carmen

The ship wasn't arriving until 11:00, so I decided to indulge in a lay-in and didn't get my sorry arse out of bed until 04:30. I know, I know—lazy sod. Tired of serving myself cold coffee in O'Sheehan's (which isn't always open, mind you), I grabbed a coffee from the Studio Lounge and settled into the Atrium, a quiet spot to pen this report.

With my brain running on low power mode, it took me several hours to finish writing. Once completed, I rewarded myself with breakfast at the Garden Café, as always. The rest of the morning was spent enjoying the ship's facilities while waiting for the meeting time for today's excursion: "Explora Park" in Playa del Carmen, Mexico.

The ship docked in Cozumel right on time, with passengers chomping at the bit to disembark since we were only in port until 18:30. Cozumel, one of Mexico's islands, offers plenty to do—from heading to the beaches on your own to participating in organised tours. Whether you're the adventurous type or you prefer nothing more than dipping your toes in the beautiful Caribbean sea, there's something for everyone. Tip: if you want to swim in the crystal clear blue sea, take the ferry to the mainland. The water is next-level gorgeous.

Since Explora Park is on the mainland, a ferry ride is required. It takes about 45 minutes each way. Trips to the mainland are very popular, so be prepared for a packed boat—up to 450 fellow cruisers from any ship docked at the pier. In our case, we shared the ferry with passengers from the Norwegian Star, the only ship in the fleet that greets you with a smile. Literally—it's painted on the bow of the ship (that's the pointy end for the nautical novices).

If you want to be first off at each end, here's a tip: when leaving the ship, board the ferry and head downstairs to sit near the bar, as disembarkation is from there. On the way back, sit on the top deck near the rear.

Armed with these tips and a sense of adventure, I set off for a day of exploration, ready to make the most of my time in Playa del Carmen. Cheers to another day of cruising shenanigans!

As planned, I was all set for the Explora Park excursion. The meeting point was the Getaway Theatre, where we were gathered before being led down to the ferry. There, the tour company greeted us and handed out stickers to wear. I have to say, I preferred the armbands from Jamaica—stickers make me feel like I'm in kindergarten again.

All aboard the boat for the short trip! Now, if you're the type who can't go 45 minutes without a drink, don't worry—they've got everything from coffee to hard liquor onboard. Just be prepared to pay prices that would make a pirate blush.

Upon arrival in Playa del Carmen, I finally got my wish: a wristband to replace the sticker, transforming me back into an incognito tourist. After a 15-minute coach trip, during which our guide explained the day's plan, we arrived at Explora Park.

Explora Park is an adventure paradise featuring four main activities: ziplines, amphibious vehicles, river swimming, and rafting. Plus, there are restaurants and other facilities to enjoy, all included in the price of the NCL excursion.

What I really liked about this excursion was the smooth process from booking to timekeeping, expertly managed by our tour guide Alberto and his colleague Freckles. On arrival, we were each given a personal helmet to use for the day. The helmet had a number on it so the park's cameras (and there are hundreds) could capture your glorious moments for you to purchase later.

We also got our own free locker. Alberto and Freckles, with their extensive knowledge of the park, were always on hand to ensure we made the most of our time there. Their first piece of advice was to hit the ziplines, as this activity takes the longest to complete.

So, helmet on, wristband secured, and ready for adventure, I embarked on a day filled with thrilling activities guided by two of the most entertaining and knowledgeable guides you could hope for. Here's to another day of high-flying fun and mischief!

Zip Line Adventures

If you enjoy the thrill of hurtling down a wire rope suspended 45 meters above the ground, then the zip line course at Explora Park is a must-try. Imagine the zip lines in Jamaica, but longer, higher, and way more exhilarating. Instead of having the lines one above the other, these are side by side, supposedly to prevent twisting. Unless, of course, you're me—then you're twisting all the way down like a corkscrew.

The final zip line lands you in deep water—literally. Trust me, you're going to get wet! I didn't quite make it all the way to the end of the water zip line, which was a surprise to me, given all the overeating and drinking. You'd think I'd plummet like a rock, but no. I ended up swimming on my back the last 20 meters, making quite the splashy entrance.

The whole activity is very safe, with a person connecting and disconnecting you at each tower. Once at the bottom, the ever-helpful tour guide is there to point you to the next adventure.

Amphibious Vehicles

Next up, amphibious vehicles for those who love off-road driving. Each vehicle can hold up to four people, but lucky me got one all to myself. Once everyone was loaded into their self-propelled cargo units (a.k.a. people), we set off in convoy around the 3.5 km track, led by a guide. The pace was fairly fast, but you can always get a burst of extra speed by stopping for a bit, letting the vehicle in front get ahead, and then flooring it until you catch up.

The track winds through dense vegetation and, at several points, leads underground through a cave network—a must-see and do. The entire course lasts about half an hour. Once it's finished, it's on to the next great adventure.

River Swim

This isn't your typical river swim; it's a river swim through a cave system. There are two routes: one long (about 500 meters) and one short. Trust me, if you're not a strong swimmer, stick to the short route. Both courses meander through dimly lit caves, creating an eerie yet exciting atmosphere. There's no current to help you along, so you're basically doggy paddling the entire way.

Life jackets are mandatory and believe me; you'll be glad for them. Mine seemed to have a mind of its own, constantly trying to push my head forward into the water. So, I spent a lot of time floating on my back and doggy paddling like an overgrown puppy. Fortunately, there are lifeguards swimming both ways in the river to ensure everyone's safety. It's a challenging swim, but it's definitely a must-do activity.

Rafting

Rafting here involves sitting on a wooden raft and paddling your way through an underground river using your hands. I can't say much more about this one since I ran out of time and couldn't complete it. But if you've got the whole day, it's worth giving it a shot.

After all that hard work, you start feeling peckish. And since you're from the cruise ship, it's time to eat! The park boasts an excellent buffet restaurant serving a variety of foods from Mexican to Western cuisine, complete with unlimited soft drinks. Luckily for us, this is included in the excursion price.

To sum up, Explora Park, it's a must-do if you're in the area. It's enjoyable for the whole family, from the kids to the grandparents. So, zipline, swim, raft, and eat your way through this adventure-packed park!

As I've mentioned more times than I've hit the buffet, the big advantage of taking an NCL organised tour over a private one became crystal clear today. One of the tours was running late, and the ferry waited for them. With a 45-minute crossing, hundreds of us cruisers ended up being half an hour late back to the ship. But since this was an NCL excursion, the ship had to wait. Score one for us procrastinators!

As the ferry pulled up to the jetty, I spotted some fortunate souls casually strolling down the pier toward the ship. If we hadn't been late, they would've missed the boat and faced the prospect of hitchhiking from Cozumel to Miami. Not exactly an ideal situation.

Because we got back late, I missed my booking for the comedy show. So, after a quick shower and shampoo, I headed to the bar for a glass of orange juice. Yes, you heard me right, orange juice. Followed by several cokes. Pick yourself up off the floor—it didn't last. Soon enough, I was back on track with orange juice spiked with Southern Comfort.

The next couple of hours were spent in the Atrium, entranced by a very talented group called Grove International. I blame their excellent music for me downing more beers than I should have. Eventually, it was time to wobble back to my stateroom and the land of nod, this time as a slightly intoxicated but thoroughly entertained cruiser. Cheers to another day of cruising chaos!

Day 9 - Day at Sea

As we all know, I'm not the biggest fan of sea days. Don't get me wrong, there's always a ton of stuff happening on the ship, from demonstrations to game shows for the whole family. But as a solo cruiser, there's only so much you can do before you start talking to the towel animals for company.

Take the rope course, for instance. It's perched high above deck 16 and even has a plank that extends over the ship's side. For the brave souls who dare to walk it, you can pull a cord and have your picture taken. Here's a tip for NCL: tilt the camera down to show that you're actually over the side of the ship. Maybe throw in an overhead and front camera combo for dramatic effect. If they had done that, I'd have bought the photo as proof of my temporary insanity.

Now, let's talk about the Solo Travellers meet-up. For some baffling reason, they moved it from the fabulous Studio Lounge to the smoker's paradise, a.k.a. the Sun Set Bar. This bar has been completely taken over by smokers who occupy every seat. Unless you can hold your breath while ordering a drink, forget about it.

As someone who enjoys a relaxing beer at the bar, this is a major turn-off. I prefer my lungs unpolluted, thank you very much. If they need a smoking bar, why not designate the Vibe Bar on deck 16? It's quiet and would keep the smoke contained. OK, rant over.

For lunch, I booked a spot at Wine Lover: The Musical. What can I say about this show? It's probably one of the best dinner shows I've ever attended, and trust me, I've been to more dinner shows than I can count—both for work and pleasure. The three actors on stage were genuinely talented. If I could give out Oscars, they'd get my vote, no questions asked.

The show itself is essentially a wine tasting with a comedic twist. You're served five glasses of wine, ranging from light white to dark red, and instructed to only taste when the host tells you to. They walk you through each wine, explaining the correct way to taste it. The show ends with a toast of sparkling wine. If you're on a cruise where this is an option, you'd be a fool to miss it.

Today, I spotted the Towel Pixie Death Squad patrolling deck 15 around 14:00. These heroes in uniform were checking the times towels had been left unattended and placing stickers on them, marking them for potential elimination. I didn't witness any towels being hauled off or pixies meeting their demise, but hey, it's a start. Maybe my not-so-subtle rant to the Guest Service Manager at the Captain's VIP Cocktail party paid off. It's about time someone took action against those towel-hogging miscreants!

The rest of the evening was spent exploring different areas of the ship, chatting with various people, and saying goodbye to the crew members who had been especially helpful during the cruise. Around 21:00, I stumbled upon the Headliners bar with its door open, so I popped in to watch the Duelling Pianos. I remembered this act from previous cruises, and it's always a blast.

However, this time the artists were subtly asking for money to play your song, saying, "We play all songs, but if you come up with a donation, you have a better chance of hearing yours. The bigger the donation, the greater the chance." This isn't the NCL way of doing entertainment and definitely needs to be nipped in the bud.

Finally, it was time to head back to my stateroom and pack my bags to be put outside the room. This is such a great idea; it always amazes me when I see people struggling with their luggage during disembarkation. Let's just say I prefer to work smarter, not harder.

So, there you have it: my sea day in a nutshell. Navigating between fun activities and avoiding smoker-infested bars, all while trying to keep my sanity intact. Cheers to another day at sea, where the adventure never ends, and neither does my quest for a smoke-free beer!

Day 10 - Disembarkation Miami

Well, I'm up nice and early as always, mainly because I had placed a cash deposit on day one. Since I had the drinks package and managed not to buy the gift shop's entire stock, I was due for a refund. The Onboard Credit desk opens at 06:00, so I highly recommend getting there right on time. No, scratch that—make it 06:15, giving me a head start.

The desk gets insanely busy, with the queue stretching longer than a Black Friday sale by 10:00. If you're looking for some entertainment on the last morning, grab a seat nearby and listen to the excuses and arguments from people trying to wiggle out of their bills. One couple even refused to pay their medical bill, insisting, "Sorry, you used the service, so pay and claim it back from your insurance."

I did feel a pang of sympathy for a couple who racked up a $1,700 bill for a 20-minute phone call to the States. Luckily for them, NCL sorted it out as a phone issue. Crisis averted.

With nothing to do but wait for my luggage label colour to be called, I had a front-row seat to the chaos. NCL uses a colour-coding system to make disembarkation smoother, but with 4,000 people trying to get off, it's like herding cats.

Finally, my colour was called, and I joined the massive queue stretching to the back of the ship. Surprisingly, the line moved quickly, and soon, I was in the luggage hall.

With bag in hand, I joined yet another queue, this time for US Customs. A lady in a wheelchair tried to cut to the front, but the Customs Agent was having none of it and sent her to the back of the line. Well played, Missy. I had no sympathy, as I'd seen her walking around the waterfront earlier. Makes you wonder if some folks use wheelchairs just to skip the lines and get their families off the ship first!

The Customs process didn't take long, and soon I was standing outside, squinting in the sunlight and wondering where on earth to find my transfer bus. Typically, there's a helpful NCL representative waving you in the right direction, but today? Nada.

I spotted a man being harassed—I mean, asked a question—by a fellow cruiser waving a piece of paper like it was a distress signal. I aimed myself at him, and he told me to follow the woman in front of me. Playing it safe, I asked what to do if she diverted. Good thing I did because halfway down the road, she decided to take a scenic detour. Eventually, I found the bus and was on my way to the Pullman Sofitel Hotel for my 4-night stay.

Checking into the hotel was straightforward, and this time, they had my reservation—unlike the Sheraton fiasco on the way in. I handed over $50 per night in cash for the deposit, avoiding credit or debit cards like they were carriers of some exotic disease. If you're planning a trip to America and prefer not to use plastic for deposits, bring $50 per night. Remember, you can't use this money during your stay, but you get it back at the end. It's like a forced savings plan with zero interest.

After unpacking, it was time for a granddad nap—cruising is exhausting, you know. Refreshed, I ventured out to explore the local area for myself and any future customers. Great news: within a 10-minute walking distance, there's a coin-operated laundrette and a shopping centre where you can buy drinks, both alcoholic and non-alcoholic, at prices that won't make you weep.

Continuing my theme of dodging high hotel prices, I found a McDonald's and a Burger King just a few minutes away. If you fancy a trip to Downtown Miami, a taxi will set you back around $23, plus the obligatory tips for people simply doing their jobs.

However, if you're feeling adventurous (and thrifty), exit the hotel, turn right, and then right again onto the main road past the shopping centre. At the main lights, turn left, and you can catch a bus to Downtown Miami for just $2. It's a 15-minute walk to the bus stop, but it could save you a small fortune.

And so, my land adventure begins, armed with cash, a map, and the resolve to avoid high prices at all costs. Cheers to new explorations and more comical misadventures!

Day 11 – Miami

The plan was simple: get up early, walk to the nearest fast food joint for breakfast (saving the $19 hotel breakfast cost), and then spend a couple of tedious hours at the laundromat washing a week's worth of clothes. Easy peasy—or so I thought.

Naturally, things didn't go as planned. I didn't roll out of bed until 07:00—the week's cruising had clearly taken its toll on me. How will I survive a 31-day cruise? Dirty laundry in hand, I embarked on a short walk to the laundromat; not saying it smelled, but I did acquire a following of curious cats.

Laundromats are surprisingly great places to meet locals. I struck up a conversation with a lovely Cuban lady who kindly helped me navigate the washing machines and even scolded me for not using fabric softener—then generously added some of her own. We spent the next hour chatting about everything from the local area to Cuba while my clothes were spinning away.

This "Mad Cuban Lady from Miami" (her words, not mine) gave me a crash course on the local Cuban culture, explaining why most signs in the area are in Spanish and why I hadn't seen many stereotypical white Americans. When I mentioned my previous day's walking adventures, she reacted with horror, pointing out that I had wandered into some less-than-safe neighbourhoods. Oops.

Our conversation was a delightful reminder that no matter where you go, you can always meet friendly, interesting people who are willing to chat and share their insights. Thank you, Mad Cuban Lady, for the company and the fabric softener.

The total cost of the week's laundry? $4.50—an absolute bargain compared to the hotel's laundry service, which would have set me back over $90. I did the math using the laundry list in my hotel room. Definitely worth the short walk and the company.

With my laundry done, it was time for breakfast. I took a short stroll back to the shopping centre (a mere 10 minutes) and visited Burger King for their breakfast platter. I'm not saying it's big, but it made English breakfasts look like a light snack. Perhaps this explains why there are so many rather large Americans around.

If you're staying at the Pullman Hotel, this shopping centre is a goldmine for saving money. There are at least five fast-food joints, two restaurants, a supermarket, a chemist, and much more. After my hefty breakfast, I worked it off with a five-hour walk around the local area, exploring and gathering information.

So, despite a rocky start, the day turned out to be productive, filled with interesting conversations, and ended with a full belly and clean clothes. Cheers to the unexpected joys of travel!

Day 12 - Key West

One of the must-do things when staying in Miami is taking a day trip to Key West. Like a good boy, I booked myself a one-day coach tour. The Pullman Hotel wasn't on the pickup point list, so I needed to get a taxi to the Regency Hotel. Finding a cab wasn't hard—the doorman blew a whistle, and voilà, a yellow chariot appeared. Okay, it was a cab from the car park, but that sounded way cooler.

The taxi ride took only 10 minutes, and to my amazement, the meter showed just $10. My surprise was short-lived as I had forgotten about the extras—tax, road toll, and the compulsory tip, which brought the total to $15.

The ticket stated a pickup time of 07:30, but the coach, operating on what I can only describe as "Omani time," arrived at 08:15. I thought I'd left that behind! Once onboard, it was time to sit back and relax for the four-hour drive to Key West.

Time flew by thanks to the driver's running commentary, which was odd because the tour guide on board said absolutely nothing. If you've never been to the Keys, the scenery is breathtaking, especially crossing the 12 bridges, including the world-famous 7-mile bridge.

Here's an interesting tidbit: when you see photos of the 7-mile bridge, you'll notice two bridges. The one on the right as you drive to Key West is the old bridge, which is no longer in use except for some sections used for fishing.

So, with the wind in my hair (figuratively speaking, since I was on a bus), I soaked in the stunning views and enjoyed a day out that was well worth the extra cab fare and the leisurely wait for the coach. Cheers to new adventures and the occasional hiccup!

We rolled into Key West at high noon and were given five hours to explore. Key West is bursting with things to do: from glass-bottom boat trips over a living reef to snorkeling, trolley rides around town, or, for the more adventurous, parasailing.

But beware, these activities can gobble up most of your time, leaving you little to explore this fascinating place.

I opted for the easy route, spending my time wandering around the town and quay, which is packed with bars and restaurants. The entertainment area boasts up to 60 bars and eateries. I only managed to visit two bars—Sloppy Joe's and another spot that featured a fantastic old-fashioned Happy Hour lasting four hours.

I settled in for two beers, which paired nicely with the alligator nuggets I had for lunch. Sorry, Snappy, but you were delicious. After lunch, I went gift shopping for the grandkids and picked up three T-shirts emblazoned with "That's it, I'm Calling Grandpa." With shopping done, I continued my sightseeing.

Then, I encountered the other side of cruising: the Carnival Magic was in port, making everything, like the trolley ride, busier than a beehive. The queues wrapped around the shops, so I decided to skip it. Never mind, I'll get my own back next week.

All in all, a delightful day in Key West filled with delicious food, good drinks, and plenty of laughs.

Visit over, I hopped back on the coach for the return trip. The driver, not the guide, provided the commentary, probably angling for his obligatory tip. The trip back seemed quicker, or maybe I caught a few ZZZs.

Remembering the Mad Cuban Lady's advice about not walking the streets at night, I asked the hotel to call me a taxi. The receptionist did so politely, but after a couple of minutes of standing there like an idiot, I realised I should have been clearer. "I need a cab to take me back to my hotel, and my name is Steve, not Taxi." Unfortunately, the Regency didn't have the magic whistle like the Pullman, so the cab took 15 minutes to arrive.

An interesting twist on the ride back was a sign in the cab stating that if you paid cash, you'd get a $2.70 discount. Not wanting to miss out, I asked the driver, who confirmed it. Yay for me!

Upon arrival at the Pullman Hotel, the fare was $10.70. After the $2.70 discount for paying cash, I figured my total would be... still $15. It turns out the tip must have been inflated to cover the discount. Sneaky, sneaky.

So, another day of cruising adventures wrapped up, full of laughs, quirky encounters, and the occasional pricing surprise. Here's to more hilarious misadventures!

Day 13 – Miami

Today was a lazy day with nothing much to talk about, so I won't.

Just kidding! Even on a lazy day, the cruise life has its quirks. Picture this: me, lounging by the pool, perfecting my art of doing absolutely nothing. I did manage to summon the energy to lift my cocktail, so let's count that as a win.

Honestly, it was one of those gloriously uneventful days where the most exciting thing was deciding between the lounge chair on the left or the one on the right. I ended up in the middle, naturally.

I'd love to say something thrilling happened, like an impromptu conga line breaking out or a rogue seagull stealing someone's sandwich, but alas, it was just me, the sun, and a parade of snacks delivered right to my lounger.

So, here's to a lazy day at the hotel, where the biggest decision is whether to nap now or nap later. Cheers to doing nothing and loving every minute of it!

Cruising onboard the Norwegian Pearl

Day 14 - Embarkation

The bags were packed nice and early since the coach to the ship was set to depart at 11:30. One thing that sets NCL apart from the rest is their level of service. They have a representative at the hotel the morning of departure and even the evening before to answer all your questions and provide the health screening questionnaire and luggage tags if you need them. Well played, NCL.

I decided to check my NCL account online this morning, and, success! I've achieved Gold Latitudes Member status. And I did it the hard way, mind you, not like those who book the Haven nine months in advance for a 16-night cruise and become Gold members after one trip. Looking forward to my room key with "Gold" on it and the welcome gift—always wondered what that would be.

I checked out of the hotel at 10:30 to avoid the rush. Check-out was straightforward, and my cash deposit was returned without any issues, proving you can indeed travel without the dreaded credit card. I found an empty chair and took up residence to await the coach.

As I sat there, I noticed that most of the other people waiting for the bus were, shall we say, part of the over-60 club. I must have been the youngest person there, and I'm 26... plus 324 months. I started to worry that the ship had been chartered by Saga Holidays (the over-60 holiday company). I planned to check the sign on the side of the ship when I got there.

Never mind, I boarded the coach with 20 other people and three disability chariots. On route, we stopped at what must have been a posh retirement home called the Marriott Courtyard to pick up 20 more coffin dodgers.

When the bus arrived, I saw one of the small things that annoys me and diminishes respect for genuinely disabled people. A large man—large in width—on an electric mobility scooter was taken past all the people queuing for the bus to the front. He then stood up so the scooter could be loaded and walked back to the hotel. He was seen walking around the whole time the bus was being loaded with bags and people, a good 10 minutes. He then walked to the bus. Does he really need the scooter?

So, here I am, surrounded by a sea of grey hair and questionable scooter usage, ready to embark on another cruise adventure. Here's hoping the ship isn't a floating retirement home, and I find some fellow 26-and-324-month-olds to share a drink with!

Check-in was even quicker than last week, thanks to my shiny new Gold Latitudes status. It would have been even faster if it weren't for the parade of disabled people checking in and slowing the line down. Now, before you start groaning, let me explain.

Here's the thing: in everyday life, people with disabilities rightly fight to be treated the same as everyone else (which I fully support). But when it comes to jumping queues and having tables or seats saved for them on board, that equality seems to vanish.

So, I've devised a cunning plan: if you don't want to queue up, just tag along with a person in a wheelchair. It doesn't matter if there are two or ten people in your party. You'll glide right past the line. Maybe NCL should limit the number of people who can escort a wheelchair (which is being pushed by NCL staff anyway) to one. The rest can queue up with everyone else. Or better yet, let's have everyone treated the same and everyone queues.

Once on board, I noticed several people who had queued to get on suddenly regain miraculous mobility. One person using a walking frame couldn't squeeze through some tables, so they stood up, lifted the frame over their head, and walked through the tables before putting it down again. Another person carried his wheelchair down the stairs before sitting back down. As I said before, this kind of behaviour is frustrating because it takes away respect from those who are genuinely disabled.

Fortunately, there wasn't much waiting time in the lounge, likely due to the arrival time of the coach at the port. So, I was soon exploring the ship, which is very similar to the Norwegian Star since they are of the same class.

And so begins another chapter of cruising adventures, filled with laughs, quirks, and the occasional questionable queue-jumping. Cheers to the journey ahead!

For example, on my last cruise, which feels like eons ago (okay, last week), I made a cash deposit instead of using a credit or debit card. Once again, there was no issue with NCL. I just strolled up to the Customer

Service desk, handed over my $1,000, and received a piece of paper in return. Fair trade, right? That piece of paper equated to $1,000 on my account.

Here's the thing: if you use a credit or debit card, multiple holds can be placed on it, sometimes lingering for up to thirty days after the cruise. This could mean you don't have access to your own money. So, avoid the hassle and leave a cash deposit. Plus, it helps you control your spending better.

Looks like someone at NCL finally listened to me. Proudly displayed on the Customer Service desk was a sign stating that passengers aged 18-21 require an Alcohol Waiver to drink on board. Additionally, signs around the ship's bars announced that you needed to be 21 or over to drink alcohol. Victory is mine! If you want to know why I'm so triumphant, check out my last review or just see the previous chapters.

The cabin was available as soon as I boarded, which was great because I didn't have to lug my bag around for hours. It's been a while since I've been in an inside cabin and I'd forgotten how spacious they are with all that storage.

Once again, NCL went above and beyond with all the extras in my cabin. From luxury toiletries to not one, but three bottles of sparkling wine, and my favorite—two plates of chocolate-covered strawberries.

Picture this: me, tomorrow, lounging by the pool in my plush dressing gown (also provided), sipping sparkling wine, and nibbling on chocolate-covered strawberries. How posh is that? Thanks, NCL. No wonder I cruise with no other company. This more than makes up for my room key still saying "Silver." Who needs a welcome aboard gift with all these treats?

When exploring the ship, you can't help but notice how much the new ships have improved in layout. Everything seems to flow so much better. On older ships like the Norwegian Pearl, you feel like you're on a quest, constantly going up or down to get to a place that's supposedly on the same level.

You also notice that many of the cool technologies on the newer ships haven't filtered down to the older ones, like interactive TVs. Plus, during the emergency drill, instead of using a handheld device to check people in, like on the Getaway, some poor crew member is still sifting through sheets of paper. In a real emergency, that could be more time-consuming than binge-watching a whole season of your favourite show.

Speaking of the emergency drill, it definitely didn't match the Getaway's standards. The only information given was how to put on a life jacket—nothing about what to do in an actual emergency. Maybe someone from The Getaway could swing by and give them a masterclass.

Ship tour over, it was time for lunch in the Garden Café. Just like every cruise, you can expect the buffet restaurant to be busier than a bee in a flower shop on embarkation day. But if you want to beat the crowds, there are other dining options available.

I stuck with the Garden Café, and as always, the food was top-notch and plentiful. The rest of the afternoon was filled with the usual first-day activities: unpacking and checking out the onboard entertainment from the Welcome Aboard show to the sailaway party.

For those who hadn't eaten in the past hour, there was a BBQ on the pool deck with live music—a definite highlight and a fantastic way to kick off your cruise holiday.

As this ship doesn't boast all the entertainment venues of the larger resort-type ships, the main action happens in the theatre, which operates on a first-come, first-served policy with no booking required. I was glad to see in the Freestyle Daily that reserving seats isn't allowed—finally, a lesson learned from the Getaway.

Tonight's show featured the senior officers, combined with music, dance, and a comedy performance by Jim McDonald. It was hilarious and thoroughly enjoyable.

Are you sitting comfortably? Yes? Good. Now brace yourself. I've been on the ship for at least 8 hours, and it's now 21:00, and not a drop of alcohol has passed my lips. Time to rectify that! Off to O'Sheehan's for a little drink or two.

It must be the itinerary or the fact that about 80% of the cruisers are Coffin Dodgers, but at 21:30, I found myself the only person in O'Sheehan's bar. I felt like a dirty little stop-out.

Compare this to O'Sheehan's on the Epic and the Getaway, where you can't move for the crowd all night long. This requires further investigation.

Despite the ship being at full capacity, by 21:30, it was like a ghost town. With very few people around, they must all be tucked up in bed with their cocoa.

This was excellent news for me—no long quests at the bars at night. I found many American guests in the casino, but the pool deck and outside bars were empty and dark.

With tomorrow being a sea day, the big question is: will the towel pixies be reserving deck chairs with towels, blankets, or comforters? Only time will tell.

Having finished my stint as a stop-out, it was time for the land of Nod. Cheers to more cruise adventures, quirky experiences, and the occasional empty bar!

Day 15 - Day at Sea

As nearly always, I was up at the crack of dawn, 04:00, searching for a quiet spot to write my report. Usually, this is a breeze—just me, a few crew members, and the occasional drunken passenger. But today, thanks to the ship's clientele, there were people everywhere. Finding a quiet place was like looking for a needle in a haystack. I might have to reconsider my early bird routine.

While patrolling the ship, scouting for a tranquil corner, I came across a lovely security guard named Laxmi. She was also patrolling but for entirely different reasons. Laxmi was a delightful lady who stopped for a chat about nothing in particular and then pointed me to her favourite quiet spot. Thanks to her tip, I found my new writing haven, Deck 6, at the back of Maltings Beer & Whiskey Bar.

After three hours of hard work catching up on the report, it was time for breakfast. Today, that meant another round at the Garden Café if I could find a table.

With a plate full of dead animals and dead vegetables in hand, I embarked on the quest for an empty table. Success! I spotted one in the distance. Now, all that stood between me and breakfast was an obstacle course of crammed tables and chairs.

With the stealth and cunning of a tiger, I weaved my way through, reaching the table just in time. I placed my plate down before the woman doing the OAP shuffle could claim it. Sorry, Granny, this table is mine.

As always, after any meal on board, it's a good idea to go for a walk. Trust me, if you don't, your waistline will expand faster than you can say "buffet." Plus, walking gives you a chance to explore more of the ship, and there's always something new to discover.

For example, I've been on the Norwegian Pearl since yesterday, and it wasn't until 18:00 today that I stumbled upon an enormous entertainment area called the Spinnaker Lounge.

So, here's to early mornings, delightful security guards, victorious table battles, and never-ending ship explorations.

I noticed on today's walk that this ship is ready for her refurbishment. She's starting to look a bit worn out, bless her. There are grubby marks on the ceilings, torn and damaged furniture in my stateroom, a large crack in the toilet bowl (I'm praying it holds up under my fat arse), and a big chip in the sink. But I'm sure once she comes out of dry dock, she'll look as good as the Epic did after its facelift.

I also found evidence that I was right—this is indeed a "Waiting for God" cruise. SAGA has set up a Help Desk for their guests in O'Sheehan's. NCL, you really need to work on your communication skills. Just imagine if a young couple or a family had booked this cruise expecting a lively, party atmosphere like last week on The Getaway. They'd be sorely disappointed.

Maybe NCL should rate their cruises like they do with excursions. For example, a 5N for Fun & Party Cruises, down to a 1N for Cruises for the Older Generation (over 60s).

Being a sea day, NCL always packs the schedule with activities. Just check out the Freestyle Daily. Judging by the number of people crammed into the theatre, one of the most popular activities today was the presentation on ports and tours. It's a must for everyone, even if you've done your homework before boarding, like me. The Shore Excursions team gives a great insight into the ports of call.

Getting out of these events is always slow going, but with 60% of the passengers doing the OAP shuffle, it makes moving anywhere painfully slow. So, plan for alternative routes. Sometimes it's quicker to go up or down a floor to get from the theatre to the Garden Café. Trust me, it's faster to go to deck 13, walk across the top of the ship, and then come back down.

I had a tough decision to make: either drag myself to the gym for a fitness program or watch a cooking show. In the interest of future cruisers (and definitely not because I wanted to avoid the gym), I decided to attend the cooking demonstration. Now, after watching the show, I can confidently say I have the knowledge and skill to make sushi and cook lobster while twirling spatulas and knives around my head like a culinary ninja.

One of my favourite onboard activities is visiting the Art Gallery, so I couldn't miss the Park West Art Auction, especially with the enticing offer of free champagne. The place was packed, and I'm not saying it was just because of the free bubbly, but after they introduced the auctioneer, half the room didn't even glance at the art.

I drooled over two originals by my favourite artist, Linda Le Kniff, dreaming of the day I have $10,000 to spare. Speaking of free drinks, once the glasses were handed out, the crowd dwindled to about thirty people. Point proven: offer free drinks and watch people evaporate once they're in hand.

I even won a prize in the raffle—a pack of the pictures/photos they usually give out after each auction. Still, it's a win, and I might even frame them.

The art auction wrapped up at 15:00, leaving me the rest of the afternoon to leisurely stroll around the ship. I stopped at different spots to watch and listen to the live music being played, which was a delightful way to pass the time.

Dinner was supposed to be at Maderno, but I wasn't that hungry. The friendly folks at the Restaurant Reservations Desk kindly cancelled it for me. Remember, folks, if you've booked a speciality restaurant and don't show up, you could still end up paying, so cancel your booking if plans change.

Deciding a Chinese meal was calling my name today; I headed to the restaurant for a lovely dinner and some friendly banter with the waiters and waitresses. However, some people truly take the biscuit when it comes to dining behaviour. Take the very grumpy man at the table near me: he was rude to the waiter, ordered several plates of food, took one bite from each, and then left without even a thank you. Honestly, if you're not sure what you want, ask for a sample—simple, as those two funny cartoon rodents would say.

Having discovered the Spinnaker Lounge earlier in the day, I decided to check it out in the evening. It's such a fantastic place, with high windows all around looking over the front of the ship, an ideal spot to watch the world go by.

I did feel a bit sorry for the entertainment department. They were presenting The Weakest Link game show, and to start with, there were more crew members than cruisers. Eventually, a few people did show up so the show could go on, but once it finished, everyone except a handful of people vanished, leaving the bar nearly empty. Perfect for me—no queue at the bar again!

I finished the night off with the 21:00 show in the theatre, mainly to see if anyone was still around. Surprisingly, the theatre was nearly full. I'll have to investigate tomorrow why all the bars are deserted while the theatre is packed. The bar staff must be very bored on this cruise.

So here's to encountering grumpy diners, finding the perfect lounge, and enjoying another quirky day at sea. Cheers to more cruising adventures and plenty of laughs!

Day 16 - Day at Sea

Well, today's been a whirlwind of firsts for me, folks! First off, I achieved the miraculous feat of sleeping past the crack of dawn, a monumental achievement for this nocturnal creature. I must've been out cold because, by the time I finally pried my eyelids open, it was a scandalous 8:30 in the morning!

Feeling like I've stumbled into a retirement home breakfast nook, I made my way down to O'Sheehan's, conveniently only a stumble away on the same floor. I was ushered to a table by the delightful Precious, who promptly delivered the elixir of life itself: my first gallon of coffee.

Breakfast, or should I say the "country platter," was a culinary adventure. Forget bacon; this platter came adorned with the noble pork scratching! It was a nice change from the morning melee at the Garden Café, let me tell you.

With time ticking away faster than my sanity on a cruise ship, I descended upon the Maltings bar to chronicle yesterday's escapades. And let me tell you, the ship was buzzing with activity, including a cake-decorating extravaganza. Now, these chefs could whip up a masterpiece with frosting like Picasso with a pastry bag. Too bad their English was as scrambled as their eggs.

The presentation wrapped up with a mad dash for cake, with the Atrium resembling a scene from "The Hunger Games." Who knew people would sprint for dessert faster than they would for a lifeboat? And all this despite the Garden Café practically oozing with free cake!

Speaking of feeding frenzies, it was high noon, time for lunch at the Market Garden. Now, some may bemoan the size of these behemoth ships, but let me tell you, there's never a dull moment in the buffet scrum. Dodging elbows and jockeying for position, I finally secured my plate like a seasoned linebacker. Move it, Granny, this seat's reserved for this hungry hipster!

Ah, the joys of cruising! Nothing like being greeted in my stateroom by a bottle of insect repellent, courtesy of NCL. Because nothing screams "vacation" like preparing for a potential mosquito uprising in South America,

Puerto Rico, and Mexico. Thanks for the heads up, NCL, but I'd prefer my surprises to be of the piña colada variety.

But wait, there's more! Along with the bug spray came a delightful letter about the Zika virus and a word deciphering game. Because what's a cruise without a bit of brain-teasing fun? Although deciphering their instructions was like decoding hieroglyphics after one too many piña coladas. "Limiting timespendinginplaceswheremosquitosmaybepresent..." Wait, what? I think I need another drink to unravel this mystery.

And speaking of drinks, it's time for the Captain's VIP Cocktail Party! Ah, the glamour, the prestige! I may be just a mere mortal among the sea of passengers, but for one shining moment, I feel like the king of the high seas. Thank you, NCL, for making me feel like a million bucks. Or at least like a hundred bucks in cruise credit.

Now, onto more firsts! Like spending consecutive days at sea and learning the fine art of sipping a mocktail on a dry cruise ship. Yes, you heard that right—no alcohol in sight! But fear not, my fellow parched passengers, for where there's a will, there's a bar. And apparently, there's also a library. Who knew people still used those things on vacation?

But I digress. Back to the VIP life! After a quick session of the 3 - S's (you know, shower, shave, and... well, use your imagination), I suited up for the Captain's shindig. And what do I find upon my return? A cheese platter courtesy of Concierge Suzanna. Bless her cheese-loving heart!

Now, let's talk fashion faux pas. I waltzed into the Spinnaker Lounge feeling all fancy in my polo shirt and trousers, only to find a mix of ball gowns, tuxedos, and... wait for it... T-shirts, shorts, and flip-flops! Oh, the horror! But hey, at least I wasn't the only one who missed the memo on proper attire.

Despite the wardrobe mishaps, the VIP party was a blast. Rubbing elbows with senior officers, hobnobbing with fellow VIPs, and maybe even slipping a business card or two—it's all in a day's work. And thanks to the generosity of the Captain and NCL, the drinks flowed freely, and the snacks were aplenty. Ah, the perks of VIP status!

With the party winding down, I sauntered over to the bar for a nightcap before catching the evening show. Because why stop the fun when there's still a theatre full of entertainment waiting?

Tonight's main event: a mentalist. Sounds like a mind-bending, jaw-dropping extravaganza, right? Well, let's just say it was more like a mind-numbing, eyebrow-raising experience.

As I sauntered into the theatre, I couldn't help but notice the mentalist huddled with a trio of guests. There's a young lady receiving some mysterious object, along with a glimpse of paper. And lo and behold, there's a dude with a video camera perched in the wheelchair section, looking suspiciously like he's streaming to his buddies in the NCL squad. Because why just enjoy the show when you can livestream it, right?

The performance kicks off, and wouldn't you know it, the "random" volunteers are none other than the folks the mentalist was just cosying up to. What are the odds, huh? And those numbers supposedly called out? Well, they're nowhere to be found on the paper projected on the screen. But hey, who needs logic when you've got magic, right?

Then comes the pièce de résistance: a grand finale involving a sum on a board and a miraculous transformation of a $1 bill. And who does he randomly select for this mind-blowing feat? You guessed it, the same lady from the beginning! Talk about a small world, or maybe just a very predictable one.

Now, I'm not saying there's foul play afoot, but if you're gonna pull someone from the audience, maybe do it when the spotlight isn't shining so brightly on your shady dealings. Just a thought.

But fear not, fellow cruisers! Tomorrow brings new adventures, new laughs, and hopefully, entertainment that's slightly less... eyebrow-raising. Until then, it's off to the land of nod for me. Goodnight, and may your dreams be as baffling as tonight's mentalist performance!

Day 17- Cartagena – Colombia

Waking up before the roosters, I wasn't about to repeat yesterday's blunder. So, with the alarm set for a ludicrous 4 AM, we were primed for our grand entrance into Cartagena, Colombia, at 7 AM. Let me tell you, arriving in Cartagena by ship is like stepping into a postcard—picture this: the crack of dawn, mist swirling over the sea like a dramatic entrance, and in the distance, the twinkling lights of Cartagena peeking through the haze. It's like the ocean itself is whispering, "Hey there, welcome to the stunning city of Cartagena!"

After navigating through the necessary legal hoops, we were finally free to set foot on solid ground after what felt like eons at sea (okay, maybe just a couple of days). The options were plentiful: join one of the NCL-approved tours or boldly venture out on our own with the promise of complimentary buses to ferry us around. My pick of the litter? A guided jaunt through the Spanish Fortress & Old City.

Boarding our cosy 43-seater air-conditioned chariot (bless those chilly vents!), we were whisked away to the fortress, with our guide Lee (a true Colombian gem) regaling us with tales of Cartagena's storied past. His advice? Don't even think about buying trinkets from the street vendors—apparently, they're all about as authentic as a three-dollar bill. But I couldn't help but feel there was more to Lee's warning than met the eye.

The fortress itself was a sight to behold, perched high above the city like a brooding guardian. The climb to the top had some of my fellow cruisers sweating bullets, but fear not! Lee, our trusty guide, graciously paused halfway up to share some history and trivia, sparing our less athletic companions from a full-blown cardio catastrophe. Oh, the things we do for a glimpse into the past!

The shortstop then turned into a long-winded tour of the Fort, which, let me tell you, was more labyrinthine than a rat's maze. We traipsed through tunnels that seemed to stretch on forever, with Lee leading the charge like a drill sergeant on a mission. Honestly, I think he lost track of time down there, or maybe he just wanted to see how long it would take for us to start sweating like pigs in a sauna.

By the time we emerged from the depths of the fortress, half the group looked ready to pass out from heatstroke. Note to self: next time, bring a portable fan.

Sure, the fort was fascinating and all, but there's only so much history a person can handle before their brain starts to feel like mush. I mean, don't get me wrong, I love a good history lesson as much as the next guy, but where were the Instagram-worthy photo ops?

Back on the bus, we trudged, bracing ourselves for what promised to be the most thrilling part of our day: a tour of the former dungeons, now masquerading as local vendor shops. Nothing says vacation like getting trapped in a dungeon with a side of retail therapy, am I right?

But wait, it gets better. As if being coerced into buying knick-knacks wasn't bad enough, we had Lee, the master of merchandise, giving us the hard sell like a used car salesman on overdrive. I swear, he knew more about those trinkets than the poor souls trying to peddle them. Suspicious? You betcha!

We were generously granted a whopping half-hour to navigate the labyrinth of souvenirs, but who in their right mind has time for that when there's a beach calling your name? So, like any rational human being, I made a mad dash for freedom, leaving behind the siren call of cheesy keychains and tacky t-shirts. Ah, the sweet taste of liberation!

Back on the coach we piled, ready for round two of old city exploration, complete with more riveting commentary from our buddy Lee. Then, just when we thought we were safe from the clutches of consumerism, we were herded towards the Spanish Inquisition Palace/Museum.

But instead of delving into the dark depths of history, what do we get? A crash course in finger painting courtesy of a local street vendor. Because nothing screams "authentic cultural experience" like smudging paint on a piece of paper, right?

To add insult to injury, Lee morphed into a full-blown salesman, pushing us to buy not one but two paintings for the low, low price of $10. I mean, come on, Lee, are you running a museum or a flea market?

With wallets lighter and spirits slightly dampened, we trudged onward, wondering if Lee would be making a return trip to collect his commission or if we'd been duped into funding his next vacation. Oh, the joys of cruising!

Next up, we had the Spanish Inquisition Palace/Museum on the itinerary, which sounded like a real hoot on paper. I mean, who wouldn't want to get grilled by some historical inquisitors?

But alas, reality slapped us across the face like a wet fish. Apart from a few cheap knock-offs, it turns out that all the juicy artefacts from the museum had been swiped by some local bigwig. Talk about a historical heist! So, what are we left with? A couple of dusty trinkets and some half-baked descriptions of what used to be here. I've seen more excitement at a bingo night in a retirement home.

Honestly, if you were thinking of checking this place out on your own, do yourself a favour and save your pesos. It's about as thrilling as watching paint dry on a Sunday afternoon.

After that disappointment, we did a whirlwind tour of the new town, which was about as exciting as watching grass grow. Then it was back to the ship quicker than you can say "adios," because let's face it, there's only so much lacklustre sightseeing one can handle in a half-day port call.

Such a shame, though. With Cartagena offering up more attractions than a theme park on steroids, it felt like we were just getting a tiny taste of what this place had to offer. But hey, at least we'll always have the memories of that riveting finger-painting demonstration, right?

Ah, back to the good ol' ship and its standard security shenanigans. You know the drill—NCL's version of Santa Claus, making sure you haven't been naughty and snuck any contraband booze on board. Tip of the day: unless you enjoy playing sardines in a can, steer clear of the restaurants when everyone's clamouring back on board. Trust me, you'll thank me later when you're not elbow-deep in a buffet brawl.

Instead, I opted for a more civilised approach: a nice, frosty beer to take the edge off the chaos. Then, it was off to the theatre for a riveting documentary on the Panama Canal because, apparently, that's the hot ticket on this cruise. Let me tell you; the theatre was packed tighter than a can of sardines. See, I told you it's a theme.

Now, onto the main event: food time! Feeling fancy, I decided to cash in on some of those free speciality credits courtesy of NCL and hit up the sushi joint. With Michal as my sushi spirit guide, I embarked on a culinary journey of raw fish and rice rolls. Spoiler alert: it was delicious!

The rest of the evening was spent kicking back in O'Sheehan's, soaking in the tunes of 2Shay and enjoying some good old-fashioned relaxation. Because let's face it, after a day of dodging buffet mobs and navigating packed theatres, we all deserve a little R&R.

But alas, duty calls! With an early morning rendezvous with the Panama Canal on the horizon, it's time to claim my spot for the show. Best bring a lawn chair 'cause you can bet your bottom dollar that every other cruiser on board will have the same idea. Ah, the joys of cruising! Off to the land of Nod, I go, dreaming of canal crossings and sushi rolls.

Day 18 - Panama Canal

Well, folks, it's the moment we've all been waiting for the grand voyage through the Panama Canal, aka the world's most significant shortcut. Up bright and early, I staked my claim at the back of the ship, ready to snag the primo view as we sailed through those iconic locks.

But lo and behold, as I sauntered up to the Great Outdoors at the crack of dawn, what do I see? Every table was already taken, like a game of musical chairs gone wrong. Not to worry, though, because I had a secret weapon up my sleeve—literally. You see, I had a clandestine rendezvous with the Towel Pixie Mafia Boss the night before, securing myself a coveted spot at the back of the ship. Hey, don't judge; you gotta do what you gotta do in the cutthroat world of cruise ship seating politics.

So there I am, feeling like the king of the world, until I realise my seat has vanished into thin air. It must've been the work of the dreaded Towel Pixie death squad, those sneaky little rascals. Note to self: next time, speak in an American accent to throw 'em off my scent.

Now, for those of you who've never experienced the Panama Canal firsthand, let me paint you a picture: it's like Mother Nature's ultimate shortcut, slicing through Central America from the Atlantic to the Pacific like a hot knife through butter. None of this East-to-West nonsense—this bad boy runs North to South, covering a whopping 44 miles. It started way back in 1880 and finally finished in 1914, and it has saved countless sailors from the headache of sailing around the treacherous Cape Horn.

Our cruise? Well, we were on the express lane from Atlantic to Pacific (yep, it runs both ways), starting with a jaunt through the Gatun Locks, the first of three on our adventure.

Now, let me tell you about the unsung hero of our journey: the Narrator. This guy was a walking encyclopedia, spouting off facts and figures over the ship's intercom like a seasoned pro. With the average passage taking a cool 10 hours, this dude was yakking away for nearly the whole time. Talk about dedication to the cause! So here's to you, Mr. Narrator, for keeping us informed and entertained every step of the way. You're a true legend of the seas!

Ah, the life of a self-proclaimed fidget extraordinaire—constantly on the move, searching for that perfect vantage point. So, there I was, prowling the decks like a restless sea lion, when I stumbled upon none other than Ships Security Officer Neil. And let me tell you, this guy was like a walking treasure trove of insider tips for navigating the Panama Canal passage. So, being the generous soul that I am, I'll share his nuggets of wisdom with you fine folks:

First off, if you want the primo view and a shot at spotting some local wildlife (cue the crocodiles!), head on down to deck 7. Close to the action and far from the maddening crowds—what's not to love?

Now, here's the real kicker: while everyone and their grandma will be jostling for space at the first set of locks like it's Black Friday at Walmart, you savvy cruisers should hang tight. Wait it out until you reach Miguel or Miraflores Locks, and voila! You'll practically have the place to yourself. It's like getting front-row seats to the best show in town without the hassle of elbowing your way through the masses.

But wait, there's more! Ever dreamt of becoming an internet sensation? Well, now's your chance! Head to the small area at the front of the ship, usually off-limits to passengers, and strike a pose for the webcam. Your adoring fans back home can tune in live to watch you cruise through the canal, and if you time it just right, you might even score a virtual wave. Talk about fame and fortune, baby!

So, a big shoutout to Neil for the top-notch advice—spot on, my friend! And here's a little tip from yours truly: don't be a ship potato, planted in one spot for the whole journey. Get moving and explore every nook and cranny of the ship—you never know what hidden gems you might uncover. Just be prepared to elbow your way through the crew deck crowd if you want a glimpse of the front of the ship. Those seafaring folks don't budge for anyone, not even for the promise of a panoramic view.

Ah, Neil, the sage of the seas, strikes again with his wisdom! If you're aiming to capture the money shot of the ship shimmying through the locks, here's the insider scoop: save your energy for the grand finale. Plant yourself smack dab in the middle of the rear deck for the last lock, where the action is just a stone's throw away. Trust me, it's like finding a deserted island in a sea of selfie sticks—pure bliss!

Now, if you're the type who doesn't mind peering at the world through a thick pane of glass (or two), then have I got a treat for you! Option numero uno: snag a spot on deck 13 at the front of the ship, but be prepared to stake your claim early, like pre-dawn-early. Option two: mosey on over to the Spinnaker Lounge, where you'll be treated to a 180-degree view through giant windows. But wait, there's more! Picture this: you're lounging in comfort, sipping on your favourite cocktail, while NCL's finest waiters cater to your every whim. It's like being the captain of your own luxury yacht, minus the pesky responsibility of actually steering the ship.

And here's the pièce de résistance: the Spinnaker Lounge has these secret wings—think Captain America but with better views—that stretch outwards, giving you the ultimate panoramic vista down the side of the ship. It's like having your cake and eating it, too, with a side of bottomless mimosas. So, mark my words: if I ever find myself cruising these waters again, you can bet your bottom dollar you'll find me planted firmly in the Spinnaker Lounge, cocktail in hand, living my best life. Cheers to that!

Ah, the epic saga of cruising through the Panama Canal—like a real-life version of "Indiana Jones," but with more buffet lines and less treasure hunting. So, there I was, armed with my trusty video camera and a dream of capturing the journey for future generations of cruise enthusiasts.

Once we'd conquered the mighty Gatun Locks, I stationed myself at the back of the ship like a captain of the high seas, ready to document every twist and turn of our aquatic adventure. With the camera set to time-lapse mode, I embarked on a cinematic odyssey through Gatun Lake, capturing the essence of jungle life as we sailed towards the Miguel locks.

But, as luck would have it, disaster struck in the form of a dead battery. Cue the frantic dash to my stateroom faster than you can say, "Abandon ship!" After a quick recharge and a fumbling grab for the spare battery (note to self: always check the battery levels before embarking on a recording marathon), I was back in action, ready to immortalise our passage through the Miraflores locks and beyond.

Now, you might think standing at the back of a ship for over five hours sounds like a recipe for boredom, but let me tell you, my friends, there's nothing quite like the mesmerising beauty of a jungle passing by to keep you entertained. And hey, when in doubt, why not try your hand at birdwatching? I mean, how hard can it be, right? Spoiler alert: not very. Spot a bird, spot another bird, rinse, repeat. Though I must admit, not everyone was as adept at bird identification as yours truly. Case in point: the poor soul who mistook a passing pelican for Big Bird from Sesame Street. Bless their clueless heart.

And just like that, before I knew it, we'd emerged victorious into the vast expanse of the Pacific Ocean, a first for yours truly. Consider me converted—I'd recommend the Panama Canal cruise to anyone with a penchant for adventure and a love of sea days. Sure, there may be more downtime than a sloth on vacation, but crossing that canal is like checking off a major item on your cruising bucket list. So grab your sunscreen and your sense of humour, folks, 'cause this is one journey you won't want to miss!

Ah, the eternal struggle of deciding what to wear for dinner—a tale as old as time, my friends. But fear not, for the nice people at NCL had a little surprise waiting for me in my room: a fruit and veggie dip plate. Because nothing says "you're special" like a platter of crudites, am I right? Take note, folks, this is how you win over a cruiser's heart.

Now, onto the main event: dinner. I opted for the Garden Café because, let's face it, decision-making is overrated, and the food is always top-notch. But lo and behold, what do I find? A group of table squatters who've set up camp since I left for my Panama Canal filming extravaganza. I mean, seriously, folks, it's called a "cafeteria" for a reason—eat and skedaddle!

With dinner out of the way, it was time to crack open one of the bottles of Brut Sparkling Wine graciously bestowed upon me upon my arrival. Cold bottle in hand, I enlisted the help of my trusty stateroom steward to clear out the minibar remnants. Hey, I may be a champion wine consumer, but I draw the line at being mistaken for a booze-hoarding maniac. With glass in hand, I settled into O'Sheehan's, soaking in the tunes from the atrium and sipping away until that bottle was but a distant memory. Ah, the joys of cruising!

Next up on the agenda: the main event, the pièce de résistance, the comedy stylings of Jim McDonald. Now, this guy knows how to tickle a funny bone, let me tell you. Sure, some of his jokes might've sailed over the heads of us non-American folk, but when it came to observation comedy, Jim was the king. And let's not forget his trusty slide show—because nothing screams "comedy gold" like a good old PowerPoint presentation.

And with that, dear friends, it was time to bid adieu to another day at sea. Off to the land of Nod, I go, with dreams of fruit platters, table squatters, and comedy gold dancing in my head. Until tomorrow, cruise on, my friends, cruise on!

Day 19 - Day at Sea

Yet another day at sea, and you'd think this ship has a hot date in Alaska. It's like it's racing to get there before someone else claims the best igloo. I decided to make the most of this leisurely pace by not setting an alarm. I'd wake up whenever I woke up. Naturally, that meant 6:30 AM, so much for my grand plans of sleeping in.

This morning, I decided to go all-out fancy for breakfast and headed to the Summer Palace. This place is decked out like the Russian Czar's summer getaway, with walls covered in paintings that could give the ocean view a run for its money. Plush tables, freshly pressed tablecloths, gleaming cutlery—it's like a scene from a movie, unlike the Garden Café, where I'm pretty sure my tablecloth tried to eat me yesterday.

The star of the show, though, was the amazing Jeanette. She greeted every guest with such an enthusiastic "Good morning!" that I was half-expecting her to follow up with a Broadway-style song and dance. It didn't matter if you were a half-asleep zombie or Mr Grumpy Pants; she greeted everyone the same way. I checked her for batteries because I'm convinced she's related to the Energizer Bunny.

I snagged a seat by the window, perfect for enjoying my breakfast and the ocean view. Oatmeal, Eggs, Benedictine, baked beans, sausages, hash browns—all washed down with enough coffee and orange juice to power a small village. The service was top-notch, and the waiters were so attentive I felt like royalty.

But the real magic was happening outside the window. The Pacific Ocean was calm, and then, like an unexpected guest at a wedding, flying fish started leaping out of the water, gliding gracefully through the air. It was the first time I'd ever seen flying fish, and let me tell you, they were showing off. It was like nature's very own acrobatics show, and I had front-row seats.

Feeling like a stuffed turkey after breakfast, I figured a walk around deck 7 was in order. One of the perks of the Norwegian Pearl is that you can walk all the way around the ship. So, off I went, full of ambition and oatmeal. After one lap, I got caught in a traffic jam of leisurely strollers at the front of the ship. It was like trying to navigate through molasses. I gave up and accepted my fate as a sedentary sea creature for the day.

Say what you will about the older generation; they've got their exercise routine down. I've been on cruises with younger folks, and on sea days, you'd be lucky to find a handful of them alive and kicking before noon, let alone exercising. I think they've mastered the art of hibernation at sea.

Sea days, for me, are a golden opportunity to kick back, catch up on paperwork (who am I kidding, it's all doodles), and transfer the millions of photos and videos from my camera to my hard drive. I spent the morning lounging and scrolling through my holiday snapshots. Judging by the sheer volume, you'd think I was on an expedition to document every seagull in the Pacific. Spoiler alert: there are a lot of seagulls, and they're all equally unamused by my presence.

As I sifted through my digital memories, it struck me how many exciting places I've been to on this cruise. At least, that's what the photos suggest. There are still plenty more adventures to come, and by the end of this trip, my hard drive might need its own lifeboat.

I've been invited to the Latitudes party this afternoon. Don't know about you, but every invite to either the Captain's VIP or Latitudes party makes me feel like I should be wearing a crown and waving like I'm on a parade float. I've been to a few on this cruise, and I'm starting to think they should just name a lounge after me.

If you've never been to an NCL Latitudes party, it's basically NCL's way of saying, "Thanks for not jumping ship!" You get automatically enrolled after your first cruise – no secret handshakes required. The perks? Snacks and free drinks, but only for about half an hour. So, set your watch and make friends with the waiters like your life depends on it.

The highlight is always the raffle, with bottles of bubbly up for grabs. But, come on, NCL, can we mix it up a bit? It's always, "Who's been married the longest?" which is a bit of a downer if you're single or cruising to recover from a breakup. Maybe raffle off something more inclusive, like a golden lifejacket or a year's supply of Dramamine.

Latitude parties are also a fantastic place to swap sea stories with fellow cruise addicts. Most of them have been on more cruises than I've had hot dinners. The party ended, and I parked myself in one of those dangerously comfortable chairs. Next thing I know, I'm waking up with a sore throat that feels like I've swallowed a cactus. Turns out I'm not the only one. Looks like someone might have fibbed on their health questionnaire. Thanks, buddy, for the parting gift of germs!

On my way back to my stateroom, I stumbled upon the ship's best-kept secret: the elusive Party Line Class lesson. According to the Freestyle Daily, it was supposed to be in the Bliss Lounge, but the electronic screens claimed it was in the Barcelona Meeting Room—wherever that is. Tomorrow, I'll embark on an epic quest to track it down. Move over, Indiana Jones.

Just when I thought my luck had run out, I spotted housekeeping heading into my room with another complimentary gift of chocolates. I've said it before, and I'll say it again: it pays to stay loyal to your cruise company. I'm practically swimming in chocolate at this point.

With just enough time for the three S's—shower, shave, and strategise—I prepped for my dinner booking at the Indigo restaurant. Now, some folks think Indigo is the overflow for the Summer Palace, but I disagree. It's got its own unique charm, like that cool, artsy café you stumble upon and instantly fall in love with. Bright-coloured paintings, a sleek, modern layout, and an indigo carpet practically whisper sophistication.

And guess who was there to greet us? Yep, Jeanette, the Energizer Bunny's long-lost cousin, still beaming with the same cheerful attitude she had at breakfast. The food and service were top-notch. Friendly waiters buzzed around, always ready for a quick chat about how your day went. A special shout-out to Jha, my server for the evening, who made me feel like the guest of honor.

Dinner was delightful, and as I enjoyed my meal, I couldn't help but feel grateful for the little quirks and surprises that make cruising such an adventure. Whether it's tracking down secret classes or being showered with chocolates, life on the high seas is never dull.

I'm not sure how NCL does it, but keep it up! There I was, enjoying my dinner, when I glanced out the window and saw a pod of dolphins breaching near the ship. Is this the same dolphin pod you hired in the Med? Seriously, if they're on your payroll, give them a raise—they're nailing the synchronised swimming routine.

I've been walking past the Maltings/Shakers bar every night, and it's always packed when Jim is performing. Tonight, curiosity got the better of me, so I decided to investigate. To make sure I got a seat, I plopped myself down at 8:00 PM, ready for the 9:00 show. Lucky I did because three-quarters of the seats were already taken. This looked promising.

The hour leading up to Jim was filled with great music by 2Shay. The young lady in this duo has more energy than a toddler on a sugar high. Just watching her made me tired. She never stops moving, and her beautiful voice could probably charm the dolphins outside.

Then it was Jim's showtime. Now I understand why this place is packed, even with people standing. Meanwhile, over at the Spinnaker Lounge, which has enough room for hundreds, the band was playing to an audience of two. Jim's act is a delightful mix of piano playing, singing, audience interaction, comedy, and a sing-along. It's like the social clubs back home, which seems to be exactly what the older crowd on this ship wants. With the average age being 62, he's the perfect act for this cruise.

The show was so entertaining that I stayed for the whole hour before heading off to the land of Nod; my sore throat was now really painful. Funny enough, Jim announced he had the same problem. Maybe we've both been overusing our charm and vocal cords.

Day 20 - Puntarenas – Costa Rica

A new day, a new place, and a new country! Today, we're in the charming town of Puntarenas in Costa Rica, where the beaches stretch for miles along the Pacific coast. It's like nature decided to throw a beach party and invited everyone but the crowds. Add in the beautiful mountains covered in tropical forests, friendly locals, and houses with that old-world charm, and you've got a recipe for paradise.

Our ship docked at one of the longest piers in Central America, practically delivering us right onto the sandy shores. Just a short walk down the pier, and voila! Beach time. Since the ship didn't dock until 8:00 AM, and my excursion—the Skywalk and Eco Cruise Tour—wasn't until later, I decided to indulge in a leisurely breakfast at the Market Café. I had plenty of time before I had to report to the theatre for the tour, so I did a few laps around the ship to warm up for the walking tour. Yeah, I'm serious about my calorie balance.

Skywalk time! We hopped on a coach for a short one-hour drive to the start of the Skywalk, made even shorter by our tour guide's excellent rundown of Costa Rica and our destination. I did hold my breath and start looking for a seatbelt when our coach overtook a truck. I'm not saying it was close, but we clipped the truck's mirror and sent it flying. Nothing like a little adrenaline to start your day!

We stopped for a short break at a lovely hotel nestled in the tropical forest halfway to the mountains. This place was a gem, and even here, our guide kept us entertained with explanations of the local wildlife. According to the excursion description, we'd be seeing all sorts of wildlife, from birds to mammals. The guide, however, quickly set us straight, explaining that spotting any animals other than birds would be like winning the lottery. But hey, hope springs eternal.

The Skywalk took us through a lush tropical forest, crossing several suspension bridges between hills, with dense vegetation 50 meters below. It felt like being in an Indiana Jones movie, minus the boulder chase. The scenery was breathtaking, and the bridges added just the right amount of adventure to keep things interesting. This, my friends, is what cruising is all about—unexpected thrills, stunning views, and a little bit of danger to spice things up.

On every tour, there are always a few folks who apparently missed the memo about what the trip involves. This one was no different. In our group, we had two women who struggled with the first twenty steps off the coach. I could practically hear their internal monologue, "Twenty steps? Why didn't anyone tell us we'd need a Sherpa?"

The route lasted about half an hour, with our guide stopping to talk about the wildlife and various types of vegetation. We were lucky enough to spot several poison arrow frogs. The guide, channelling his inner Steve Irwin, chased one halfway down a steep slope and triumphantly caught it. We all got a chance for a close-up, though the frog didn't seem too thrilled about its modelling debut.

This part of the tour was fantastic, with nothing but the sounds of nature to disturb the tranquillity of the tropical forest—except, of course, for our chattering group. My only minor gripe was the blue rope lining the entire route, which sort of clashed with the whole natural vibe. It felt like we were hiking through an obstacle course set up by Smurfs.

Then it was back on the coach and off to the next adventure: an eco-cruise down a crocodile-infested river. This part did not disappoint. On the way, the bus stopped so everyone could hop off and snap photos of some bright red birds in a tree. Don't ask me for the species—I just know they were red, they had feathers, and they seemed important enough to warrant a photo op.

We soon arrived at the staging point for the boats, where we had a little time to explore the souvenir shop. Our guide explained that most people in Costa Rica aren't wealthy and that buying souvenirs helps support the local community. So, I had no complaints as I picked up a few trinkets, knowing my money was going to a good cause. Plus, it's always nice to have something to show off back home—"Oh, this? Just a little something I picked up in a crocodile-infested river in Costa Rica."

All aboard the small boat, designed for a cosy group of twenty, ensuring everyone gets front-row seats to Mother Nature's wildest reality show. Within minutes, our tour guide was pointing out various lizards and iguanas lounging on the riverbank like they were on a reptilian vacation. A little further up the river, we saw an impressive array of bird species, making every bird lover's heart flutter. But the true stars of the river were the crocodiles, the largest and most toothy residents.

As these crocs swam alarmingly close to our boat, everyone made sure their hands stayed firmly inside the boat. The boat's driver, in a cheeky move, sported a t-shirt that read, "No Swimming." Really? Like I needed that reminder. Just looking at those Crocs had me clutching my life jacket like a security blanket.

Speaking of life jackets, I had one pressing question: why were they even on the boat? Were they so the crocodiles could spot us more easily if we fell in? If the boat started sinking, I'd be doing my best impression of the Jesus Christ Lizard, which can sprint across water. Trust me; I'd break water-speed records if it meant outrunning a Croc.

Despite my mild panic, this boat tour was a must for anyone who loves crocodiles and other wildlife. The trip ended with some much-needed refreshments. It wasn't the heat that got to me—it was only in the thirties—but the humidity was like being wrapped in a warm, damp blanket. The cold drinks and fresh fruit were a lifesaver.

All too soon, we were back on the coach, heading back with our guide filling us in on more fascinating facts. As we bumped along, I couldn't help but think about how lucky I was to be on this adventure, even if it did involve a little too much close-up time with crocodiles.

The tour wraps up a few hours before the ship is scheduled to depart, leaving ample time to explore the area around the beach and pier. As you wander, the first thing that strikes you is the blissful lack of crowds. This place would be teeming with people if there was more than one ship in port, but today, it's just us on the Pearl.

For a deeper dive into Costa Rican culture, take a stroll through the local market along the seafront. Pick up a souvenir, but remember to channel your inner haggler. They expect you to barter, so don't just settle for the first price unless you're in a hurry or allergic to discounts.

Back on board with time to spare, I indulge in one of my favourite pastimes: watching the pier runners. These are the folks who misjudged their time and are now sprinting down the pier, wild-eyed and panicked, while the ship waits for them. It's like an impromptu comedy show. The best part? The ones who think they can casually stroll, snapping photos along the way, even though the ship's officers are waving frantically at them. Their heads are so far up their own self-importance, they might need a map to find reality.

After a day in the sun, it's time for a cold one or two at O'Sheehan's, followed by some Fish & Chips. Today's verdict: absolutely delicious. Even the mushy peas had the right texture, and the fish was perfectly crispy with fluffy white insides. I've had Fish & Chips on board before that were soggy, like they'd been cooked by someone who thought "crisp" was a type of lettuce.

A couple of cold ones later, it's already time for the evening show at the theatre. Tonight's entertainment is Sideshow Bert, a comedy-juggling act that was hands down the best show of the cruise so far. Bert's blend of humour and jaw-dropping juggling skills was a must-see, although the show only lasted 45 minutes.

Feeling a bit under the weather, I contemplated an early night but found my room wasn't ready. So, it was back to O'Sheehan's for me. The Atrium was an option, but I swear some people park themselves there in the morning and never move all day.

My decision paid off as I spent the next hour appreciating the talents of Avalon. The young lady has a voice that could make a statue weep. The guy playing the electric organ while singing? Not so much. He should definitely leave the singing to her. Here's a thought: how about a duet with the two ladies from Avalon and 2Shay? Now, that would be worth listening to.

With that, it's finally time for the land of Nod.

Day 21 - Another Day at Sea

Alright, picture this: It's 08:00, and I'm finally dragging myself out of bed. Whether it was the swaying of the ship or just my innate ability to be a professional sloth, who knows? Anyway, I manage to shuffle my way to the garden or market café – honestly, they could call it "The Breakfast Nook of Mystery" for all I care. Coffee and croissants, here I come!

Have you ever lounged on your patio, soaking up the sun and the sweet symphony of nothingness? Multiply that by a thousand, and you might get close to the experience of sitting on an open deck, basking in the glow of the morning sun, the ocean's gentle whisper in the background, and the faint hum of the ship's engine. It's breakfast cruise style, baby. And there's a waiter who seems to have a sixth sense for when your coffee needs a top-up. Perfection.

So, it's another day at sea with more activities lined up than a hyperactive summer camp. We're headed to the ancient realms of Guatemala and Mexico, where the Mayan civilisation once thrived. I decided to catch a talk by Gabi, one of our ship's entertainers and self-proclaimed Mayan expert.

While waiting for the presentation, I engage in my favourite pastime: people-watching. It's a goldmine. I spot a couple of generously-sized folks attempting to wedge themselves into the theatre seats. And then it hit me – faster than an NCL waiter spots an empty glass – a brilliant thought, one for the cruise industry record books: Why doesn't NCL lead the way in creating rows of seats 1 ½ times the standard size?

Imagine a designated section with seats proudly boasting signs like "Reserved for the Larger Than Life." It would be the ultimate social experiment, akin to the reserved seating for the disabled but right in the middle of the ship for added ballast! Who would own up and sit there? All jokes aside, watching those folks squirm in the regular seats is a real knee-slapper, but I bet it's less funny when you're the one with numb buttocks.

So, there you have it, another day at sea filled with laughter, sunshine, and the occasional bout of deep philosophical musings about ship seating arrangements.

So, after some technical shenanigans that would make even a tech-savvy millennial cringe, Gabi finally kicked off her presentation. And let me tell you, it was obvious this topic was her jam. No script, no slides—just pure, unfiltered Gabi passion. The talk was like a Ted Talk meets stand-up comedy, lasting a full 1 ½ hours. Hats off to Gabi!

If I had to nitpick (and who am I kidding, I always do), it would be the America-centric focus. I get it; it's an American Cruise Line, but hey, we've got a mini United Nations on board. Not everyone gets the endless references to baseball and apple pie.

I had planned to hit up a lecture in the art gallery, but Gabi's deep dive into Mayan civilisation had me hooked. So, I spent the next hour doing what I do best: absolutely nothing. And let me tell you, I nailed it.

Next up was a presentation on NCL Mega Ships. As a seasoned cruiser with a soft spot for the Epic, I rolled into O'Sheehan's around 13:15 for a good spot. That's when I encountered the dark underbelly of cruising: seat savers. Someone had tried to reserve prime real estate by placing a piece of fruit with a cover and a note that screamed entitlement: "We'll be back." The note said 'they' not 'we,' so clearly, a crew member was involved in this fruit-based conspiracy.

NCL's policy on seat saving? It's about as clear as mud. By 13:35, with no sign of the seat hoarders, I did what any self-respecting cruiser would do: I relocated the fruit. Fifteen minutes before showtime, the culprits returned, outraged that their fruity placeholder had been ousted. They spoke English with an American accent—surprise, surprise—and left in a huff after the Mega Ships talk wrapped up.

The presentation itself was fascinating, and I spotted the hidden quiz of the day. The Cruise Next Manager, while showcasing the Epic and Studio Lounge, had a little slip-up. The photo labelled as the Studio Lounge on the Epic was actually from the Getaway. A small detail, but hey, I'm three for three on spotting these hidden quizzes this week.

And speaking of quizzes, it raises an important question: if she's the Cruise Next Manager, who's menanging the Cruise Now? Just a thought. But I digress. Onward to more cruising adventures, where the fruit is for eating, not for seat-saving!

So, I fully embraced the freestyle cruising life this afternoon, which basically means I did a whole lot of glorious nothing. Just me, a comfy chair, and a glass of champagne graciously provided by NCL. The backdrop to my laziness was the sweet serenade of 2Shay at the Maltings bar, and let me tell you, that's how you do cruising right.

On my way past the theatre, I noticed tonight's show was a tribute to Frankie Valli and the Four Seasons. Music from the middle of the last century? Sure, why not! It's freestyle cruising, after all—if I didn't like it, I could always make a dramatic exit.

Turns out, the show featured some seriously talented male singers. I couldn't recognise most of the tunes, but who cares? It was a delightful way to spend the evening. The audience, a collection of enthusiastic coffin dodgers, were having the time of their lives. This is what you call entertainment—giving the people what they want!

Still not feeling 100%, so I decided to call it an early night and drift off to the land of Nod. Because even on a cruise, sometimes the best activity is no activity at all. Cheers to that!

Day 22 - Puerto Quetzal – Guatemala

Is sunrise your favourite time of day? Then you've got to experience it from the back of a ship. Picture this: the moon slowly lowering, casting a silvery glow through the morning sea mist on one side, while the first rays of the sun peek over the horizon on the other. It's like nature's way of showing off, and trust me, there's no better way to greet the day.

Today's port of call is the magnificent city of Puerto Quetzal on the Pacific coast of Guatemala. With the ship scheduled to arrive at 09:00 and my coffee plantation tour not until 10:15, I had plenty of time for a leisurely breakfast and some prime ship-watching as we docked.

Now, the Freestyle Daily says we'll be docking at 09:00, but remember, that's the "estimated" time. We could be cruising into port up to an hour earlier. Puerto Quetzal's cruise port is an interesting sight—a sprawling industrial hub with a tiny patch of green oasis in the middle, no bigger than 200m by 200m. It's like someone forgot to finish their SimCity project.

Tour time rolled around, so I headed to the theatre to meet my fellow coffee aficionados. We were sternly instructed not to stop for shopping on the way to the buses, lest we delay our departure. I wondered how many self-important folks would ignore this and stop anyway. Miraculously, everyone on my bus showed up on time and with no shopping bags in sight. A minor cruise miracle!

So, off we went, ready to dive into the caffeinated wonders of Guatemala. Because if there's one thing that pairs perfectly with a sunrise at sea, it's a fresh cup of local coffee. Cheers to the adventures ahead!

The coach trip to the coffee plantation took about an hour, which, in theory, is a perfect chance to soak in the local countryside and immerse yourself in the culture. However, instead of quaint villages and lush landscapes, my view was mostly piles of rubbish. Imagine trying to capture a picturesque river winding through a valley, only to find your shot photobombed by mountains of trash.

This wasn't just a one-off eyesore either—the entire route was like a guided tour of Guatemala's landfill collection. It shattered my dreamy image of the place. Curious (and slightly horrified), I asked our guide about the trash problem. He shrugged and chalked it up to a lack of education, claiming it was cleaner than other Central American countries. I silently disagreed, having just been to some of those countries, and mentally scratched Guatemala off my list of potential land-based holiday spots.

But then, salvation! The coffee plantation was like stepping into another world—immaculately clean and pristine. Maybe it was the armed guard lurking about, discouraging would-be litterbugs with the power of intimidation. Nothing says "don't litter" like a guy with a gun.

Once off the coach, we were introduced to our tour guides: the lovely Anna and her boss (I think), who swooped in whenever Anna struggled with an explanation. The tour kicked off with a brief history of the Finca Columbia Coffee Plantation, followed by a short twenty-minute walk around the growing area.

Now, NCL goes to great lengths to prepare you for these tours. They put information on every tour description and even on your trip ticket. Despite this, some folks just can't be bothered to read. On our tour, we had a woman who needed assistance walking and people wearing flip-flops despite being told to wear sturdy shoes. Ignoring this info isn't just a minor oversight; it's a major inconvenience for everyone else who has to keep stopping to wait.

So, if you're planning a cruise and think you can wing it by ignoring instructions, remember: your flip-flops might be comfy, but they're not going to make you any friends when the rest of us are stuck on a leisurely tour-turned-hiking-trip because of your poor footwear choices.

I met this lovely Australian couple on the cruise who shared a gem of a story. They had signed up for a tour called "Hiking up a Volcano." Now, which part of that title hides any mystery? Despite the glaringly obvious nature of the excursion, they had people on their tour who couldn't walk to the mailbox without assistance, let alone hike a volcano. These folks ended up needing horses!

NCL excursions are a fantastic and fun way to explore, but come on, people—read the description before booking. Don't be a selfish tourist; be a "Traveller, not a Tourist."

Back to my Coffee Plantation tour, Anna stopped at several points to explain the different planting processes and stages of coffee bean maturity. At one point, some of the larger members of our group apparently decided they were starving and started munching on the coffee beans right off the plants. Who needs breakfast when you have raw coffee beans, right?

Back at the ranch, Anna explained the entire process, from picking the coffee beans to packing and shipping them. One of the many interesting facts she shared was that the beans are shipped green before roasting because they last longer this way.

Then came the highlight: tasting the homemade coffee. You can't get a fresher cup of joe—it's grown and brewed right on the plantation. True to their word, the coffee was divine. I bought a bag of coffee beans to take home; just don't tell Customs.

This tour is a must if you're a coffee lover like me. You'll be amazed at how many steps go into producing your morning cup. It's not as complicated as the big coffee manufacturers would have you believe, just incredibly time-consuming. And hey, now you can savour your coffee with a newfound appreciation—and maybe a laugh or two thinking back on the bean-munching tourists.

Back on the coach for the hour-long trip back to the port, we were treated to even more scenic views of... you guessed it, rubbish. It was like the trash parade decided to follow us. But remember that little oasis in the harbour I mentioned earlier? Turns out it's a hidden gem, with loads of souvenir shops and stalls scattered around. It's a beautiful spot in its own right, a perfect place to snag some mementoes. So, let me drop some souvenir-shopping wisdom on you:

- These are souvenirs, folks. Don't expect a Gucci handbag at a flea market price.

- Haggle like your life depends on it. Seriously, the first price is just a suggestion. They expect you to negotiate.

- For the ultimate deal, scope out what you want, ask the price, and then walk away. Come back about half an hour before you need to board the ship and haggle again. The stallholders know the tourist dollars are about to sail away, so they're more likely to cut you a sweet deal.

Following my own advice, I managed to get bags for my daughters. Initially priced at $25 each, I got them down to $12 each just before the ship was set to leave. That's better than half-price, folks! So, not only did I return with bags of goodies, but I also returned with bags of pride in my haggling prowess.

Talking of great deals, let me spill the beans about the red tent-like structure near the gangway entrance. It's like a magical oasis, offering cold beers for $3—a whopping $5 less than the ship prices. Plus, it comes with free internet! This little spot saved me $30, thanks to my heroic consumption of six large beers. Doing the math? Yep, I boarded the ship after downing six brews.

Back on board, I headed straight to O'Sheehan's for another beer. What can I say? Once you've got the taste, there's no turning back. I parked myself overlooking the gangway, ready for a riveting game of "spot the pier runners." Sadly, no runners today—boring!

You never know who you might end up chatting with on an NCL cruise. Turns out, I spent twenty minutes talking to Elton John! Well, at least the guy who will be Elton John in the Legends in Concert Show. He let slip some insider info about an upcoming show called 'Throwback to 1969,' where he'll be performing. He asked me to keep it hush-hush, so mum's the word—until now, but the show's long gone, so no harm, no foul.

A few more drinks later, I decided it was time for a snack at the Garden Café. For some inexplicable reason, I was utterly exhausted tonight. It must have been the high altitude of the coffee plantation and all that caffeine. It definitely had nothing to do with the copious amounts of alcohol consumed. So, off to the land of Nod early for this little cruiser.

Day 23 - Puerto Chiapas – Mexico

Well, up at the unholy hour of 'why-am-I-awake,' the internal bickering began between my body and mind. In a brilliant strategic move of divide and conquer, the body opted to stay nestled in the cosy embrace of the bed, wrapped up in a warm quilt like a burrito, while the mind decided to go on an early morning adventure around the ship.

Not to worry, the mind eventually returned about an hour later, full of excitement and ready to kick the body out of bed to share its early morning discoveries. The first revelation happened during a lonely wander down the empty corridor of deck 9, where it deciphered the true meanings behind those mysterious door signs outside every cabin:

- Welcome: Please, come in and clean up my catastrophe.

- Makeup Cabin: I've finished creating chaos, so please come in and tidy up.

- Turn Down Cabin: I've made such a disaster I can't find the bed; please, save me.

- Do Not Disturb: Busy, generating more mess for you to clean later.

The second epiphany occurred in the Garden Café around 5:30 AM. There, five husbands were stationed near the window, dutifully reserving tables for their wives' future breakfast endeavours. You could tell these men were not naturally early risers—they were practically snoozing over their half-filled coffee cups, each table meticulously set for their better halves.

To paint you a picture, imagine your granddad slumped in a chair, precariously holding a cup of coffee that seems destined to spill as he dozes off. One brave husband appeared to have made a daring escape, leaving a perfectly set table for two, complete with full cups of coffee, likely hoping to return before his wife arrived for breakfast.

With body and mind finally reunited, it was time for my own breakfast—a heroic effort to refuel before another day of cruise ship shenanigans. The ship was scheduled to dock at Puerto Chiapas at 08:00 in the Soconusco region of southern Chiapas, Mexico. And thus, another day of cruising adventures and inevitable misadventures began.

The meeting point, as usual, was the theatre, which had turned into an impromptu game of "Guess the Tour." Today, though, it was too easy. When they announced the "Chocolate Discovery" tour, half the oversized population in the theatre stood up, along with the chocolate addicts like yours truly. Of course, we crafty snack enthusiasts had cleverly disguised our tour selection among other activities to avoid detection.

The tour involved a coach trip from the port, and I had the brilliant idea of sitting near the exit so I could nab a prime front seat on the bus for some stellar video footage of the local area. Being the overachiever I am, I was one of the first people off the ship for this tour. So imagine my surprise when I reached the assembly point and found a queue that could rival Disneyland's.

These folks either had Olympic-level sprinting skills to beat me there or had simply bypassed the meeting point instructions, probably parachuting off the ship. Their plans backfired spectacularly when the line moved from the rear first. Ha! I ended up near the front of the bus, right behind some savvy young German lady who had commandeered the bus the moment it arrived. Now that's playing the game smart.

As I settled into my seat, ready for a day of chocolate-induced euphoria and cultural enlightenment, I couldn't help but chuckle at the antics and absurdities of cruise life.

After a brief jaunt through the Mexican countryside—remarkably free of the rubbish-strewn landscapes of Guatemala—we rolled into the quaint village of Chiapas. The streets here were so narrow that they seemed more suited for a parade of unicyclists rather than our lumbering bus. My hat goes off to the driver for his expert manoeuvring, a performance worthy of its own reality show, "Bus Drivers Got Talent."

Our bus finally shuddered to a stop in what appeared to be the local village square. Picture this: a small market bustling with vendors, a grand stage complete with a lively band, local dancers, and a cooking demonstration that promised to be more exciting than any cooking show on TV.

At this point, I was still on the lookout for a chocolate factory, imagining a scene straight out of Willy Wonka's playbook. But no chocolate rivers or Oompa Loompas were in sight. Instead, we were herded off the coach and onto the stage. Laid out before us were the different stages of chocolate production, each more intriguing than the last.

It slowly dawned on me—we weren't heading to a factory at all. We were in for something far better: a hands-on demonstration by the local artisans themselves. A couple of local ladies, decked out in traditional costumes, took the stage and embarked on a full-scale chocolate-making demonstration. They showed us how to transform cocoa beans into the divine confection we all know and love.

We got to taste the chocolate at every stage, starting from its bitter beginnings to the sweet finale that left us all drooling. It was a revelation! Turns out, the road to chocolate nirvana is paved with cocoa beans and the expert hands of these wonderful local chocolatiers. Who needs a factory when you've got the magic right here?

Chocolate demo over, we were treated to a spectacular show by the local villagers, featuring everything from ancient Mayan tribal dances to more modern moves by local women. Now, I knew these performers were true locals and not professionals because I had just bought chocolate from a stall-keeper who was now on stage, shaking a leg like nobody's business. Talk about multitasking!

After the dance extravaganza, we had some time to browse the stalls near the stage and contribute to the local economy. I did my part, mostly by buying more chocolate, because who can resist?

Next, our guide for the day, Mara, led us on a tour of the domestic market and the church. Mara was like the walking Wikipedia of Chiapas, providing fascinating tidbits about the local culture. After the guided tour, we were set loose for half an hour to explore more of the village on our own.

For those wary of exploring small towns solo due to crime concerns, fear not! The place was swarming with police, all making sure we felt safe and sound. The last thing these villagers want is an incident that scares away future tourists. Personally, I felt safer here than in my own kitchen during a cooking mishap. And I'm the type who loves to wander off the beaten path.

Talk about hospitality! It felt like the entire village had come out to welcome us. Chiapas truly knows how to make you feel like a rock star. If you ever get the chance, don't miss out on this charming village. You won't regret it, and you might just end up dancing on stage with a chocolate seller.

Time to visit the Mayan ruins at Ipataz, a cosy little collection of ancient structures that, according to our guide Mara, was a bustling market area back in the day. It was discovered when someone decided to clear some trees, probably thinking, "Hey, let's see what's under this jungle!"

The Mayan ruins were a big draw for many of us cruisers, the ancient equivalent of Disneyland. Once we got off the bus, everyone fell into a reverent silence, hanging on Mara's every word as she regaled us with tales of the Mayans. She also emphasised the importance of staying together until the end of the tour, at which point we'd be free to explore on our own.

One of the many fascinating tidbits we learned was about a square on the ground. Apparently, back in the day, you'd start at one corner and sacrifice a small animal like a rabbit to make sure your prayers were heard. If that didn't work, you'd move to the next corner and keep going until you reached the centre. Quite the process! Unless you're a rabbit!

But wait, there's more! The Mayans had a sports field where they played a game that makes soccer look like a gentle pastime. Instead of a ball, they used a human head wrapped in a leaf. The objective was to keep the head from hitting the ground, using only your shoulders and hips. And the stakes were high—lose the game, and your next stop was the top of the tallest building for a one-way ticket to being sacrificed. Talk about motivation to win!

Despite Mara's advice to stick together, most of us scattered like confetti the moment we had the chance. Who could blame us? With so much to see and photograph, it was every cruiser for themselves. I was no exception—after coming this far, I wanted to soak in as much history and adventure as possible.

Like most tourist spots, there's always a few photo hoggers who seem to think they've booked the place for a private photo shoot. Take, for instance, the prime structure in the middle that everyone was eager to snap. One guy planted himself at the top, fiddling with his phone for a solid 15 minutes, desperately searching for a signal as if he were expecting a call from the Mayan gods themselves.

Without a tranquiliser dart to assist, I resorted to the next best thing and hollered, "Move your arse! People want to take photos!" Miraculously, it worked. He shuffled off, possibly to find a better signal—or a less vocal audience.

For those into Mayan history, this place is a gem. It's believed to be the birthplace of the Mayan Calendar, the one that famously predicted the world would end in 2012. Spoiler alert: they got that wrong, thank goodness.

After a day packed with ancient ruins and impromptu shouting matches, we hopped back on the coach and headed to the port. The small shopping area nearby beckoned, promising souvenirs and an even more enticing offer—a small bar selling cold beers for just $3 a pop. A steal compared to the ship's prices and a perfect way to end a day of cultural immersion and comedic encounters. Cheers to that!

Early evening on a cruise ship is the perfect time to unwind before the nightly festivities. So, after a bit of relaxation, I headed off to dinner, followed by tonight's entertainment in the theatre. The highlight? A ventriloquist, or as I like to call it, a guy who sticks his hand up a puppet's backside and makes it talk.

Now, I have to say, the show was only about 75% funny. The first part was chock-full of American references that flew over the heads of the hundreds of international guests. Some folks even got up and left, presumably to find entertainment that didn't require a cultural decoder ring.

Just as I was about to make my own escape, the ventriloquist wised up and switched gears, moving away from the America-centric jokes. Suddenly, the show became more universally funny, and I decided to stay.

NCL here's a tip: yes, you're an American cruise line, but you have thousands of guests who aren't American. How about booking performers who can entertain an international audience? Have I mentioned this enough yet? Seriously, it's not rocket science—just good business!

Day 24 - Huatulco – Mexico

Up before the crack of dawn again, but today, folks, I'm the captain of my own destiny. After an intense hour of pretending to be productive with my little report, I indulged in a leisurely breakfast. Picture this: I'm at the back of the ship, savouring every bite while the sun decides to make a grand entrance over the horizon. Pure bliss.

Now, my morning routine involves several laps around the ship, where I occasionally stop to do absolutely nothing but stare at the sea. It's a profound activity, let me tell you. During this cruise, I've become quite the marine life connoisseur. I've seen dolphins doing their best acrobatics, a sea turtle giving me the side-eye, flying fish defying gravity, and a stingray that seemed to have a vendetta. Beats staring out my window at home where the most excitement is a stray cat or dog doing their business on the lawn. Seriously, try it sometime. The sea, not the lawn-watching.

Today, we dock in the stunning resort town of Huatulco, Mexico. Nestled where the Sierra Madre Del Sur Mountains casually meet the Pacific Ocean, it's a paradise with nine bays and 36 beaches. Yes, you heard that right, thirty-six. If you love the sun, this is your mecca.

With no tour excursions or mandatory fun on the agenda, I had the luxury of taking my sweet time to disembark. Here's a pro tip: always pick at least one port of call where you skip the official excursions and just explore. But choose wisely, my friends, because some ports are as lively as a snooze button convention. Seek advice if you're unsure.

Luckily, Huatulco is not one of those snooze-fests. There's a smorgasbord of activities, from lounging on the beach, cocktail in hand, to walking around the marina admiring boats that are definitely compensating for something. Shopping addicts, rejoice! There's everything from luxurious splurges to cheap trinkets for those folks back home who demand souvenirs.

As for me, you'll find me nursing a cold beer at one of the many beachside bars. They're conveniently located just a five-minute stroll from the ship. And did I mention the beaches? Thirty-six to choose from! If that doesn't scream "holiday," I don't know what does.

Well, after waddling off the ship—because apparently, the cruise turned into an all-you-can-eat-and-drink marathon—I decided it was time to stretch these legs. I embarked on a two-hour trek through some gorgeous parks and country roads, surrounded by trees and serenaded by birds. Who says exercise has to be tedious? Not me. After my nature jaunt, I needed a bottle of liquid oxygen, which conveniently came in the form of a cold Corona.

Now, the funniest thing here is the waiters. Spotting potential customers, they sprint towards you from all directions like snakes after a lizard (seriously, watch Planet Earth 2). They're desperate to get you to sit at their tables and spend your money. I swear, they must be on commission. I saw a couple of ladies try to make a break for it, but their waiter corralled them back like a determined sheepdog. Territory wars, my friends.

Totally refreshed, it was time to do something I hadn't done in about twenty years—go swimming in the sea. Yes, I know I live by the sea and have been on numerous cruises, but let's just say I have a healthy respect for the things that swim in there. Have you seen where sea creatures go to the loo?

Today was different, folks. I had a brand new GoPro camera, which is waterproof and absolutely screaming to be tested.

Now, the big question: where to stash my bag and clothes so they wouldn't be permanently "borrowed"? The idea of walking back to the ship in just my swimmers wasn't exactly appealing. Thankfully, almost anywhere on the beach was safe, thanks to the kind Mexican government. They had three armed military personnel and two policemen stationed at the end of the pier, eyeing down the beach like hawks. Not to mention a Navy boat anchored just off the coast and plenty of police patrolling the streets. This was a "steal something if you dare" situation.

So, after a quick striptease on the beach—making sure Greenpeace wasn't about to mistake me for a beached whale. Slowly, I walked into the sea, bracing myself. The last time I tried this, the water was freezing, but not here. The water was pleasantly warm, and I could see the bottom. If any sea nasties came my way, I'd spot them and make like a torpedo out of the water.

Carefully, I lowered the GoPro into the water to check for leaks. All clear, so down it went until it was a good two meters under, filming crabs crawling along the rocks. And yes, there's evidence I was in the water too. I spent the next few hours playing with my new toy, capturing some fantastic video of Huatulco both on land and from the sea.

And let me tell you, it was an absolute blast. The GoPro worked like a charm, capturing epic underwater footage, all while I expertly avoided any encounters with aquatic toilet-goers. If you ever get the chance, dive right in. Just remember to have a cold beer and a quick exit strategy handy.

As the ship was docked so close to the beach, I decided to stop playing around and head back to our floating hotel for lunch. Just my luck, as I was making my grand exit, I stepped on a sharp rock, resulting in a nice, long gash on the bottom of my foot. Note to self: next time, wear something on your feet, you idiot.

First things first, I hobbled back on board to my stateroom for a shower to wash out all the sand from my new battle wound. I felt sorry for my stateroom steward, Abdullah. Now, my stateroom looked like a mini replica of the beach outside. Sorry, Abdullah.

I still had hours before the dreaded "get your arse back on board" time, so after a quick lunch, I headed back out to explore more. This time, I stayed away from the sea, as it clearly had it in for me. Instead, I spent more time exploring the shopping area and the marina. I discovered that if you don't go on an organised tour from the ship, you can pay locally, but remember: they don't come with the added security that the ship will still be there when you get back.

I made sure to be all aboard in plenty of time, unlike some people who were twenty minutes late and provided everyone with the entertaining spectacle of the pier runner's game. Nothing like watching someone sprinting towards the ship with a mix of panic and desperation.

So, as has become a regular practice for me on this cruise, I plopped myself down in O'Sheehan's for a few cold drinks, watching the port disappear into the distance. Only one minor issue: can someone please decide what O'Sheehan's Bar & Grill is? Is it a bar where you can get food or a restaurant where you can buy drinks?

I was moved twice so people could sit down for food like it was a restaurant. Not like any other O'Sheehan's I've been to on any other NCL ship. Eventually, I got fed up and left.

Ah, cruising life. It's all fun and games until you step on a rock and get shuffled around like a piece of luggage at a bar that can't make up its mind. But hey, at least there's always a new story to tell and another laugh to be had!

The evening was winding down, so it was back to the room for the essential 3 S's. After that, I was off to grab a cold beer before heading to the theatre for the advertised variety show featuring Sideshow Bert & Richie M. I'd seen Sideshow Bert before—an excellent performance—but Richie M was a new one for me. Here's hoping for a great show.

No need to worry. This show had me laughing for the entire 45 minutes. New material from Bert and Richie M was a riot. What made this show even better? It was aimed at an international audience, which Richie pointed out with no jokes or references that only Americans would get. More shows like this, please!

Nearly made a fatal mistake on leaving the show. I mistimed my exit from the row of seats and stepped directly into the path of a stampeding herd of OAPs (Old Age Pensioners, for the uninitiated). They were moving faster than they had in the last 12 days, all heading to the Spinnaker Lounge for the throwback to the 1969 show.

The lifts must have been working overtime. In the interest of future cruisers, and because I was only seven in 1969, I decided to see what nearly got me crushed. This was the show Elton John (not the real one) had informed me about. It consisted of the legend stars and the production staff performing several songs and dances from the time of Flower Power, Love, and Hippies. The audience was loving it, with people joining in the fun.

The show ended, and I played it safe, remembering the ferocity of the stampeding OAPs getting here. The exit could be even uglier now that it was after 9 PM—some might realise it's way past their bedtime. So, I decided to stay for another beer just to be safe before heading back to my room and the Land of Nod.

Cruising life, I tell you. It's all fun and games until you get caught in the rush of seniors reliving the '60s. Cheers to another day of laughs, near-death experiences, and, of course, cold beers!

Day 25 - Day at Sea

Well, another day at sea and time to tackle that endless list of cruise promises. You know, get up early to watch the sun appear over the horizon while enjoying a light breakfast or two (come on, it's a cruise; who's counting?). Then, soak up the sun by the pool, complete with a leisurely soak in one of the many hot tubs for an hour or two. Maybe even treat yourself in the luxury spa with a relaxing massage or beauty treatment, or spend several hours in the thermal suite enjoying the sauna and steam room, followed by a long soak in the warm baths.

Attend one of the many events happening on the ship—surely there's something you'll like. How about dressing up for a romantic dinner in one of the speciality restaurants, followed by a show in the theatre? Finish the night with a moonlit stroll around the promenade deck.

Well, here's what actually happened. I woke up at 8:30, shuffled to the Garden Café for a full English breakfast, and then attended an event about Aztecs given by the very talented Gabi in the Spinnaker Lounge. The rest of the day? Spent with several cold ones, a luxurious snooze, and more cold ones before dinner.

The evening was dedicated to the fine art of doing absolutely nothing, just watching the world go by. But hey, welcome to Freestyle Cruising!

Day 26 - Puerto Vallarta – Mexico

Back to dry land today with a visit to the stunning port of Puerto Vallarta, a Mexican beach resort on the Pacific Ocean with tropical beaches, a rich cultural history, and local markets brimming with goodies. Something for everyone!

The ship didn't dock until 8:00 AM, giving me plenty of time to wander around the ship, soak in the sunrise, and work off a couple of those extra pounds I've accumulated over the last 12 days. And, of course, making room for today's breakfast indulgence.

I initially aimed for a healthy breakfast of cereal, fruit, and coffee. Well, that was the plan until I reached the Garden Café. Healthy intentions flew out the window, and I ended up indulging in an unhealthy feast. Never mind, I'll start the diet on May 15. Have you seen aeroplane food?

Today was the much-anticipated All-Terrain Vehicle (ATV) tour. Like a good boy, I headed to the theatre meeting point and waited for the tour to be called. Good news: it looked like a small group, especially compared to the crowd for the bike tour. You know, those silly bikes with no engine.

Off the ship, I met our tour guide and hopped onto the awaiting bus. Well, for a short ride, anyway. Ten minutes later, all five of us were dropped off at the local office of the company 'Canopy River,' the masterminds behind the ATV Adventure & Village Tour. After a short wait, we boarded an open-sided truck along with others who were already on board. We made several more stops to pick up folks from other companies.

I started to get worried. The group for the ATV tour was growing larger by the minute. This was the first tour with NCL that included people from other companies. It was turning into an ATV convention!

As we bounced along in the truck, I couldn't help but laugh at the absurdity. Here we were, a ragtag bunch of adventurers, all eager to tear up the trails on our ATVs. Who knew what lay ahead? One thing was certain: it was going to be one heck of a ride!

Once the last stragglers were picked up, we headed up to the base camp of Canopy River, nestled in the mountains. The drive itself was an adventure, winding through small villages with lush, dense tropical forests on both sides.

It was a delightful 30-minute journey, perfect for snapping photos of the scenery to remember forever.

Relief washed over me as the other people on our transport veered off in a different direction at the base camp, leaving the five of us from the Norwegian Pearl in our own little group.

Next up, the paperwork marathon. Form after form of waivers to complete, a check of driving licenses, the usual formalities. We were then fully kitted out with bandanas to prevent us from inhaling half the mountain (lucky me, I brought my own) and safety helmets.

Then came the safety introduction, where we got the lowdown on our new toys, the ATVs, which we'd be playing with for the next couple of hours. Safety first! A quick check to see if we could handle the machines involved following our new tour guide (the old one stayed on the bus) around one lap of the yard.

Safety check over, we were off! Lucky me, I got to follow the guide, with a young English couple from Birmingham behind me and bringing up the rear, an American couple well past retirement age who looked ready to redefine "adventure."

The moment we hit the trail, it was a mix of exhilaration and sheer comedy. Picture it: the guide tearing ahead, me trying to keep up without eating too much dust, the English couple whooping with excitement, and the American duo bravely bringing up the rear, looking like they were on a leisurely Sunday drive rather than an ATV adventure.

The scenery was breathtaking; the air was filled with the sound of engines and laughter, and I couldn't help but think: this is what cruising is all about. Adventures, laughs, and memories that will last a lifetime.

Now, this is what you call Off-Road ATV riding! Picture this: the track was a roller coaster of small mountain trails cutting through dense tropical forests with steep inclines, declines, and surfaces bumpier than a teenager's first shave. After about half an hour of tearing through streams and kicking up dust like a Hollywood car chase, we arrived at a stop to hike down to a stunning waterfall.

If you had your swimming kit, you could take a dip. Not for me, though, or the young couple Nicole and Craig. Meanwhile, our two more mature companions decided to stay up top, likely debating the merits of walking down a steep path versus the comfort of just staying put.

We had plenty of time to snap photos of the water cascading over rocks before disappearing into a stream winding through the forest. When we trudged back up, we discovered our two companions had thrown in the towel and headed back to base camp. It turns out they had envisioned a gentle ATV ride, not a jungle edition of an extreme sports show. But hey, respect to them for giving it a shot!

Back on the ATVs, we ramped up the pace, zipping along the trails for another adrenaline-fueled half hour before stumbling upon a bar in the middle of the tropical forest. Thinking this was the end, we happily guzzled a cold beer and spent ten minutes chatting with the guides and a mysterious man who seemed to appear at random points snapping photos.

Break over, we got back on the bikes for what we thought would be a short jaunt to the finish line. Wrong! Another half hour of wild riding ensued before we finally made it back to base camp.

The grand finale of our ATV adventure was a lesson on tequila making, which, let's be honest, was just a prelude to the tequila tasting. And by tasting, I mean straight to the tequila shots. Some of them were surprisingly delicious, and a few even had me considering a new career as a tequila connoisseur.

After a short wait, we boarded the transport back to the port, retracing the same scenic route we took up. All in all, it was an unforgettable day of thrills, spills, and a healthy dose of tequila. If you ever get the chance, don't miss it – just make sure you know what you're signing up for!

If you're even thinking about taking this tour, let me tell you—this is the off-road adventure you've been dreaming of. Forget those lame "off-road" tours where you just bump around a flat field. This is the real deal, where the terrain is as wild as your imagination. Just a heads-up: if you're expecting a leisurely Miss Daisy drive through the countryside, this is not the excursion for you. But for all you thrill-seekers out there, this is a must-do.

Puerto Vallarta is a bustling port city, and there's no shortage of local stores, restaurants, and bars right next to the dock. Perfect for some last-minute shopping or enjoying a cold drink while soaking up the local vibes. Naturally, I took full advantage of this myself and found a cosy spot next to the local market to nurse a beer. Pro tip: if you need to exchange currency, there's a spot for that here. And yes, there are free Wi-Fi hotspots, but don't expect lightning speeds—you might be better off sending a carrier pigeon.

Back on the ship, it was straight to O'Sheehan's for a couple of beers. The highlight of the evening? Watching the classic Pier Runners show. Today's episode featured two frantic travellers being herded by security towards the gangway with just minutes to spare. It's like the cruise ship version of "Survivor," and trust me, it never gets old.

So, whether you're tearing up the trails or just enjoying a cold one while people-watching, Puerto Vallarta has something for everyone. And remember, the adventures on land are just as wild as those at sea!

Fun and games over, it was off to my stateroom for a quick change before dinner at the Lotus Garden, the ship's Chinese restaurant. The food and service were, as always, top-notch. My chow mein, or what looked like enough for two portions, was soon delivered by the kind waiter.

Now, on each table, they place comment cards for people to give feedback on the service they've just received. Naturally, being the curious type, I decided to read what someone had written on the card at my table. Some people either lack common sense or just want to fill the space with nonsense. The comment read, "Restaurant too expensive and not worth the money, Saki." Why are these people stupid? Well, it's a FREE restaurant! Duh!

Tonight's entertainment was a talented all-male string quartet called Well-Strung. They put their own spin on the music of Mozart, Beethoven, Madonna, U2, Disney, and much more.

One granny in the audience must have been on the sherbets all day because, after the first song, she was shouting, "More!" Now, let me think. These four musicians flew from the USA to Puerto Vallarta, rehearsed, and came on stage just to play one song and leave. You silly personage, of course, they are going to play more. The show lasted the same as all the other shows, around 45 minutes, but this group was definitely worth watching.

Day 27 - Mazatlán – Mexico

Day 14, and another port! Today, we dock in Mazatlán, the Mexican resort that could give Paradise a run for its money. We're talking 21 kilometres of sandy beaches, the kind that makes you question your life choices if you aren't there right now. Mazatlán is famous for its big-game fishing, which is a fancy way of saying, "Come here and catch fish the size of your car." Perfect for fishing fans and those who just want to tell exaggerated stories at dinner parties.

The morning routine is the usual: get up, attempt a walk that feels like a triathlon, breakfast (more like an all-you-can-eat endurance test), and then before you know it, I'm standing on the pier, squinting into the sun, waiting for today's tour. This adventure is billed as 'Nature Exploration by ATV & Boat,' which sounds exciting until you read the fine print. Apparently, the boat part has been swapped out for a village tour due to "local conditions." Translation: someone forgot to reserve the boat.

We hop onto a bus, a tiny group of 10 brave souls, off to our nature exploration. After a drive that felt shorter than a sneeze, we arrive at a government-run Turtle Sanctuary. It's not exactly the wildlife safari I envisioned, but hey, turtles are cool, too, right?

We shuffle into a small lecture room for a presentation on turtles. Our host, the turtle guru, speaks passionately in Spanish, and our guide translates. Or at least that's the theory. Turns out, our guide is fluent in Spanish but only semi-fluent in turtle facts. The rest of the staff? Nada English. So when the guide steps out for a break, asking questions becomes a game of charades, with lots of pointing and confused looks. Spoiler alert: "Why does this turtle look like it's plotting world domination?" does not translate well through interpretive dance.

By the end of the day, I've learned two things: turtles are fascinating creatures, and there's a lot more to "nature exploration" than just ATVs and boats. And who knows, maybe tomorrow they'll surprise us with something even wilder. Like, you know, a working boat tour.

The turtle talk finally wrapped up, and it was time to board the ATVs. Now, here's the kicker: they don't mention on NCL.com or in the shore excursions brochure that all the ATVs are for two people. So, if you're in a group of six (split in two), congratulations, you get to make a new best friend whether you like it or not. I was bracing myself for this awkward buddy system, but lucky me, there were only five people in my group. I got my own ATV, and I felt like the king of the beach.

If you were hoping for a heart-pounding, adrenaline-fueled ATV adventure like the day before, prepare to be spectacularly underwhelmed. This was a leisurely drive down a nearly deserted beach to a lagoon that looked like it was practising social distancing. The reason for the boat tour cancellation became glaringly obvious.

We had a riveting ten minutes of wildlife spotting, which consisted of me squinting at fish and birds while trying not to fall asleep. Then, it was a slow ride back to the office, making sure to follow the guide closely because the beach was littered with turtle nests. At one point, the guide spotted fresh turtle tracks, so we all stopped for an impromptu turtle egg show-and-tell. He carefully uncovered a nest, showing us the eggs like a proud parent at a science fair, then covered them back up to keep them safe from predators.

Back at the office, we swapped with the other half of our group, who had been chauffeured in a pickup truck to another beach. They got to admire the local scenery while we got to ride our ATVs like turtle-friendly sloths. Honestly, it might have been more exciting to send the ATVs to their beach and have the pickup do our turtle crawl.

Once we all regrouped, the center had a "once in a lifetime" opportunity for us. They collect all the turtle eggs after the moms leave and incubate them in a room that's basically a turtle maternity ward. After about forty-five days, the baby turtles are released back onto the sand near the sea, which is adorable and a little like a graduation ceremony for tiny reptiles.

So, while it wasn't the thrill ride I expected, it was a day full of surprises, new knowledge, and way more turtles than I ever anticipated. And who knows, maybe tomorrow's adventure will involve a boat that actually works.

As we've now learned, they release baby turtles on the beach instead of directly into the sea so they can imprint on the smell and sound of the beach. This way, they can find their way back to the same beach seven years later. Pretty smart for little turtles. At 45 days old, I could barely find my way to my milk bottle, never mind navigating halfway across the world.

Now, it was time for the "lifetime opportunity." Today, a group of turtles was scheduled for release, and we were the lucky folks who got to do the honours. First, we watched the centre staff show us how it's done in the wild: they dug a small hole in the sand with their hands, placed several baby turtles in it, and buried them alive. Don't panic—within seconds, little heads popped out of the sand like a scene from a cute horror movie.

We each got our own baby turtle in a plastic tub to avoid any squishing accidents. I named mine Steve Junior. A line was drawn in the sand with strict instructions not to cross it. We all stood there like anxious parents on the first day of school, waiting for the countdown. And then, all at once, we released our baby turtles.

Mine must have developed a bond with me because it was the last to say goodbye and scuttle into the sea. "See you in seven years, Steve Junior!" I called after it, already planning our reunion.

After the turtle release, we boarded the bus for the next part of the tour: the newly introduced city tour. Our guide drove us around, pointing out various exciting landmarks and even stopping at the local shrimp market for photos. Some folks opted to stay for a meal at a local restaurant, but I chose to head back to the ship.

Puerto Vallarta is a bustling port with plenty of shops and restaurants to explore before our ship was set to sail at 16:30. With a day like today, I spent the rest of the evening relaxing and enjoying the variety of music on board. It was an early night for me, reflecting on the day's unique and unexpectedly hilarious adventures.

Day 28 - Cabo San Lucas – Mexico

Today's early morning plan was simple: get up when the alarm sounds, perform the sacred 3 S's (Shower, Shave, and you can guess the third), chug a gallon of coffee, find a quiet spot, and catch up with my review. Easy, right? Except the alarm sounded like a fire drill at 04:00, and my body waged a full-scale rebellion. For an hour, I wrestled with my desire to stay wrapped in the warm quilt, but by 05:30, I finally managed to drag my sorry self into the shower.

Sitting on the bed to put on my shoes, my traitorous body made one last attempt to crawl back into bed. But I wasn't having any of it. Have you ever had one of those mornings where you feel victorious just for getting your shoes on, only to look down and realise you forgot your pants? Yeah, that was me. Dammit!

With time running short, my plans to update my review were thrown out the window. The ship was arriving in Cabo San Lucas at 07:30, or at least anchoring outside and using the tenders to go ashore. Some people gripe about this, but I see it as a great opportunity to confirm the lifeboats actually work. Hey, we might need them one day.

Cabo San Lucas is stunning, perched at the tip of the peninsula with the Pacific Ocean on one side and the Sea of Cortez on the other. The entrance to the port is a dramatic sight, with high cliffs on one side and a long, stretching beach on the other. Being a hub for sport fishing, we were greeted by a flotilla of fishing boats heading out to sea. It was genuinely spectacular.

The ship uses a ticketing system to manage the flow of people heading to shore via the tender boats. Unless you have a shore excursion, your tour ticket doubles as your tender ticket. So, with my tour lined up, I reported to the theatre, as usual, waiting to be called to the tender boats.

And thus began another day of cruising adventures, filled with unexpected hilarity and the kind of mishaps that make for great stories later. Who knows what other shenanigans await me today? Stay tuned!

The first thing I noticed when boarding was how small the tender boats were, holding only 94 people. I must have been spoiled by the Epic, which carries 200. But hey, as they say, a second-class ride beats a first-class walk—or, in this case, a swim.

Here's a tip for when you choose where to sit: avoid the spots under the driver's seat or the crew's seats, which are higher up. There are a lot of loose items—water bottles, hardback folders, and other random stuff, including hard hats for crew safety. If the boat hits a wave hard, you could end up wearing one of those hard hats. Hopefully, it lands the right way up; otherwise, it's going to hurt. If you're really unlucky, you could get bonked on the head by the other items.

One thing I will say: it's a good thing the housekeeping staff, along with other hotel staff, shows you how to put on your lifejacket. The sailors, bless their hearts, seem to have no clue. I noticed some wearing theirs incorrectly, which would hinder rather than help in an emergency.

All ashore and off to today's adventure: a 4x4 mini Jeep experience. Don't let the word Jeep fool you; we're talking off-road buggies here. Our group was small, so we all piled into a minibus to get to the site.

I think Mexico has a new racing driver in the making. Our driver seemed to be going for the land speed record for minibuses. We arrived in one piece, greeted by a beautiful sight (at least to me): rows of quad bikes and off-road buggies. This was going to be fun.

As with all motorised activities, we had several waiver forms to fill out before being given bandanas and safety helmets. As before, I used my own bandana—cleaner and more stylish.

So, buckle up and get ready for more laughs and lunacy as we dive into today's escapade. Who knows? Maybe we'll discover the next great racing legend or just get a good story out of dodging hard hats and speeding minibuses. Either way, it's bound to be memorable!

Off to meet our vehicles, and I quickly realised I was the lone ranger in a sea of couples. They paired off and shared their buggies while I claimed one for myself and made sure to snag a spot at the back. No way was I getting stuck in the middle, driving at a snail's pace. The beauty of being in the back is you can keep slowing down and then zoom to catch up. And that's exactly what I did. Hoo, what fun!

Time for the adventure to begin. We all set off, following the guide. As expected, a few buggies ahead decided they were auditioning for the role of Miss Daisy in "Driving Miss Daisy Goes Off-Road." They were puttering along like they were out for a Sunday drive. Move it, Grandma! So, I reverted to plan A: drop back, then zoom forward.

The route took us over a dried-up lake bed, packed with challenging spots, jumps (I know I wasn't supposed to, but hey, no one was looking), and steep inclines. We also drove along sandy beaches, which was as glorious as it sounds. We made several stops along the way for photos and to change drivers, though not for yours truly. This whole driving extravaganza lasted about an hour and a half, making it the second-best excursion of the cruise, just behind the ATV adventure in the mountains.

For all you thrill-seekers out there, this is a must. It's an adrenaline-pumping alternative to the usual sightseeing tours. If you want excitement, this is the excursion for you. And remember, always claim the buggy at the back.

Boo, the tour's over, and now I find myself back at the port. After a quick orientation, I'm dumped on the quayside surrounded by souvenir shops, bars, and restaurants offering free Wi-Fi. A word of caution about that free Wi-Fi: it's about as secure as a cardboard safe.

I spent an hour wandering up and down the quay, watching pelicans brawl over fish scraps tossed into the sea by the fishermen. There was even a sea lion getting hand-fed by some tourists right on the jetty. The pelicans looked like they were plotting a mutiny. I could practically hear them squawking, "Hey, fat boy! How about sharing?" and "Hey, humans, we're here too! Big beaks, love fish, remember?"

Feeling a pang of sympathy for the feathered freeloaders, I decided to drown my sorrows in some cheap pier-side beer. I found a nice bar next to the sea and settled in to watch boats coming in from the ocean while people in the other bars seemed to be having the time of their lives. Sampling the local brew while soaking in the scenery was definitely worth it.

Eventually, it was time to get back on the little rowing boat—sorry, I meant tender—for the trip back to the Pearl, which sat all majestic out in the bay. Once back on board, it was time for the Everest challenge: climbing from deck 4 to deck 12 for a coffee. Yes, I said coffee. The elevators had been packed the whole trip with cruisers who apparently have a deep-seated aversion to stairs. As one woman succinctly put it, "Use the stairs? Hell no."

Let's look on the bright side. If this had been the Epic or the Getaway, the climb would have been up to deck 15. I made the rookie mistake of walking through the Garden Café, only to be nearly mowed down by a stampede of hungry cruisers. They'd been off the ship for a whopping six hours and were in full-on food hunt mode.

Miraculously unscarred, I made it to my coffee in the great outdoors, where I spent the next hour chatting with fellow cruisers before it was time to feed myself at the buffet bar. Nothing like a little buffet bonding over a plate piled high with questionable culinary choices.

Tonight's entertainment in the theatre was "Legends in Concert," featuring Elton John, Michael Jackson, and Madonna. I'd seen this show before on my favourite NCL ship, the Epic, and it's always a hit. Tonight was no exception.

The show kicked off with Elton John belting out several of his famous hits. The audience was right there with him, singing along and getting into the groove.

Next up was Madonna. Now, I felt a little bad for her because about 80% of the older crowd wasn't quite connecting with her songs or style. But when she took her jacket off, suddenly, a lot of men leaned forward with renewed interest—until their wives' elbows quickly reminded them to sit back. People-watching truly is a sport.

The final act was Michael Jackson, who had the audience clapping and singing along again. But don't tell anyone—my favourite was Madonna. She not only sounded like her, but she looked incredible.

The only hitch in the evening was the sound. I know it's ironic for someone who's tone-deaf and hard of hearing to critique the audio, but halfway through Madonna's act, the sound went wonky. Michael Jackson's performance was almost drowned out by the drummer, who seemed to think he was the star of the show. Maybe the sound engineer is a frustrated drummer who likes to crank up the percussion. Someone should remind him that this is "Legends in Concert," not "Rock of Ages."

Well, excellent show, a must to see on any cruise, thanks, NCL I managed to see Elton John, Michael Jackson & Madonna all in one night shame there was no photo opportunity with the stars of the show as the other ship would have purchased the pictures of me with them.

Stopped in the Magnum bar for a while and listened to the unique style of Jim. Until it turned into a mass Karaoke, then made a run for it. If you saw a flash running down the corridor, it was me, arrived in the sanctuary of O'Sheehan's with the tranquillity of no screeching, just excellent music by Avalon. Soon, time for the land of Nod for this boy, so not to upset the guardians of the land of Nod off, I popped.

And so, another day of cruising comes to a close with a mix of laughter, near collisions, and a bit of off-key entertainment. Who knows what tomorrow will bring? Stay tuned for more adventures on the high seas!

Day 29 - Day at Sea

Day 6 at sea, the final stretch. I decided to embrace the art of doing absolutely nothing. No plans, just vibes. Well, except for updating my review—I've been a lazy sod some mornings and fallen behind. I devoted the entire morning to catching up. But as they say, the best-laid plans of mice and men often go awry. Here's how my day unravelled.

The first part of the plan went smoothly. Woke up—always a promising start to any day. Had breakfast in the Garden Café. Then, the plan went straight out the porthole. I was supposed to whip out my computer and start typing away. But no, I convinced myself it could wait. There was a presentation at 10:00 in the Spinnaker Lounge: a Q&A with the Captain, Chief Engineer, and Hotel Director about the technical operations of the ship.

Now, this turned out to be fascinating, apart from the occasional ridiculous question from certain...let's call them "unique thinkers." One gem was about the Costa Concordia. Really? What's that got to do with the Norwegian Pearl? Kudos to the Captain for gracefully sidestepping that landmine.

So, there I was, enthralled by the technical jargon and tales from the bridge. My review updates? They could wait. Besides, who can resist the lure of potentially learning about the inner workings of a floating city? Especially when you have an audience member comparing it to a shipwreck. Ah, cruising life—never a dull moment.

Right, it's time to get the computer out and finally tackle that review! Or so I thought. Instead, lunch beckoned, followed by a presentation on "Resolving Conflict at Sea." I wondered if the answer involved a plank and a hearty shove overboard. Intriguing, but I digress.

So, to achieve any semblance of productivity, I barricaded myself in the stateroom for a couple of hours. Partial success! I managed to update most of the review, though it wasn't without its challenges. The sea was rough, and the ship was rolling and pitching like a drunken sailor. I kept hitting the wrong keys on the keyboard, but hey, that's my excuse, and I'm sticking to it.

Picture me, swaying back and forth, trying to type coherent sentences while the room spun like a carnival ride. It's amazing I didn't end up typing out an entire novel on sea sickness remedies by accident. Still, progress was made, and I emerged victorious, if a bit seasick.

Like a bear emerging from hibernation, I left my stateroom on the hunt for food. Five hours without eating? The food police would surely be on their way. The funny thing is that NCL must have anticipated the rough seas because they placed sick bags next to every elevator on every level. NCL really knows their customers.

For a change, the Garden Café was nearly empty, with plenty of places to sit. I dined with the stars, enjoying my meal along with a great conversation with Elton John. Well, we know each other now, don't we? I mean, it sounds cool to say you had dinner with Elton John. Besides, the performer who plays him is a great person.

With some time to kill before the 21:15 show, I decided to waste it wisely with a few beers and a bit of exploring on the open decks. The ship was like a ghost town due to the weather, which made for some really great video footage of the swimming pools misbehaving! Waves splashing everywhere, loungers abandoned like a scene from a maritime apocalypse. Just another night on the high seas, filled with unexpected hilarity and the kind of mishaps that make for great stories later. Stay tuned!

Time for the theatre! Clearly, I must be becoming cultured. Tonight's lineup featured a variety show with Well-Strung and a new act called Fountains. Well-Strung played almost the same songs as their first performance. Seriously, do they not know any other tunes?

But the real show-stealer was Fountains. Imagine several people dressed in togas—who turned out to be the Cruise Director and his staff—acting like human fountains with all sorts of hilarious consequences. Picture water spewing from unexpected places. It was an excellent and side-splitting way to finish the cruise.

What surprised me was how some people seemed to lose the ability to read or follow basic instructions upon entering the theatre. Every show starts with a clear announcement: "Videoing or taking photos during performances is forbidden," and it's also written in the Freestyle Daily. Yet, the number of people recording or taking pictures was unbelievable. I was even temporarily blinded by the flash of some cameras. How did the cast manage to perform with all those lights flashing like a paparazzi frenzy?

I counted at least five people recording the entire show. If they thought they were being discreet, they were sorely mistaken. Phones light up, and in the dark, it's like a beacon calling for attention. Alright, rant over. You can continue reading.

Well, it's time for bed and the end of this part of the cruise. Tomorrow, another adventure begins.

5 Day Pacific Cruise

Day 30 - Disembarkation & Embarkation in Los Angeles

Well, that's the end of our grand Panama Canal escapade. Now, we're off to the Pacific, cruising from Los Angeles to Vancouver. Enter Dan the Man, our Cruise Director, whose entertainment line-up is firmly aimed at the retirement crowd. We're talking knitting workshops, joint pain seminars, anti-ageing lectures, bingo marathons, ballroom dancing sessions, and music nights featuring hits from the 50s, 60s, and 70s. It's a miracle I didn't leave the ship with a new crochet project and a back brace. But hey, nice try, Dan! Remember, not all of us are auditioning for the next episode of "Waiting for God."

Just because it's the last night of the cruise doesn't mean the fun has to end. Cue the Customer Services department with today's mystery quiz: spot the mistake, or as I call it, "spot the connection" (spoiler alert: there isn't one). We landed in the good old U.S. of A., renowned for its hospitality and ridiculously tedious customs checks.

Now, picture this: I'm subjected to more immigration checks than a herd of cattle at a border crossing. Next time, I'm pretending to be an American – they seem to breeze through with a wave and a smile. Meanwhile, I'm practically undressing in the security line. It's high time the EU adopted a similar policy: all Americans go through a million checks, and everyone else gets a free pass.

Rant over, back to the quiz. What's the connection between Dan's entertainment choices and U.S. customs? They both make you question your life choices and long for the sweet release of disembarkation.

Ah, the joys of cruising. Nothing says "relaxation" like being handed an I-94 and a Customs form by the ever-so-kind folks in Customer Services. And by "kind," I mean they have a sadistic sense of humour. They even threw in a daily mystery quiz on how to fill out the I-94. Let me walk you through this comedic gem.

The attached letter had instructions for each section. For instance, it told me that Section 8 should have my country and place of residence. Naturally, Section 8 on the I-94 asked for my passport number. A few more delightful discrepancies like this, and I felt like I was starring in a bureaucratic version of "Survivor."

But, determined as ever, I managed to get all the questions right. I marched triumphantly to the Customer Service desk to claim my prize. My reward? "Too late, we've already sent it out." This was the second hiccup from Customer Services. Seriously, does nobody proofread these things before they land in our staterooms? Come on, NCL, you're making yourselves look like amateurs here. A little quality control wouldn't hurt, you know?

Now, doing a back-to-back cruise in this part of the world is a pain in the bum. And that's putting it mildly. NCL does try to smooth things over bless their hearts, but let's compare this experience with Europe:

Back-to-back in Europe:

- Wear this "In Transit" sticker if you feel like getting off the ship. Your choice.

Back-to-back in America:

- Complete a Customs form.

- Complete the I-94.

- Get off the ship and be banned from returning for several hours.

- Wear the "In Transit" sticker as if it were a badge of honour.

- Endure the Customs procedure, which is designed to make a line of sheep look efficient.

It's like being part of an elaborate practical joke, except the punchline is your own exasperation. Thanks for the memories, NCL. I'll cherish them right alongside my collection of misprinted Customs forms.

Finally, off the ship and through what felt like an FBI interrogation, I found myself outside waiting for the mythical free trolley that was supposed to whisk us from the dock to Ports of Call. Surprise! Someone at NCL made a major oopsie and forgot to inform the port folks about the trolley schedule. No trolley for us. This helpful bit of info was shared by the kind soul working at the port, who probably had the same level of exasperation as the rest of us.

Well, no trolley, no problem! Looks like a walk is in order, which is actually a good thing since I've been overindulging in the all-you-can-eat buffet on the ship. I suspect the Shore Excursions department has been engaging in some mild fearmongering, claiming we needed to book their tours because the Ports of Call was supposedly a million miles away, and traffic in LA is perpetually gridlocked. Spoiler alert: neither of these claims is remotely true.

Ports of Call is an easy 15-minute stroll, even at a snail's pace. And as for the traffic, I've seen more congestion in my local village during a Sunday afternoon bake sale.

So, after my "gruelling" trek, which took all of, oh, 15 minutes, I arrived at Ports of Call. Now, what exactly is Ports of Call, you ask? It's a quaint little shopping and souvenir area along the port. Or at least it was until it got bulldozed into oblivion.

It used to be a charming collection of small shops in picturesque surroundings, where you could buy all sorts of trinkets you neither need nor want. Adjacent to this was a fish market and restaurant area. Not to say the food was fresh, but the fish were practically doing laps next to the counter. I swear, you could almost hear them say, "Don't pick me; pick the chubby one next to me. He's got more meat." And if you did choose one, you'd hear a disgruntled "Bastard, hope you choke" as it met its fate. Feeling guilty, I only ate the one that pointed to his friend.

The area was so delightful, I spent the next couple of hours wandering around, taking videos to share. Because nothing says "wish you were here" like footage of a demolished tourist trap and a fish market with a side of aquatic sass.

The Port of Los Angeles is nestled in San Pedro, the charmingly aged part of LA. Never been here before, so I figured I'd spend a couple of hours exploring the old town of San Pedro. I mean, how rude would it be to skip out on that opportunity?

So, what's the scoop on San Pedro? It's not exactly packed with Hollywood landmarks; this is the "other" LA. If you're dying to see the glitzy stuff, you'll have to sign up for an excursion. But fear not; there's plenty to see here. The local streets and shops are spotless, and contrary to what the Shore Excursions desk would have you believe, there's hardly any traffic. I even had time to practice my multilingual skills while buying a soft drink. Spoiler alert: "Coca-Cola" is universally understood.

For the history and naval buffs, our ship was berthed right next to the USS Battleship Iowa. Worth a visit, though you only get to see a small part of the ship. Still, it's impressive enough to make you want to salute someone or something.

With my port visit wrapped up, it was time to see if reboarding the ship was as painful as getting off. Surprise, surprise—it wasn't! All you have to do is slap on your Paddington Bear sticker on the top left of your shirt (for easy identification, obviously), and you get to skip all the queues. I was back on board within 20 minutes, feeling like a VIP.

San Pedro may not be the star of LA, but it sure knows how to treat its visitors right. Now, back to the buffet to undo all that walking!

Back on board, I made a beeline for the Customer Service desk to swap my room key for the one with those three magical letters: PBP. Yep, free beer for the next five days. Brace yourself, liver; it's going to be a bumpy ride.

With my PBP card in hand, I headed straight to the bar—for scientific testing purposes, of course. Several beers later, I figured it was time to feed the fat face, so I staggered over to the café for some food. Here's the problem with daytime drinking: it makes you sleepy. So, naturally, lunch was followed by a granddad nap that lasted several hours.

I was rudely awakened by the ship's intercom blaring about a lifeboat drill in 15 minutes. Half-asleep and confused, I decided to attend—better safe than sorry, right?

I must say, it was one of the better drills I've attended. They even explained what to do if we were docked—now that's a first. The only hiccup was the demonstration of the emergency signal: seven short blasts followed by one long one. Our drill master must have worn out the button because we only got seven short blasts. Where was the long one? This could have confused the first-time cruisers. Then again, I was too groggy to care much.

Back to the stateroom for a quick shower, and I felt refreshed and ready to enjoy the ship's entertainment. I spent the rest of the evening in Magnum's Bar, chilling out to the smooth sounds of the Pearl Show Band playing jazz. It must have been all that walking, and absolutely nothing to do with abusing the beverage package, that knocked me out by 10 PM. Off to the land of Nod, I went.

Oh, and I almost forgot to mention—thanks to the lovely folks at NCL, I was presented with two bottles of sparkling wine, a box of chocolates, and chocolate strawberries. I've said it before, and I'll say it again: it pays to stay loyal.

Day 31 - Day at Sea

Welcome to the first day at sea—or day seven if you're counting from Miami—the second day of this cruise leg. The swap-out of passengers has worked wonders. With a younger(ish) crowd on board and fewer people in general, we're not running at full capacity. The result? The Garden Café actually has available tables for breakfast! No more playing "Hunt the Free Table" with people who've turned table-reserving into an art form, complete with early-rising granddads and dodge-the-granny manoeuvres on the promenade deck.

As for me, I'm all hyped about the start of my third cruise on this grand adventure. I woke up bright-eyed and bushy-tailed at 4:30 AM. Yes, I know, quite the lie-in. After a big yawn and stretch in front of the mirror, it hit me: my food intake had overtaken my exercise output. I had officially become a sea fatty.

Wracked with guilt, I headed to the promenade deck for a few laps (3 1/3 laps equals 1 mile, in case you're wondering). Let's see how long this fitness kick lasts! After my exercise session, I felt justified in heading straight to breakfast. Hey, exercise makes you hungry! I opted for a healthy breakfast of Raisin Bran, followed by a not-so-healthy dead pig sandwich.

So here's to a new day at sea, with more room to breathe, fewer table wars, and the eternal struggle to balance indulgence with a semblance of health. Cheers to the sea life!

It didn't take long before I stumbled upon the hidden quiz of the day, courtesy of the ever-mischievous Shore Excursions desk. This time, the challenge was to identify the correct price of the Hop on Hop Off bus returning to the ship in Vancouver. According to the electronic display boards near the lifts and the one conveniently located right next to the Shore Excursions desk, the price was $49.

But wait, the plot thickens! The information and booking forms next to the Shore Excursions desk and the ones kindly left in your room by the always-helpful stateroom steward listed the price as $59. Guess which price I'm going to pay?

Armed with this intel, I marched over to the Shore Excursions desk to claim my prize/discount. The response? "Oops, we made a boo-boo." Really, Sherlock? Never mind, one ticket for $49, please. To his credit, he did honour the price, and later on, I noticed the prices on the screens had been changed. Case closed.

Feeling the need to make a significant dent in my Beverage Package, I headed to the Maltings Bar for my very own beer-tasting session. This was made even more entertaining and informative by the knowledgeable young lady behind the bar, Soini (I hope I got your name right!). I tried to catch her out several times, but to no avail—she knows her beer. Well, except for English Real Ale, but maybe NCL should send her on a tasting session to complete her education.

Five or six pints of beer later, I decided to pause the beer tasting for now. It was time for the Latitudes member cocktail party in the Spinnaker Lounge. As I've mentioned before, it's a great place to meet people and have a good old chat about nothing, all while enjoying the best-tasting drinks on the ship—since NCL is picking up the tab.

Feeling a bit cheeky, I decided to test the officer-to-crew feedback system. I made a point of telling Rumi, the Food and Beverage Director, and Joe, the Bar Manager, about Soini's excellent beer knowledge and asked them to pass on my compliments. Just to see if they would. Time will tell, and I'll check back on the second sea day of the cruise.

As usual, the cruise kicked off with the classic freebies: sparkling wine and a $100 off Photo Studio Package. The catch? Guess how long a couple's been married. Yes, it's the same tired shtick as last time. Can't they think of something new?

In a moment of brilliance (or sheer cheek), I scored a $100 Photo Studio voucher by declaring I'd been happily divorced for 20 years. The look on their faces? Priceless. With the party done, I moseyed over to the atrium for the NCL cruise presentation, hoping to uncover a nugget of wisdom I missed last time.

Nada. Just another friendly reminder that solo travellers get the short end of the stick. Starting May 1st, the Beverage Package promotion is off the table for Solo Studios or Inside Cabins. So, if you're a lone wolf, get ready to cough up double for a Balcony Stateroom. It's like they're saying, "Congrats on your independence! Now, pay up!"

The rest of the day? A masterclass in doing sweet nothing, or as NCL calls it, "Freestyle."

For the evening, I decided to go fancy with dinner and a show. Well, "fancy" might be pushing it since dinner was at the Garden Café. But hey, it was followed by a theatre show and topped off with after-show drinks.

Where else can you dine in a restaurant that's trying too hard to be posh, watch a West End-style show, and finish the evening with drinks in a Champagne Bar—all without worrying about cabs or driving? Only on a cruise.

Tonight's entertainment was comedian David Naster. Hilarious guy with some quirky viewpoints. Some parts of his show felt like an after-dinner speech, but it was delightful nonetheless. I rounded off the night with a tour of the ship's bars. There's always something happening until the wee hours for the night owls.

Having been up since 04:30, I was ready to hit the sack and sail off to Dreamland.

Day 32 - San Francisco – USA

Today, our magical port of call was the ever-exciting San Francisco, the glittering gem of America's west coast. This city's got it all: the Golden Gate Bridge, Pier 39, Lombard Street, Alcatraz Prison, and those iconic cable cars clattering up and down its steep hills like they're auditioning for a retro action movie.

Just like everyone else, I was up at the crack of dawn because passing under the Golden Gate Bridge was scheduled for 06:15. My body was unceremoniously kicked out of bed, the essential 3 S's were completed, and I avoided the mirror like a vampire remembering yesterday's fright. Like a dutiful cruise soldier, I was off to deck 7 for my mile walk. Yes, that's two days in a row—stop the presses! I even skipped breakfast, just grabbed my cameras from the stateroom and claimed my spot on deck 13 at the front of the ship.

Being the genius that I am, I bought a clamp for my GoPro. I clamped that bad boy to the top of the barrier at the front of the ship, set it to record, and voila! I had a continuous video from the Golden Gate Bridge all the way to Pier 35. Meanwhile, everyone else was contorting themselves like amateur yogis, trying to take photos through the glass or standing on tiptoes with cameras raised high, hoping for a decent shot. Tip of the day: Get yourself a GoPro with a clamp and save yourself the hassle.

If you've never cruised to San Francisco, let me tell you, the approach is a visual feast. The Golden Gate Bridge looks fantastic in the morning light, and Alcatraz Island—up close and personal—gives you a peek at the infamous former prison that once held legends like Al Capone and the Bird Man of Alcatraz. As you get closer to port, you're greeted by the noisy, lovable colony of seals on Pier 39, barking away like they're hosting a marine life talk show.

Once we docked and the customs folks gave us the green light, it was decision time. You could either join one of NCL's organised tours or unleash your inner explorer and go it alone. If you ask me, San Francisco is best-enjoyed solo—unless you're aiming for the Golden Gate Bridge, which is more of a scenic distance thing. Everything else? Just a stroll away from the port.

First stop: Pier 39. This place is like Disneyland for shoppers, foodies, and bar-hoppers. The shops and eateries are painted in every colour of the rainbow, stretching along both levels of the wooden pier, connected by quaint little bridges. It's prime territory for some epic photos. And trust me, the seals at the end of the pier are a must-see (or must-hear, if you were already serenaded by them upon arrival). Forget the selfie sticks—grab a fellow cruiser and get a proper photo.

Next up, Fisherman's Wharf. Just a bit further down past the eclectic fleet of fishing boats is a seafood lover's paradise. Fish restaurants and stalls galore, selling every sea creature you can imagine—and some you'd rather not. These critters are so fresh they're practically staging a jailbreak, slithering and crawling in a desperate bid for freedom.

And then there's Alcatraz Prison Island, looming ominously in the middle of San Francisco Bay. It looks just as foreboding as it does in the movies, with swift currents surrounding it. I swear I even spotted a shark casually cruising by, probably doing its own sightseeing tour.

For Alcatraz, you've got options. You can join an NCL organised tour, or you can book it yourself at Alcatraz Landing, where all the tours depart. You might save a few bucks going solo, but remember, the ship won't wait if you're stuck counting shark teeth. Price-wise, there's not much difference, so choose your adventure wisely. Once on the island, you get a pair of headphones and a self-guided tour in your chosen language. I skipped this tour myself but gathered all the intel during my last visit. If setting foot on the island isn't your thing, there's always a boat trip that circles it.

Lombard Street—ah, the windiest road you've seen in every Hollywood flick set in San Francisco. Now it's your turn to tackle this iconic zigzag, whether you're strolling up or down its famous curves. Spoiler alert: the street isn't actually that long, though it feels like it when you're trudging uphill. Officially, you're supposed to use the stairs on either side, but rebels and thrill-seekers often ignore this and walk right up the road. I can't exactly endorse that, but if you do, watch out for cars—they only go one way, but trust me, you don't want to be in their path.

Lombard Street is a tourist magnet, so brace yourself for some serious photobombing. You'll get folks standing in your shot for what feels like an eternity, but patience is a virtue, or so I've heard. Here's a pro tip: the road at the top of Lombard is a hot spot for those famous streetcars, which come by every 20 minutes or so. Stand there, and you can snap a killer photo or video of the streetcar bouncing over the first bump halfway down. They also make a pit stop at the end of the road.

If the thought of a steep, lengthy walk up Lombard Street doesn't thrill you, don't start from the bottom. The famous part is just the top section, not the entire stretch. Save yourself some sweat and hike up one of the adjacent streets instead. From Pier 35 to the top of Lombard Street, it's about a half-hour trek, depending on your fitness level and whether you get sidetracked by a coffee shop or ten.

Streetcars—riding one is on everyone's San Francisco bucket list. The starting point is on Taylor Street, conveniently close to the port. Tickets range from $7 for a one-way trip to $20 for a day pass. Make sure to brush up on the safety rules before hopping on since these vintage beauties are as open as they look in the movies. If you can, stand at the back for the best photo ops, even though sitting on the side might tempt you.

Beyond the iconic sights, there's plenty to do right near the port. You can easily spend the entire day exploring without venturing far. Pier 39, for instance, boasts bars that offer FREE Wi-Fi. I personally tested the connection at Beer39, and it was fast enough to upload all your seal selfies and then some.

Before you know it, it's time to head back to the ship. Be smart and plan to be back on board at least an hour before the all-aboard time—don't become one of those notorious Pier Runners, flailing down the dock in a desperate sprint.

Getting past port security is a breeze. Just flash your room key and a photo ID (a photocopy of your passport will do) to the gatekeeper at the main entrance. After that, it's a short stroll to the standard security checkpoint, where your bag takes a thrilling X-ray ride, and you get to strut through a metal scanner. Voilà, you're strolling down the gangway, greeted by the NCL security folks ready to scan you back on board.

Being back on the ship early gives you a prime opportunity to snap some killer port photos from your built-in vantage point, the Norwegian Pearl herself. After many early mornings and countless bad shots, I've learned to take my harbour pictures in the afternoon when we're leaving rather than arriving—much better light.

I then met up with Geoffrey, aka Elton John, in the Garden Café for a quick coffee chat. It's amazing how well he pulls off that disguise—no one ever recognises him! He had to dash off for rehearsal, prepping for his onstage karaoke later. One thing I love about him: unlike many artists who are overly full of themselves, Geoffrey is down-to-earth and a riot to hang out with.

So, take it from me—give yourself plenty of time to get back on board, enjoy the afternoon light for your photos, and don't miss the chance to chat with a legendary rock star in disguise. Cruising doesn't get better than this!

Not long before the Legends in Concert at the theatre, so I grabbed a few preshow drinks and tested Soini's knowledge at the Maltings bar. I caught the show last week but decided to give it another go—and boy, am I glad I did. It just keeps getting better and better. Sure, I spotted a few trade secrets, but let's keep those between us.

This time around, the sound system was finally fixed, allowing the artists' talents to shine through. You could actually hear them over the band's music and the other singers. Someone must have had a word with the drummer because he was no longer overpowering the show, instead, he was nicely faded into the background.

Madonna got the recognition she deserved from the younger crowd, and you could tell—it really boosted her performance and interaction with the audience. Elton John was on fire, even better than last time, with a crisper voice and more lively audience engagement. As for Michael Jackson, I could finally hear what he was singing, which made me appreciate his talents more, even though I'm not exactly a fan.

After the show, I followed the crowd out through the casino. Honestly, I don't know how people can sit in there, let alone work there. The place reeks of stale tobacco. On my way out, I passed the OAP sing-along area, where poor Jim was valiantly trying to get people to join in with classics from the last century.

Deciding I hadn't drunk enough to make the Unlimited Beverage Package worthwhile, I stopped by the Maltings and Atrium for a few nightcaps before heading off to the world of Nod.

So there you have it—another glorious day on the high seas, wrapped up with the spectacular sights of San Francisco. Now, if you'll excuse me, I have some seal selfies to perfect. It's not easy getting a seal to strike a pose, but I'm determined.

Now go forth and conquer the city, fellow cruisers! Just keep an eye on the clock, or you might end up starring in your very own "Lost in San Francisco" sequel. Trust me, the seals aren't great with directions.

San Francisco—a city where even the streets have a sense of humor. Enjoy every twist, turn, and unexpected photobomber!

Day 33 - Day at Sea

I'm getting used to these sea days, where no alarm clock dares to interrupt my slumber. This morning, I woke up gradually, sneaking a peek at my watch, only to be pleasantly surprised by the late hour of 05:00. My body, however, decided to stage a mutiny, getting out of bed one part at a time. Apparently, my body knew something my brain didn't.

Turns out, my watch had been conspiring against my desire to sleep in. It was an hour fast, which meant it was actually 04:30. No wonder my body was protesting. As I finally stood up, I swayed into the walls, wondering if I had been sleep-drinking. Good news, though, a quick check on deck 7 confirmed I hadn't been hitting the booze in my sleep.

It seems the Captain and the kind folks at NCL had been gently rocking the ship all night to ensure everyone got a good night's sleep. Thanks for the effort, but could you maybe stop now? I nearly spilt my beer—I mean, coffee. It's way too early for beer!

My early morning grumble session on deck 7 turned into a moment of pure magic when I saw my very first wild whale. He flicked his tail in the air, seemingly saying, "Morning, Steve!" Of course, I didn't have my camera on me. Note to self: always carry a camera in these waters.

I've been a lazy sod, honesty time—I haven't written anything for the past two days. This seems to be a recurring issue on my adventure. So, I spent most of the morning, right up to 12:00, catching up on my writing. Later, I'll take myself aside for a stern motivational pep talk.

David Naster, the comedian from the other night, was doing a talk on how comedy can be the cure for major illnesses like depression. Since I know someone who's had more close encounters with depression than a cat with curiosity, I decided to check it out. Fascinating talk, with humour, sprinkled in like confetti at a clown convention—what do you expect? He's a comedian talking about humour in medicine.

I did learn some interesting tidbits, though. David mentioned some bridge, and a woman near me started clapping. Are there bridges in America that sing and dance? The ones I know just stand there, doing nothing, occasionally groaning if you dare drive over them. Maybe I need to travel more.

One point that really stood out was when he said, "When you're in a dark place, did anyone tell you that you had to stay there?" A much better message than the usual, "Get over it, move on, does it really matter?" I even had a fascinating chat with David after the show. The guy really knows his stuff.

Time was ticking away, and my stomach was sending out SOS signals. I hadn't eaten since breakfast, and that was at least six hours ago. I wouldn't want to waste away on a cruise ship, of all places. So, I found myself dining in the great outdoors with two pigeons who had decided to join the NCL Freestyle Dining experience. It was a bit much when they waddled over to borrow the ketchup.

Only made it halfway around the world the other day on my beer tasting session, so back to the Martini bar to continue the rest of the journey. After all, who wants to be stranded in a foreign land with no way back, right? Finally, I made my way back to the starting point, and I couldn't tell if the ship had stopped swaying or if I'd just synchronised my wobbling. Pretty sure it was me, so I went for a walk and some fresh air.

My little stroll took me past the gift shop, where I stumbled upon today's mystery quiz: Guess the price of the items in the store that started and ended in 'A'. Tiny hint: we're on our way there. Not a single price tag in sight, so I cornered a young shop assistant for answers. His response? "We just got them in." Time must move slowly in the shop because those items had been sitting there since LA.

Decision made to embrace more freestyle cruising, which involved waking up thirty minutes before tonight's performance by Jeri Sager, a Broadway veteran from shows like Cats and Evita. Definitely worth a look. Talented lady, channelling the spirit of Elaine Page with her Broadway hits. What let her down were the long-winded chats between songs and her attempts at comedy. Let's just say she should stick to singing. Still, it's an entertaining show, worth the stop.

You can tell we're moving north because the days are getting longer, with the sun refusing to go to bed until around 9 PM. Not ready to call it a night,

I wrapped up the evening in the Atrium with a few nightcaps, listening to the guitar and vocals of Denis, or as Jim likes to call him, the Drunken Guitarist.

Day 34 - Victoria – Canada

I drag myself out of bed at an ungodly hour, driven by the memory of yesterday's whale sighting. I stumble onto deck 7 at 06:00, keeping up with my so-called exercise routine. Let's just say it was so cold this morning that a Brass Monkey at the bow was clutching his privates for dear life! Sadly, no whales in sight today. Maybe they decided to sleep in.

Needing to thaw out, I head to O'Sheehan's for a piping hot coffee and decide to linger for breakfast. Chatting with the waiters, I realise they are a treasure trove of travel tips. Seriously, these folks have been to places that Google hasn't even heard of. Who needs a guidebook when you've got these seasoned globetrotters?

With no plans to dock in Victoria, Canada, until 14:00, I've got plenty of time to kill. I sit through a few presentations and take full advantage of my Beverage Package. Gotta get my money's worth today because tomorrow, the free ride ends, and I start paying for my drinks. The horror!

First up is a presentation by David, the ship's resident knowledge dropper. His talk on dealing with bullies is riveting. Now, considering my main bully is the unholy trinity of Me, Myself & I, it's not exactly groundbreaking advice for me. But hey, it's still worth a listen if you ever get a chance.

Tomorrow marks the end of this cruise and the start of the next leg of my grand adventure. The lovely folks at NCL have put together a presentation to make sure we all know how to get off the ship and re-board without ending up in Timbuktu.

So here I am in Canada, scratching my head in utter bewilderment because we have to go through American Customs clearance. Yes, you heard that right. We're in the land of maple syrup and moose, but we're being processed like we're trying to sneak into the States. The ever-cheerful NCL crew explained that this little charade is so we don't have to deal with American Customs when we reach Juneau in two days. Makes total sense, right? Wrong.

Why does America insist on this rigmarole every time you so much as glance in its direction? I've been cleared more times than a traffic jam in the last month alone. Ever since I left Miami, I've somehow transformed into an illegal alien—or maybe just an alien from outer space. Beam me up, Europe, where this kind of bureaucratic madness doesn't exist. I can only imagine what Canadian customs will have in store for us. A polite interrogation over a cup of Tim Hortons, perhaps?

We finally arrive in the stunning city of Victoria around 14:00, greeted by brilliant sunshine and postcard-perfect views. Getting on and off the ship here is a breeze. Just flash your stateroom key and some form of photo ID—heck, a photocopy of your passport will do. It's like they're not even trying to be difficult.

The ship docks a mere 40-minute walk from the town centre. No biggie since the walk is packed with sights and activities. Just follow the signposted footpath that meanders along the coastline, and you'll be there in no time. It's like a scenic stroll with a destination bonus. Easy peasy, lemon squeezy!

Within the first 10 minutes of my stroll, I find myself at the delightful Fisherman's Wharf. Now, unlike those massive, over-commercialized wharfs in other cities, this one's a charming little gem. Picture this: brightly coloured houseboats lined up like a rainbow parade on one end of the floating pontoons, and local fishing boats on the other. It's like a scene straight out of a whimsical storybook.

Of course, what's a wharf without a few eateries and fish stalls scattered about? But what truly makes this place special are the local sea lions. These clever critters have figured out that if they look at you with those big, puppy-dog eyes, wave a flipper, or give you a playful splash, you'll toss them a fishy treat. And wouldn't you know it, you can buy that fish right from the local stalls. Now, that's what I call local enterprise! It's a win-win situation: the fishermen sell their catch, the stalls make a profit, the sea lions get a free meal, and tourists like me get a kick out of the whole spectacle. Man and nature in perfect harmony!

If you're not up for walking the rest of the way to town, no worries. For a modest fee, you can hop on a water taxi. These little guys are painted just like regular taxis—yellow and black—only they're pint-sized and float! It's like hailing a cab, but way cooler because, you know, it's on water.

Still waddling off the buffet-induced excess, I continue my coastal walk, soaking in the stunning scenery and watching life on the water, including the local flying boat service. Yes, planes with floats, for those of you not up on your aquatic aviation.

Pro tip: During your walk to town, you'll stumble upon the local ferry terminal. Guess what? Free toilets! An oasis of relief in a sea of scenic splendour. The coastal walkway meanders along but splits just past the ferry terminal, leading you to the public offices before spilling you into the heart of town.

The city itself is like most cities, with shops, bars, and restaurants lining the streets, but it's infused with that unmistakable Canadian charm. What really stands out is the cleanliness of the streets, the friendly locals, and the delightfully unhurried pace of life. It's just beautiful.

Strolling down the main high street, you'll discover a magical thing: FREE Wi-Fi the entire length! Perfect for catching up with folks back home. I used it to make a WhatsApp call, but a word of advice—unlike me, remember the time difference. Calling your daughters at 1:00 AM their time might not win you any "Parent of the Year" awards.

After a pleasant five hours wandering this picturesque city, it's time to head back to the ship, which departs at 22:00. Give yourself at least an hour for the return walk—you'll want to stop and snap those last few photos. And always aim to be back on board at least an hour before the all-aboard time, if for no other reason than to avoid the security check queues. Trust me, no one likes a last-minute mad dash through customs!

With a quick flash of my stateroom key and photo ID, I breezed through security, heading back to the ship where the hard-working security personnel checked me in with their usual flair.

Following my own sage advice, I returned before the crowd and decided to treat myself to an elegant dinner tonight. I booked a spot at the Summer Palace Restaurant, which was my first time dining there during this entire cruise. Tonight's culinary delight? Surf & Turf. And let me tell you, this isn't your run-of-the-mill shrimp and steak combo. Oh no, we're talking half a lobster paired with a succulent steak, plus all the glorious side dishes. The meal set me back an additional $29, including taxes. Yes, even on the ship, they sneak in those taxes separately. Daily rant: Why can't NCL just list the price with everything included? It's basic math, folks. Help us budget better! End of rant.

The meal was delightful, and as always, there was no rush. You can savour your dinner at your own leisurely pace. After the scrumptious feast, I aimed to unwind in one of the bars with a nice cold beer or two, making the most of my last night with the Beverage Package. Horror of horrors, the bar was closed! This needed further investigation.

I tracked down a still-operating watering hole and learned that the bar was closed because we were in Canada, and apparently, only one bar can be open per floor. Intriguingly, O'Sheehan's, the only bar on deck 8, was shuttered despite this rule not applying in Vancouver, which, last I checked, is also in Canada! So all I have to say is, "Hmmm."

For the first time ever, I spent the night drinking in the Atrium bar before eventually heading off to the land of Nod. Here's to cruising, confusion, and cocktails!

So, here's to another day of cruising shenanigans and avoiding self-inflicted bullying!

Day 35 - Vancouver – Canada

Today, we docked in yet another stunning Canadian city—Vancouver—just a hop, skip, and a splash across the water from Victoria. Now, here's the burning question: given that these two cities are only 90 miles apart, what on earth has the ship been doing for the last 9 hours? Sailing in circles? Holding a secret shipboard marathon?

The entry into Vancouver is a sight to behold. On one side, the city skyline dazzles with towering, glittering buildings, while on the other, snow-capped mountains stand majestically. The ship glides under a towering green suspension bridge, like some grand entrance to a fairy tale. As we sail in, we're greeted by a flotilla of small boats and buzzed by low-flying seaplanes taking off from this bustling port. It's like a maritime circus out there!

We gently dock at the cruise terminal of Canada Place, an impressive and picturesque dock that's arguably one of the best-looking cruise terminals in the world. It's conveniently located on the city's edge, surrounded by restaurants, bars, shops, and even the local hop-on-hop-off buses that depart right from the front door. Talk about convenience!

Since Vancouver is a turnaround port, I decided to play it safe with all the added security and opted for an NCL Tour. Here's where it gets interesting. NCL loves to brag about how, if you book a tour with them, the ship will wait for you if you're running late. It's their big selling point for shore excursions.

I've read everything about Norwegian Cruise Line and their shore excursions, and here's a fun fact: NCL is increasingly using hop-on-hop-off tours as part of their organised excursions. So here's my question: if I take that hop-on-hop-off bus tour and decide to take a detour for, say, an emergency maple syrup run, will the ship really wait for me? Or if it sails off, will NCL whisk me to the next port at their expense since it's technically their organised tour? Because, at the end of the day, rules are rules, right?

Ah, the mysteries of cruising! Now, if you'll excuse me, I have a city to explore and a few buses to hop on and off.

Here I am, sitting in the Stardust Theatre as instructed on my tour ticket (see above for the riveting details). The Shore Excursion staff keep repeating like a broken record, "For all the people on the Hop-On Hop-Off tours to the airport and returning to the ship; we are waiting for your bags to be offloaded. Once we get confirmation, we'll call the tours." Now, getting back on the ship, I can only hope my stateroom steward isn't the one offloading my bags. So, what exactly am I waiting for again?

Never mind. Soon enough, the lovely Monica is leading us off the ship, through Canadian immigration (which, surprise, didn't exist), and all the way to meet the tour company representative. Thanks for the seamless transition, NCL.

The buses are conveniently parked right outside. After exchanging our green vouchers, we're given yet another sticker to wear all day, along with two large labels from NCL. One says "In Transit," and the other says "Hop-On Hop-Off Tour." I'm starting to feel like a walking billboard.

For anyone out there who didn't already realise I'm a tourist—blind or stupid people, I'm looking at you—these stickers practically scream, "Terrorists, aim here!" since we're supposed to slap them on our left chest area. Pro tip: wear them on your sleeve. Guess who peeled them off the moment I got on the bus? This guy.

And so begins the hop-on-hop-off adventure, with me looking like a human pinata of tourist identification. Let's see what kind of trouble I can get into now!

Now, faced with a crucial decision, you must choose between the City tour or the Park tour. Take it from me, go for the park tour. Let me explain: the city tour is essentially a grand showcase of Vancouver's finest roadworks. Unless you have a burning desire to tour the construction sites of Vancouver, it's not exactly a thrilling option.

As for snapping photos along the city route, forget about it. You'll mostly be up close and personal with buildings and rows of parked cars. Your photo album will end up looking like a tribute to urban parking. The only decent shots you might get are when the bus passes side roads, and that's if you're quick enough to snap them through the bus's closed windows.

I chatted with a few folks who took the park route, and they were positively impressed. So, my advice? Definitely go for the park tour. At least you'll get to see some greenery and nature, which beats asphalt and orange cones any day.

Now, one thing in favour of the city tour is that the driver will dish out loads of interesting facts about Vancouver and point out cool places to explore further. It is a hop-on, hop-off bus, after all. But in my experience, most people hop on and then cling to their seats like they're on a roller coaster, not hopping off until it's time to return.

Vancouver is a stunning city with plenty of impressive buildings, so I spent the rest of my time wandering around and soaking in the sights before heading back to the ship. Much better than playing peek-a-boo with parked cars!

Getting back on the ship is as straightforward as assembling IKEA furniture without instructions. Let me explain: first, you have to navigate your way to the cruise booking centre. Tip: just take the escalator to the lower level and find someone who looks like they know what they're doing.

Once you've stumbled upon the terminal area, slap that 'In Transit' sticker back on your chest. This magical sticker will make re-boarding easier as it directs you through the same route as the crew. Feel like a VIP for a moment, but don't get too excited.

Next, you'll encounter American Customs in Canada. Yes, you read that right. Here, you'll be rechecked like a library book overdue by six months. Further along, you'll also have to be verified by the booking staff again, but at least you get a fast pass to the front. Hooray for small mercies!

Eventually, you'll make it back on board, but it's a bit of a pain in the arse. And remember, once you're back, the ship is now crawling with newbies who've just joined. Avoid the public areas like customer services, shore excursions, and the Garden Café—they'll be packed like sardines.

Be smart. If you need to book shore excursions, use the electronic signboards or drop a request in the dropbox. For food, head to places like O'Sheehan's or the main dining rooms instead of the overcrowded buffet. Trust me, a little planning can save you a lot of frustration. Now, time to find a quiet corner and relax before the next round of cruising chaos!

Back in my stateroom, and oh boy, surprises galore for little old me! More chocolate strawberries, champagne, sparkling wine, and my Latitudes Platinum welcome pack. I became a Latitude Platinum member after the

Panama cruise, but better late than never, right? This means I now get even more goodies—a free bag of laundry, which might not seem like much, but after a month at sea, I've got enough smelly socks to start a science experiment.

Dinner for two at either La Bistro or the Italian restaurant? The big question is, since it's just me, do I get two free meals? Plus, a behind-the-scenes tour of the ship! I've wanted to do this for a while but didn't want to cough up $79. Call me cheap; I don't care.

Also waiting for me were the Shore Excursion tickets, only to find out that the two tours I was most excited about had been cancelled. The Icy Strait Point Kayak was nixed due to "Local Logistics." Really? Local logistics? What's so logistically challenging about two people in a kayak? Another blow to us solo travellers.

The other cancellation was the Mendenhall Glacier Adventure Hike, again due to "Local Logistics." At 16:10, I got a voicemail saying the hike was back on. So, no more local logistics issues, huh? Someone's not telling the whole truth, and it's frustrating.

Determined to get answers, I went to interrogate the Shore Excursion staff. After several minutes of what I can only describe as verbal waterboarding, they still wouldn't reveal what the mysterious "local logistics" issue was. I left, grumbling all the way back to my stateroom.

Call me old-fashioned, but just putting "Due to Local Logistics" isn't enough. People deserve to know the real reason. We're old enough and brave enough to handle the truth. If it's because they didn't sell enough tickets, just say so!

Dinner was a delightful affair, taken while enjoying the magnificent scenery sliding past as the sun slowly set. If you've never seen a sunset in Alaska, what are you waiting for? It's a must-see! There's nothing more spectacular than watching the sun disappear over the mountains while at sea.

Tip: Most people scamper back indoors after leaving the port of Vancouver. Resist this urge! Stay on deck, preferably at the rear of the ship, and watch the snow-capped mountains parade by. Trust me, it's worth battling the chill.

PS: Still grumpy. I'm a platinum member now, but my card still says Gold. Maybe on the next cruise, they'll get it right.

As I spent most of the evening on deck, it wasn't long before the call of the Land of Nod became irresistible. So, nighty-night, folks!

The Alaskan Cruise

242

Day 36 - The inside passage

As today was all about cruising the Inside Passage, I had grand plans to get up early and catch the sunrise. You know how it goes with plans, though! I woke up at 06:30, with the sunrise having strutted its stuff at 05:00. So I missed that spectacular event. Breakfast be damned; I needed to get on deck to see the passing mountains.

From the moment I rolled out of bed, things went haywire. My body and legs apparently conspired to keep me horizontal. I'd been standing for about a minute when my left leg decided it had had enough and crumpled beneath me. No big deal, I thought, I've got another leg. But, surprise, surprise, my right leg—ever the mimic—decided to do the same. Down I went in a heap, doing my best impression of a poorly constructed human Jenga tower.

The worst part? I hadn't even been drinking the night before. Unless, of course, I've taken up sleep drinking—a sport similar to sleepwalking but with a higher likelihood of waking up in a ditch with a traffic cone as a hat. Eventually, I managed to peel myself off the floor, grabbed my camera, and headed up to deck 13, wheezing like I'd just finished a marathon. Who needs the gym when you've got a built-in StairMaster in the form of a ship's staircase?

Once on deck 13, camera at the ready, I quickly realised someone had moved the mountains. If, like me, you were expecting them to be as close as the Norwegian fjords, prepare for disappointment. You'll need binoculars or Superman's eyesight to see them.

I resigned myself to the fact that the mountains weren't going to move closer just because I wanted a better view. So, I decided to hit up the presentation on ports and tours in the Stardust Theatre. Here's hoping they don't tell me the mountains have packed up and left altogether.

I still can't wrap my head around why people sit at the end of an empty row of seats and then get all huffy when someone dares to ask them to move. Did they think their presence alone would magically keep the row exclusive, like some sort of human velvet rope? It's like they believe they're on an aeroplane, where an empty seat is an urban legend.

After enduring several of these presentations, I've had a light bulb moment: why are there so many folks on walking tours who look like they should be on a 'Sitting Tour'? Maybe it's because no one ever mentions the activity levels for these tours. It's as if saying, "Hey, if walking to the fridge is a struggle, maybe this isn't for you," is taboo.

Case in point: the other day, a Shore Excursions staff member was selling a walking-heavy tour to a couple who clearly had issues walking. Their solution? "Give it a go, and if it's too much, just stay on the bus." Brilliant! Because nothing says "enjoyable tour" like being the bus mascot. Pro tip: read the tour description before booking. If it says level 3 and you're a level 1, maybe reconsider.

I decided to take refuge in O'Sheehan's, armed with my laptop and several cups of coffee. Just as I was settling in, a family plopped down at the table next to me. No problem, until the human megaphone of a dad started shouting. Naturally, I couldn't resist a little social experiment. I told him, "You're not allowed to shout here." Predictably, they cranked up the volume, now with a full chorus of American accents. It's almost comforting how predictable some nationalities can be.

The whole scenario was like an impromptu performance of 'Shout: The Musical'. Meanwhile, I'm just trying to get some work done, thinking, "Is this what they meant by the 'cultural experience' on the brochure?"

Today was the day of the Latitudes cocktail party, so I donned my finest glad rags, invite in hand, and sashayed over to the Spinnaker Lounge to mingle with fellow passengers and the senior officers. Note to NCL: please fix the microphones! Sitting at the back near the bar, I couldn't hear a word the Captain was saying. And I wasn't the only one—it was like a silent movie but less entertaining.

As usual, there were more prizes to be won, but I didn't even bother. The same people who had been married the longest seven days ago won again, and the prize for the most cruises? Yep, you guessed it—the same couple as last week. Déjà vu, anyone?

On the bright side, I scored several free drinks, so I left happy and slightly tipsy, with my collection of six bottles in the stateroom growing nicely. The Cruise Next Manager delivered the same presentation, word for word, joke for joke. I checked outside to see if someone had put the hills back, but no luck—I still needed binoculars to see them.

I now understand why they build mega-ships. All the public spaces were jam-packed with people, and finding a seat was like a game of musical chairs without the music. Even the window sills were occupied. So, being the clever cruiser I am, I retreated to my stateroom for a couple of hours before dinner. Ah, peace and quiet, at last!

On the way to dinner, it hit me why all this overeating had been necessary: I was making like a seal, layering on blubber to stay warm in Alaska. It must be working because here I am, strutting around the deck in shorts and a T-shirt, thinking it's a heatwave, while everyone else is bundled up like they're heading to the North Pole. Yay, me!

I had a horrifying flashback to my reflection from a few days ago when I looked like a sea fatty, so I decided to take several laps around the ship before the night's entertainment in the theatre. Tonight's show was the Tenors of Rock.

Given the name, I was expecting some serious headbanging tunes. But within the first ten minutes, I was desperately seeking an escape route. Why? Because this rock group decided to kick things off with opera from Phantom of the Opera. Opera! Trapped by a wall of people, I had no choice but to stay put.

Turns out, it was a blessing in disguise. The act got better as time went on, showcasing some truly talented singing. And the bright lights? Not part of the show, but from the audience taking photos and videos like paparazzi. Still, it ended up being a fantastic way to spend the evening. I must admit, there have been some stellar acts throughout the cruise.

I finished the night off at the Martini Bar with a nice cold beer, enjoying some good chats and humour from the crew. Jim's music played in the background, occasionally drowned out by the enthusiastic screeching of the audience. All in all, it's a perfect way to wind down before heading off to the land of Nod.

Day 37 – Juneau

Still no whales spotted by yours truly. Up bright and early, camera in hand, I made my way to deck 12, only to be greeted by the stunning beauty of Alaska. Both sides of the ship were flanked by snow-capped mountains with waterfalls cascading down into the sea, slicing through the lush forests that draped the hillsides. Truly, it was nature's own Instagram filter.

I've now decided that whale watching—or, more accurately, attempting to watch whales—is an active pastime. I must have circled the ship about 15 times. I'm beginning to suspect the whales have an anti-Steve device. I can just imagine them spotting me and passing the word around, "Dive, dive! Steve is on deck!" Apart from the one sluggish tail, I saw the other day; they've been playing hide and seek like pros.

We weren't due to arrive in Juneau until 14:00, so I had to tear myself away from the incredible scenery for my scheduled "Behind the Scene Tour." One of the many perks of being a Latitudes Platinum Member. Normally this tour would set you back $78, but for me, it was gratis. Thanks, NCL!

The first part of the tour was a visit to the Bridge viewing room. Our guide, Lorna, gave a brief rundown of what happens on the bridge. It was quite informative, even if it didn't involve any pirate lingo or dramatic "Captain on the bridge!" moments.

Next, we descended to deck 4 and the entrance to Narnia—actually, it's called I-95, the ship's main corridor. Lorna gave us another briefing on what happens here, which was promptly interrupted by silly questions that had nothing to do with the inner workings of the Pearl. Someone actually asked about cold coffee on another ship. Really?

We moved on to the laundry, where I gained a newfound respect for the hardworking staff there. Best of all, I spotted my laundry, all neatly washed and dried. I snapped a few pics to show Abdullah, my long-suffering stateroom steward. He'll be thrilled to know that, yes, I do know how laundry works.

The tour continued to the backstage area of the theatre. I was all set to do my best Hamlet impression, but the group had other ideas. We got a quick talk from Stage Manager John about how backstage operations are coordinated. Fascinating stuff, right up until the usual suspects started asking irrelevant questions again. One person actually inquired, "How long were you married?" Seriously? How is that relevant to theatre production?

Finally, the tour concluded, and we were booted out of Narnia via deck 6. It was an interesting peek behind the curtain, even with the occasional bout of ridiculousness from my fellow passengers. Now, back to whale-watching—or at least trying to outsmart those sneaky cetaceans!

This is Alaska, folks. There's far too much to see outside to stay cooped up inside, so I'm back on deck, admiring the breathtaking scenery and, of course, continuing my elusive whale hunt. Spoiler alert: still no whales. We finally arrived in Juneau right on time, and right on cue, it was pouring rain. The rain was so heavy I was grateful the Captain could even see the dock.

Juneau's port is about a mile from the town, so if you're not on an organised tour, you have a few choices: catch the free shuttle bus, walk, or, in today's case, swim.

Lucky me, I was booked on my first hiking tour of the cruise: the "Mendenhall Glacier Adventure Hike." This grand adventure involved hiking through the rainforest next to the glacier for four hours. A perfect way to burn off those buffet-induced pounds. This tour was classified as a level 3, which translates to "sweat, groan, and maybe cry a little." Naturally, there's always someone who either didn't read the paperwork or thought level 3 meant a leisurely stroll.

The silver lining was our small group size—just 9 of us. Smaller groups always make for better tours. We assembled outside on the dock, trying to shelter from the rain under the lip of a building, waiting for the bus. One young lady in our group took one look at the weather and decided she wasn't up for swimming around the mountains. She bailed out, but jokes on her because as soon as we arrived at the hike's starting point, the rain stopped.

So there we were, ready to tackle the hike, no rain in sight, surrounded by Alaska's raw, untamed beauty. I couldn't wait to get started, even if I was still whale-less.

The hike itself was a real doozy, with plenty of steep inclines designed to challenge even the most seasoned hikers. The track is well-marked and winds through some truly stunning scenery. Just when you're getting into the groove, you're met with a long, steep set of wooden stairs that make the stairs from deck 4 to deck 13 on the Pearl seem like child's play. I swear, I'll never complain about those ship stairs again. Okay, I probably will.

We all made it to the top of the hill, gasping for breath and hunting for the nearest oxygen supply. But the view of the Mendenhall Glacier was absolutely worth the effort. As always, in a small group, there's a great team spirit. We even cheered on the folks who were struggling despite having to stop frequently for them to catch up.

I think the rest of the group, myself and our guide Tristan included, were a bit annoyed at the constant stops—this was supposed to be an adventure hike, after all—but we kept encouraging everyone to push on.

This hike is a must for anyone who loves trekking up mountains for fantastic views. But be warned: it's a level 3 hike, which means it's tough. If you're unsure about your fitness level, double-check before signing up.

After the tour, we had only two hours left before we had to be back on board. Tristan kindly offered to drop us off in town, but everyone unanimously declined. We opted to stay on the bus and head straight back to the ship, eager to rest our weary legs and catch our breath.

There isn't much to do at the cruise terminal except browse a few shops, so I hopped straight back on the ship before the rush.

You can definitely tell we're back in America because our guide was dropping hints for a tip. Now, I would've tipped him, but since the cruise started, we've been drilled to be travellers, not Tourists—take only photos and leave only footprints. So, I stamped on his foot and snapped a picture of him hopping around. Mission accomplished!

This being Alaska, I spent most of the daylight hours outside, chatting with some lovely people, both passengers and crew, while keeping an eye out for Alaskan wildlife. The combination of crisp, fresh air, a rigorous hike, and perhaps a bit too much champagne led to an early night for me. Thanks to Alaska and NCL, it was a perfect day. Let's see what tomorrow has in store. Nighty-night, off to the land of Nod!

Day 38 – Skagway

The ship was arriving early into Skagway, so my alarm went off at the ungodly hour of 04:00. Time to drag my lazy arse out of bed—not that it was a problem for my arse, but convincing the rest of my body to follow suit was another story. Eventually, I managed to get myself together, perform the morning trio of necessities, and head for my morning gallon of coffee with the lovely folks at O'Sheehan's.

With my body now fully caffeinated, I made my way to the great outdoors at the back of the ship to see what weather surprises awaited us. Good news—the rain had decided to take a holiday elsewhere, leaving us with a pleasantly dry day.

I spent the next hour chatting with Bernie, an ex-tax inspector. Now, hold your boos—he's actually a lovely man. We've spent many a morning talking and laughing before the rest of the world emerges from slumber. With breakfast and conversation wrapped up, we arrived in Skagway. Unlike yesterday's dock in Juneau, the ship docks right at the edge of town here. When you step off the ship and look back from the main street, it looks like it's parked at the end of the road.

Skagway is a place where the past lives in the present. You can almost hear the sounds of ballroom pianos and boomtown crowds echoing through the night. It's like a time capsule where two cars on the same street constitute a traffic jam. Nowhere else but Skagway!

Today, I was embarking on my second hike in two days. Yes, I must be mad, but considering I've become a sea fatty, losing a couple of tons seemed like a good idea. Today's hike had a twist: the first part was on the world-famous White Pass Railway.

After a brief stop at the Stardust Theatre, I headed to the dock to meet our guide for the day—a man named Dillon. Kudos to NCL Shore Excursions for keeping the group size small, making the experience all the more enjoyable.

Off we went, ready to tackle Skagway's trails and take in more of Alaska's stunning beauty. Let the comedy of errors, I mean, adventure continue!

Today's group started with just three brave souls, but two more intrepid explorers joined us after their original tour was cancelled. So, we became the fantastic five! You could easily spot us as the walking tour crew—we hoofed it to the train station, unlike the pampered masses who took the bus for the whole 15-minute journey. Nothing like a brisk walk to get the blood pumping for a hike, right?

The White Pass Railway is a charming relic from the Gold Rush era, with carriages that do a decent job of mimicking the originals. They've even got standing areas at the front and back of each wagon, perfect for those exclusive photos. Pro tip: wait for the train to hit a curve for that epic shot of the whole train, just like a postcard, but with more of your finger over the lens.

Safety is a big deal for the tour company and NCL, so naturally, we got a safety brief about what to do if we encountered a bear. Spoiler alert: none of the instructions included "panic and scream." As we prepped for the hike, the kind folks from the tour company handed out water bottles and some kind of energy snack. I, being the model of self-restraint, devoured mine before the train even stopped.

For those who forgot they were going on a hike and didn't bring the essentials, the tour company provided small 'bum bags' (fanny packs for my American friends) and even walking shoes. Bless their hearts.

Just like a scene straight out of "The Alaskan Railroad" TV series, the train stopped in the middle of nowhere to let us "professional hikers" off. Some might call us idiots, but hey, we prefer "adventurous." Our first stop was the tour company's bear-proof box just inside the forest, where we could stash any unnecessary items. I have to wonder, though—who shows up for a hike with stuff they don't need? But hey, it takes all kinds to fill the freeways.

So there we were, ready to conquer the wilderness, armed with our snacks (well, some of us), water bottles, and an optimistic disregard for our own lack of preparation. Let the hilarity hike commence!

Led by our fearless mountain man, Dillion, we embarked on a journey through the Tongass National Forest, an epic trek on a mostly unprepared trail. When I say "unprepared," I mean a trail where the company occasionally intervened just enough to ensure we didn't fall off a cliff or get eaten by bears. Ah, the comforts of modern hiking.

Just like yesterday, this hike was perfect for those who love strolling through dense, moss-covered forests with nothing but the sounds of the wild to keep you company. And by "company," I mean the incessant chatter of Dillion as he paused every few minutes to give us a National Geographic-worthy lecture on the local environment.

The real highlight, though, was Dillion's unexpected foray into culinary tourism. Our guide, who could probably make a gourmet meal out of tree bark, treated us to a tasting tour of the forest. He pointed out what we could and couldn't eat, inviting the brave to sample some local delicacies. Some of it was actually delicious, and some of it, well, let's just say it put hair on your chest.

Dillion, being the resourceful local he is, had an encyclopedic knowledge of how to make wine out of almost anything. It's a pity he didn't bring any samples. I'm pretty sure he had a kitchen sink in that backpack of his, though.

The hike took about two hours, including frequent stops for educational tidbits and waiting for the group to catch up. One memorable participant was a woman who confidently claimed to be an excellent hiker. Her pace suggested otherwise, but hey, enthusiasm counts for something, right?

There were plenty of photo ops along the way, especially when the forest opened up to reveal a mountain river cascading over rocks, forming beautiful rapids. It was like a scene from a nature calendar, only with more sweat and fewer perfectly groomed landscapes.

As time pressed on, we had to transform from leisurely strollers into power-walking Olympians to catch the train back from Canada. We arrived just in the nick of time, giving everyone a few precious minutes to scramble for that Instagram-worthy shot of the White Pass Train gracefully rounding the bend over the bridge. It was the kind of moment that makes you feel like a triumphant explorer, even if you spent most of the hike wondering why you ever thought hiking was a good idea.

Now, here's the kicker: since the train had crossed into Canada, you were supposed to bring your passport. Enter the Customs man, who is more spherical than tall, armed with a gun and a glare that could melt glaciers. Picture a grumpy Santa with a sidearm. If you forgot your passport, you're in a pickle. Your choices? Get shot or sat on. Personally, I'd opt for the bullet—less crushing, literally.

After bidding farewell to our mountain guru, Dillion, we had a few hours to kill before the all-aboard time, which meant it was prime time for sightseeing and the ever-important souvenir shopping.

Skagway, like most Alaskan towns, is charmingly quiet and clean, a refreshing change from the trash-ridden urban jungles elsewhere. As for traffic, seeing more than two cars on one street is considered a major traffic jam. The locals probably have traffic reports that go, "Breaking news: two cars spotted on Main Street; expect a two-second delay."

So there we were, wandering the pristine streets of Skagway, bags ready for an influx of trinkets we'd likely forget about by next week. But in that moment, every keychain and moose-shaped magnet was a treasure, a memento of our ridiculous, wonderful, and utterly hilarious Alaskan adventure.

First stop: the Brothel. Yes, you read that right, a Brothel. But don't get too excited; this one doubles as a saloon called the Red Onion, a bar/museum showcasing how saloons operated during the gold rush. The serving wenches strut around in traditional period costumes, playing their roles with gusto. The madam of the house offers a guided tour of the mock-up working area upstairs. But if history tours aren't your thing, it's also an excellent spot to grab a beer and enjoy the views!

After quenching our thirst, it was time to hunt down Robbie, the Port Shopping Consultant, for the best shopping tips. Now, if you think Port Shopping Consultants exist just to steer you to expensive jewellery stores, think again. Robbie, a top-notch guy I got to know well on the ship, was always available for a chat and offered great advice on all things portside. He's your go-to for everything from the best places to eat to public toilet locations and even the spots with free Wi-Fi (just look for the crew members glued to their phones).

Pro tip: Attend Robbie's presentations—you'll be surprised at the insider info and even learn which stores give away free gifts. Want to know about the port? Check out the port shopping guide included with your freestyle daily. Don't be like me and toss it straight in the bin. Yes, guilty as charged.

With Robbie's guidance, I found myself at Del-Sol, a fantastic shop where all the merchandise looks drab and boring in black and white or just white. But take it outside, and bam! The colours burst to life right before your eyes. At the time of my visit, they had a deal: buy two T-shirts and get a free colour-changing tote bag. As a savvy shopper, I managed to snag a discount on my two T-shirts, thanks to my own personal shopping consultant. I had to get two for the delightful boys in the family, Hadley and Joshua, plus a few extra gifts I charmed out of the shop assistant.

After maxing out my shopping time, it was a pleasant walk back to the ship, where Neil and his team of security guards greeted us. They do a stellar job of keeping us all safe. So there you have it—a day of historical tours, savvy shopping, and colourful adventures.

Bags dropped off in the stateroom; it was time to head to the Spinnaker Lounge. Dan the Man had arranged for a local entertainer to regale us with songs and tales of Skagway's history. It was all fascinating and surprisingly entertaining. But tonight wasn't just about historical enlightenment; it was also about meeting the rudest bartender in the entire NCL fleet. Let me explain:

Picture this: there are three of us at the bar, and Mr. Sunshine decides to literally throw napkins at us. In the kind of tone that makes you wonder if you've wronged him in a past life, he snaps, "And you?" I blink, thinking, "How rude." I replied with a polite "Pardon?" which only made him double down with a sharp, "What do you want?"

Well, for starters, I'd like you to take a course on basic human interaction. Then, I'll have a beer. I'm not sure what his name was, but I plan to go back and find out.

The pièce de résistance was when another gentleman approached the bar with the innocent question, "What beers do you have?" Our friendly neighbourhood bartender handed him the menu with all the grace of a grizzly bear and barked, "They're in that."

Now, I've experienced the brilliant customer service that NCL crews are famous for, but this guy was a special case of rude. And he wasn't even busy, so we can't blame it on the rush. No, this level of grumpiness was cultivated, honed to perfection.

So there you have it: a night of historical charm and a lesson in how not to win friends and influence people. Here's to hoping our next drink comes with a side of courtesy!

The evening was spent basking in the excellent service and infectious friendliness of the bartenders at O'Sheehan's and the Martini Bar. These folks were the polar opposites of Mr. Grumpy from earlier.

At O'Sheehan's, the bartenders were like your favourite sitcom characters—always ready with a joke, a smile, and an uncanny ability to remember your drink order after just one round. It was like Cheers, but with better weather and no laugh track. They had this magical way of making you feel like you were the most important person at the bar, even if you were just ordering another round of nachos to soak up the tequila.

Then, I floated over to the Martini Bar, where the bartenders mixed drinks with the precision of brain surgeons and the flair of Broadway performers. They didn't just make cocktails; they crafted them, complete with little garnishes that made you feel fancy even if you were still in your flip-flops from the pool. And the conversation! They could talk martinis, travel, or the meaning of life with equal enthusiasm, all while shaking up the perfect dirty martini.

By the end of the night, I felt like I'd made new best friends, learned a few new jokes, and discovered the secret to the perfect cocktail. The excellent service and genuine friendliness at these bars were the perfect antidote to my earlier encounter with the Bar Grinch. Here's to the bartenders who truly know how to keep the spirits high—pun absolutely intended!

Day 39 – Sitka

Today, it was Sitka's turn to dazzle us. Picture a charming island community wrapped in stunning mountain and seaside panoramic views, with enough wildlife to make Noah's Ark look like a petting zoo—whales, brown bears, deer, and sea otters galore.

We were scheduled to arrive early morning, so I set my alarm to get up and catch the review. Let's just say that plan went out the porthole. Once I was up on deck, watching the magical Alaskan landscape slide by, I was glued. Who could turn away from that, even for a second? As a result, I spent the entire morning on the open decks, mesmerised by the scenery. I even missed breakfast, but shh, don't tell the food police—I think I can manage to survive until lunch.

Today's adventure was a "Rainforest Adventure Hike" through the Tongass National Forest. Now, when they say big, they mean it—this forest is huge! Three days, three hikes. I thought it would help shed some of this sea fatty look. Well, that was the plan, but reality had other ideas. Apparently, there was a slight misinterpretation on the part of either NCL or the tour company. This hike was less "Bear Grylls" and more "Grandma's Nature Walk."

The "hike" turned out to be a leisurely stroll through the forest, perfect for those who prefer a gentle walk with plenty of stops along the way. Our guides, two sweet old ladies, provided charming little talks on various plants, trees, and even the differences between the two local types of slugs. Riveting stuff if you're into that sort of thing.

While it was all fascinating, the frequent stops every couple of hundred meters got a bit tedious. It was great for those who enjoy a slow-paced nature walk, but it was hardly the vigorous hike I had envisioned. The trail was mostly a wooden boardwalk with some gravel paths, making it an easy-going adventure.

During the walk, you'll be taken to a variety of picturesque spots—estuary, forest, beach, and swamp areas. All lovely, mind you, but let's remember this was billed as an Adventure Hike. Apparently, some folks missed that memo.

One man, bless his heart, gets a gold star for perseverance. He couldn't walk properly and needed assistance with even the smallest tree roots and the few steps on the trail. To be fair, the path was mostly flat with only one slight incline, but still, kudos to him for pushing through. Maybe if this hike had been advertised accurately, more folks like him could have joined without feeling like they were in a survival challenge.

Honestly, while the scenery was stunning, it was sometimes hard to appreciate it, thanks to the couple of Photo Snobs we had in our group. They tried every trick to stay at the rear, hoping to get the best shots without us mere mortals in their frames. So, naturally, I decided to have a little fun. I'd pretend to take a photo, just standing there looking over my camera, and they'd stop dead in their tracks, waiting for me to finish. It was like a game of photographic chicken, and I was winning.

Eventually, I got bored of my antics and decided to join the rest of the group. Turns out, they were friendly people and not just nature walk enthusiasts on a covert photography mission.

Like all good tours, everyone eventually got along, and we had an enjoyable time. So, if you're looking for a well-guided nature walk and your walking abilities are limited, this is the tour for you. Hopefully, NCL will reclassify it appropriately. I'll be sure to have a word with William, the Shore Excursions Manager.

Once the tour wrapped up, we were herded back to the ship by coach. But fate smiled upon us, and after a brief stop at the port, our driver decided to go the extra mile—literally—and took us straight to town. Talk about door-to-door service!

Sitka, charming as it is, isn't exactly a hop, skip, and jump from the harbour. Walking would be a stretch, but hey, the bus is free! Sitka's a quaint little place with a main street that you can stroll from end to end in less than 10 minutes. Think of it as the express tour of small-town Alaska.

There are a few interesting spots to check out. For instance, there's the Totem Pole Park, conveniently located within walking distance from the bus drop-off point. Pro tip: At the far end of town, you'll find an old fort tower that offers stellar views of the area. Perfect for those Insta-worthy shots, and with the whole town centre covered by free Wi-Fi, you can upload your pics faster than you can say "likes and comments."

Getting back to the ship is a breeze, thanks to the constant stream of shuttle buses ferrying folks back and forth. No need to stress about missing the boat—literally. So, all in all, it was a day well spent exploring, snapping photos, and soaking in the small-town vibes of Sitka with zero worries about how to get back to our floating hotel.

Starving after a day of non-stop exploration, it's time to dive into the feeding frenzy at the Garden Café. Have you ever noticed the distinct feeding groups in any buffet? It's like watching a nature documentary but with more carbs.

First, you've got the predators. These folks dash from counter to counter, side to side, grabbing whatever they can before prowling the seating area, hunting for that ever-elusive table to devour their prey.

Then there are the grazers. They move slowly and methodically, carefully selecting a little from each station before returning to their partner, who's been heroically defending their dining turf from the predators.

Bringing up the rear, we have the Sea Fatties. They don't bother with all that dashing about. No, they start at one end and work their way down, taking food from every possible stand. Sometimes, they need two plates just to ensure nothing is left behind, and they use their size to muscle through the shy grazers in the feeding area.

As for me, I'm a buffet chameleon—I exhibit traits from all three groups.

After surviving the feeding frenzy, I check the interactive boards to see what tonight's entertainment lineup looks like. One activity caught my eye in the 'Wave Fitness Centre.' Now, I know where the Pulse Fitness Centre is, so maybe it's near there. Or perhaps it's hidden by the Southern Pacifica Spa? Time to play a little game of "Find the Fitness Class" on this floating city.

After a day of hilarious misadventures, I decided to soak in the vibe of the magnificent NCL Pearl, hopping from bar to bar like a professional lounge lizard. Now, here's a little secret between us: the best seat on the ship is by the window on deck 6, right before the Maltings Bar. This prime spot offers stunning sea views and a cosy atmosphere. But remember, this is classified info—so mum's the word. And if you happen to see me there, well, you've been warned: "Get out of my seat!"

I've said it before, and I'll say it again: the best place to watch any sunset is from an open deck, especially with Alaska as the backdrop. So, heeding my own sage advice, I spent the last hour wandering the open decks, basking in the golden glow.

As the sun finally dipped below the horizon, it was time for yours truly to head to the land of Nod. Being this far north, the sun takes its sweet time to set, but eventually, it calls it a night. And so do I.

Day 40 - Cruising Glacier Bay

Technically, it was a sea day, but let me tell you, this was a sea day on steroids. Picture cruising up several bays where snow-capped mountains practically high-five the ocean. These views are so close you could almost reach out and give a glacier a fist bump. Watching a huge chunk of ice fall off a glacier on TV? Child's play. Seeing it live, with the glacier so near, you don't even need binoculars? Now that's living.

And get this: our kind-hearted Captain turned the ship a full 360 degrees so everyone could soak in the glory. I'm convinced he saw me setting up my GoPro on the railing and decided, "Let's give that guy a show." Thanks, Captain, you're a gem.

Whale hunters, rejoice! This place was teeming with whales; one even came so close to the ship that I swear it was trying to hitch a ride. This led to the funniest moment of the trip: as this whale surfaced, the entire bridge crew rushed to one side of the ship like synchronised swimmers. For a moment, I wondered who was steering this behemoth.

With the sun gracing us with its presence (a rare treat in these parts), the scenery was nothing short of jaw-dropping. I spent the whole day on the crew deck at the front of the ship, getting up close and personal with the glaciers. I couldn't tear myself away, not even for lunch. Eight hours later, I had a treasure trove of once-in-a-lifetime photos and videos, plus the company of some fantastic folks, including a delightful young lady whose name, embarrassingly, I still can't recall.

All good things must come to an end, so I finally peeled myself away from the deck, changed out of my shorts and jumper, and cleaned up for dinner and drinks. With nearly 400GB of photos and videos, I parked myself in O'Sheehan's to review my work of art. Some truly stellar shots, if I do say so myself.

The evening called for a nightcap at the Champagne Bar. I was escorted by the very beautiful and stunning Reba, the Tanzanite expert, who linked arms with me as we descended the stairs. The envious looks from Jim, the Piano Man, and every red-blooded male in the room made me feel like royalty. How often do you get to stroll into a bar with a stunning woman on your arm?

And so concluded another spectacular day in Alaska on the Pearl. When I returned to my stateroom, I found an invitation to attend a historic moment the next morning—celebrating being the first ship to dock at the new pier at Icy Point. Now, that's how you end a day on a high note!

Day 41 - Icy Straight Point

My body must have been more excited about the pier's grand opening than my brain, as it was up and showered before my brain even realised we were awake. With the meeting time not until 09:00, I had a leisurely three hours to wander around the ship, eat like it was my last meal, and watch everyone else disembark to explore the stunning island of Icy Point.

Finally, the moment arrived. I sauntered down to the Maltings Bar to meet the senior ship's officers and the other lucky guests. If I felt special last night, this morning, I felt like the King of the World. Out of 2,700 passengers, only eight of us, six of whom were couples, were invited to be part of this historic event. Honoured doesn't even begin to describe it—thank you, NCL, from the bottom of my heart.

Once we'd all gathered, we headed to the jetty to meet the local mayor, senior members of the Huna Totem Corporation, and other dignitaries for the official dock-opening photo session. Larry, the CEO, mentioned the pier had been finished six months ago, but the final touches on the new visitor's centre were completed just nine hours ago. Also, a fun fact: this is the only privately owned port in Alaska.

For those who haven't visited Icy Strait Point before, the ship used to anchor offshore and tender people ashore. But today, we docked in style. NCL even gave me a complimentary photo with the date and place printed on it, which was delivered right to my stateroom. These pictures will likely be displayed in the port and on the NCL Pearl for years to come.

Of course, every grand occasion has its comedic moments. One of the select guests was trying to outshine everyone by handing out her business cards like she was running for office. She handed me one, so I gave her mine right back—take that, Missy. During the photo setup, she tried to position herself in front of everyone. At the last moment, I slid in front of her, and then the photographer moved the area for the picture, putting her right back in her place. Karma, my friends, works in mysterious ways.

After this historic moment, it was time to join my fellow passengers at Icy Strait Point, where we were welcomed by local traditional dancers. A fitting end to a memorable morning and a perfect example of why cruising is an endless source of entertainment and hilarity.

Welcome to the grand spectacle that is the new visitor center, a marvel of modern architecture complete with a few shops and a cafeteria. Yes, you heard it right—cafeteria! This is the kind of awe-inspiring place where culinary dreams and retail therapy collide in a burst of organised chaos.

As you step into the central area, your senses are assaulted by the tantalising aroma of overpriced coffee and the sound of tourists trying to find the nearest bathroom. But wait, there's more! A wooden structure beckons you to dine and drink on a patio with a view that's so stunning that it almost makes you forget you're guzzling down lukewarm beer. And if you're lucky, you might even catch a glimpse of a whale—a majestic creature that, unlike you, knows exactly what it's doing in this bay.

Now, if you're one of those adrenaline junkies who think walking on the beach is for wimps, you'll be thrilled to know that Icy Strait Point boasts the world's highest and longest zipline. That's right, folks—strap in for a 45-minute bus ride to the top, only to hurtle back down in a gut-wrenching 90 seconds. It's like the universe's way of saying, "Enjoy the scenery... now scream!"

For those of us with a bit more sanity, there's a picturesque walk along the coastline leading to stores, restaurants, and a museum—all conveniently located on a wooden boardwalk. And for the really energetic (or the hopelessly lost), there's a coastal path to the local Huna village. It's a 30-minute trek filled with views so breathtaking you'll be too busy snapping photos to notice your aching feet.

If you're not in the mood for a nature hike or a death-defying zipline, you can always opt for the shuttle bus or a leisurely 20-minute stroll on the nature trail. This trail is perfect for those who want to feel adventurous without breaking a sweat.

Many visitors, like me, prefer to embrace their inner beach bum. Today, I did absolutely nothing but lounge on the beach, and let me tell you, it was the best decision ever. We were treated to a nature show that could rival any blockbuster. A massive humpback whale decided to make an appearance, surfacing so close I'm pretty sure I got a facial from its blowhole spray. Talk about front-row seats!

Curious about the whale population, I asked a local why there were so many of these magnificent creatures around. It turns out that this bay is a prime feeding ground, which is why whale-watching tours come with a money-back guarantee. Who knew whales were such reliable performers?

After the whale show, it was time to hit the shops. Unlike the mass-produced souvenirs of the big cities, here you'll find locally-made treasures that actually benefit the community. Time flies when you're having fun—or when you're frantically trying to buy last-minute gifts before heading back to the ship.

And just like that, another day in paradise comes to an end. Back to the Pearl, we go, laden with memories, souvenirs, and possibly a hint of whale spit. Ah, cruising life at its finest!

Once on board, the first order of business is the time-honoured tradition: dump the bags in the stateroom and make a beeline for the bar. Today, however, I was on a mission to find Harold, the ever-cheerful bartender who has a sixth sense for knowing when my beer needs a top-up. Beer in hand, I ascended to the open decks to marvel at the splendor that is Icy Strait Point.

Pro tip: For the sail away, stake your claim at the back of the ship on deck 7 on the shoreside. You might just spot Yogi Bear or, in my case, a majestic humpback whale passing close enough to make eye contact. Nature, you never disappoint.

Naturally, this whale-watching adventure worked up a thirst, so it was back to O'Sheehan's for a refill. With my trusty beer, I claimed a spot to the right of the bar at a table opposite the stairs and settled in for a session of intense relaxation.

While there, I couldn't help but notice the relentless flashing from the photographer's setup at the top of the stairs. After the third migraine-inducing flash, I began to wonder if I was developing a superpower. I polled a few others, including the staff at O'Sheehan's, and they all agreed—the flashing was driving us to the brink of insanity. Seriously, if someone has an epileptic fit halfway up the stairs, it's a recipe for disaster. A simple warning sign would do wonders here, folks. "Caution: Flash Photography in Progress. Proceed at Your Own Risk (and Bring Sunglasses)."

Public service announcement over, it was time to head to the Stardust Theatre. I hadn't seen a show in a while, and tonight's act featured a ventriloquist. Last time, the jokes were as flat as a pancake, mostly revolving around American culture, which flew over most of the audience's heads. But hey, hope springs eternal.

This ventriloquist, however, was a pleasant surprise. His jokes were relatable, and he skillfully balanced the act with just enough American references to keep everyone entertained. I laughed so hard that I considered starting a new exercise regimen based on his shows. If laughter truly is the best medicine, I was on the path to immortality.

After the late show, it was straight to the land of Nod. Another day in cruising paradise, successfully navigated with beer, whales, and unexpected humour. Life at sea has its perks, and tonight, my dreams will be filled with giant mammals and punchlines. Cheers to that!

Day 42 – Ketchikan

Today, the Pearl graced the legendary Ketchikan, the self-proclaimed Salmon Capital of the World. This charming little spot is famous for its Native American totem poles, the nearby Misty Fjords National Monument, and enough salmon spawning streams to make any fish blush. Naturally, there are plenty of shops, restaurants, and bars conveniently clustered around the dock, just waiting to drain your wallet.

With the ship not docking until 09:00, I had ample time to enjoy a leisurely breakfast in the Garden Café. The food was decent, the coffee was passable, and the conversation with Robbie, the ever-enthusiastic shopping consultant, was priceless. Mid-chew, it hit me: I still had a mountain of gift shopping to tackle. Thanks, Robbie, for the gentle reminder and the rising panic.

Still ticking off the minutes before our grand entrance into Ketchikan, I ventured up to the top deck to capture the arrival on film. Let me tell you, the journey down the narrow waterway into Ketchikan is the kind of jaw-dropping scenery that makes your camera weep with joy. Alaska, with its majestic beauty, will leave you breathless. Consider this your official warning: Deep breaths are mandatory.

True to form, the Pearl docked right on schedule, expertly manoeuvring into place like a pro figure skater. With my shopping list burning a hole in my pocket, I hovered near the stairs like a caffeinated squirrel, ready to bolt as soon as the local officials gave us the green light.

If you were on this cruise and saw a blur racing down the gangway, that was me executing a not-so-graceful sprint towards the shops. Turns out, my frantic dash was unnecessary—the shops are literally a stone's throw from the ship. Armed with the Port & Shopping Information sheet and a cunning plan, I embarked on my mission: hitting up every shop giving away free gifts just for saying hello. Yes, I was that person, collecting a bizarre assortment of trinkets like a magpie on a caffeine high.

And so, my day in Ketchikan began—an adventure in bargain hunting, breathtaking scenery, and the ever-present quest for the perfect piece of salmon-themed memorabilia. Cheers to cruising life, where the only limit is how much free stuff you can carry!

First stop: the nearest shop, where I launched into a friendly chat with the store person standing outside. Naturally, the conversation veered toward the most important question of the day: "So, where do I pick up my free gift?"

Minor hiccup at the first shop—it wasn't the right one. Turns out, I was next door to where I should have been. But hey, these kind folks were feeling generous and handed me a gift just for trying something on. Score one for the confused but charming tourist.

With that small victory under my belt, I set off on a mission to visit the remaining stores and collect as many freebies as possible. Before long, my bags were brimming with an eclectic assortment of goodies. With time to spare, I wandered into Del Sol to grab the T-shirts my granddaughters wanted. Naturally, I managed to snag a few more freebies there too. Winning!

Now, if you're the shy type and the thought of waltzing into stores and asking for free gifts makes you break out in hives, here's my advice: don't be. These shops are expecting you. Still unsure? Find your friendly Shopping Consultant, like my pal Robbie, and let them guide you through the process. Trust me, it's like a treasure hunt with guaranteed loot.

And thus, my day of shamelessly collecting freebies and shopping for souvenirs continued. Who knew shopping could be this entertaining? If only every shopping trip came with a side of free stuff and a dash of adventure!

With time to kill before the tour, I headed back to the ship for lunch, then made my way to the Stardust Theatre at noon for today's grand adventure. Minor hiccup: the theatre was pitch black and not a Shore Excursion person in sight. A quick glance at my ticket revealed the painful truth—I was at the wrong meeting point. The correct rendezvous was at the dock, at the front of the ship. The moral of the story: always read your ticket, folks.

Miraculously, I made it from the theatre to the front of the ship in under five minutes, a personal best. There was Alan from Shore Excursions, clipboard in hand, looking like a guardian angel of adventure. Kudos to

NCL, as only three people had booked the Rainforest Island Adventure today, making it feel like an exclusive VIP tour.

I'd previously suggested that Shore Excursions staff should join all tours to offer expert advice. Today, we had two of the ship's finest, Alan and Maria, tagging along. A short walk led us to our guide, a woman who could talk for America—charming but a talker. She doubled as our bus driver, taking us to a small marina where we'd get a safety briefing before boarding an inflatable boat for a high-speed ride to the island we'd be exploring.

Safety briefing done, we boarded the boat, where I was promptly given the "washy, washy" treatment as the spray from the waves hit us. We made one stop en route, so our captain could give us a short talk about some island rocks. I wasn't paying much attention, though, because I was on high alert for Yogi Bear. After all, you don't come to Alaska to miss out on bear sightings. Monty had already shown me a video of the bear he saw just to rub it in.

All ashore for the next two hours, and we were off for a delightful stroll through the woods on a wooden walkway that seemed more suited for a runway show than a hike. Our two guides managed to lead and follow simultaneously, creating a sort of guided tour sandwich with the group in the middle.

This wasn't some grueling trek up Everest; it was a gentle walk that even my grandma could handle, and she considers getting up from her recliner a workout. We ambled along at a leisurely pace, stopping to admire the local flora and swap jokes like we were on a stand-up comedy hike.

Halfway around the trail, there was still no sign of Yogi Bear, though I did spot a wooden bench. I wondered if it was a product of Yogi and Boo Boo's woodworking skills. But then, at the end of the trail, we were rewarded with snacks—salmon and hot chocolate. A bizarre combination, yes, but it hit the spot. Even the local birds seemed to join the party, probably hoping for leftovers.

The friendly banter continued, and I suggested that on the next tour, they should hide a picnic basket along the trail and have someone in a bear suit jump out at us. It would be the highlight of the trip! For some reason, this idea didn't take off—maybe next time.

Maria, one of our guides, decided to explore the shore, hopping over rocks and peering into tide pools to see what critters were lurking. Naturally, the rest of us, all four plus our guides, followed her lead. It felt like being kids again, playing by the shore and looking for treasure.

Soon enough, our trusty boat returned to whisk us back to the ship. A part of me was relieved because, as much as I enjoy nature, I wasn't keen on starring in an NCL version of Survivor. And so, our adventure concluded with laughter, snacks, and the lingering hope of spotting that elusive bear next time.

On our way to the port, the driver casually mentioned that the island's best milkshakes could be found here. Naturally, the beautiful Maria and I had to investigate. Let me tell you, these milkshakes were so thick that trying to drink one through a straw was like trying to suck a bowling ball through a garden hose. Spoon, anyone?

Halfway back, I was still valiantly wrestling with my milkshake. That's when Maria, bless her, walked straight into comedic history. She proudly announced she'd finished hers because she was "better at sucking," complete with a cheeky straw demonstration. The rest of the group responded with a synchronised 'No Comment,' leaving me with no choice but to document this moment of hilarity. Sorry, Maria, it had to be shared!

Another grand tour concluded, made all the better by the company of the Canadian couple, Alan and the ever-entertaining Maria. With some time to spare before all aboard, I headed to a bar whimsically named "The Asylum" for a few beers. This place was conveniently close to the ship, serving Alaskan brews at reasonable prices. The best part? Unlike my last visit to an asylum, they actually let you leave whenever you wanted!

By 18:00, back on the ship and now firmly in the mood for more beer, I made a beeline to O'Sheehan's. A few cold ones later, I was ready for a late dinner in the Garden Café. Hey, don't judge—the beer was excellent and went down smoother than a greased otter.

Later, I decided to catch the late show at the theatre featuring the Tenors of Rock and Harry Maurer. They must have been phenomenal because I didn't see much of the show—fell asleep almost immediately. Sorry, guys! I blame all the walking and fresh air, definitely not the copious amounts of beer.

After the show, it was back to my stateroom to complete my nap marathon and head to the land of Nod. The day's adventures, from the near-miss meeting point fiasco to the boat spray initiation, combined with the quirky moments and the relentless hunt for Yogi Bear, made it an Alaskan escapade I wouldn't forget anytime soon.

Day 43 - Day at Sea

Another sea day, another chance to marvel at the ocean and do... well, not much of anything. By now, I've seen most of the ship's presentations that piqued my interest, so I decided to dedicate the day to perfecting the art of laziness. My day consisted of leisurely wandering the ship, catching snippets of shows, and chatting with the many wonderful people I've met since the 14th of April.

Tonight's entertainment was "Legends in Concert," and having seen it twice already, I opted for a more laid-back evening. I stationed myself at the Maltings/Shakers/Magnums bar, chatting with Soini, the resident know-it-all on all things alcohol. Despite my repeated comments to her bosses—the Food & Beverage Director and the Beverage Manager—it seems my feedback is still floating in the void. This doesn't bode well, as many crew members have mentioned that management has a habit of ignoring or failing to pass on important information.

The night stretched into the early hours as I found myself in the Bliss Lounge with the delightful company of Trudy and Jim from the north of England—well, north of Winchester, which is practically the Arctic to me. As I've often said, you start a cruise as a solo traveller but quickly find yourself among friends from around the globe. Jim and Trudy were just two of the fantastic people I've met, along with Colin, Bernie, and the lovely folks from Oz.

The best part? The Pearl isn't scheduled to dock in Victoria until lunchtime tomorrow—or should I say today—giving me plenty of time to catch up on sleep and dream about all the antics to come.

Day 44 - Victoria – Canada

A little bit of a lie-in this morning because, let's face it, it's the day before the end of the cruise, and even my mind and body agreed to a truce and let me stay in bed until 07:30. After a rapid-fire round of the three S's (Shit, Shave & Shampoo, for those keeping track), I made my delicate way to breakfast. Somehow, I found myself on a deck too far, feeling slightly under the weather. Could it have been the vast quantities of alcohol consumed in the wee hours? Maybe. But I soldiered on with a full English breakfast, washed down with approximately a million gallons of coffee.

Today marked a first for me with NCL: visiting the same port twice on the same cruise. Technically, it's a different cruise, but since I never got off the magnificent Pearl, I'm counting it as the same one. My head needed a serious wake-up call, so I spent a couple of hours on the open decks, gulping down the fresh, brisk air like it was the cure for all my ills.

True to form, our trusty captain got the Pearl to Victoria right on time. After the usual customs formalities, the mass of eager tourists was unleashed upon the beautiful city. Having been here just 12 days ago, I played it smart and waited for the initial queue to shrink before venturing out to explore the parts of Victoria I missed the first time around.

Once I finally disembarked, I made a beeline for the town centre, knowing I could score some free internet there. This time, I didn't bother following the crew and their covert Wi-Fi operations. On the way, I got sidetracked by sea lions doing tricks for fish because, apparently, I have the attention span of a toddler.

The walk to the town centre took longer than expected, thanks to a pesky mosquito bite from Sitka that had turned my leg into a stinging mess. Pro tip: If you get bitten by something on a cruise, don't try to be a hero. Go see the medical centre if the bite still hurts days later. Yes, it's expensive, but that's why you have travel insurance.

Finally, I stumbled my way to the centre of town, looking like a drunken penguin on roller skates. There, along the quayside, I found a tiny market bustling with Native Americans selling every souvenir under the sun.

Whether you need them or not is irrelevant—they make fantastic gifts. And if you really don't want them, well, there's always the noble art of re-gifting.

As I made my way down the high street, I was serenaded by a sound that could only be described as a herd of cats being strangled. Thankfully, for the sake of my love for cats, it turned out to be a band of bagpipes and drums doing their best to stay in tune as they played for the local pubs. When they finally finished, another band jumped in, turning the whole affair into some kind of battle of the cat stranglers—sorry, I mean bagpipers.

Instead of just breezing past the money exchange at the dock, I decided to change some American dollars into Canadian dollars. This decision enabled me to grab a nice cold drink and watch the pipers' duel from the comfort of a shady spot. But alas, my curiosity and my aching feet spurred me onward. So, I resumed my stroll/limp down the high street, which eventually morphed into Chinatown. You know you've hit Chinatown because the streetlight posts are all painted red, which is apparently the luckiest colour in the Chinese palette.

I must have only spent an hour or so wandering through Chinatown because, honestly, if you've seen one, you've pretty much seen them all. Sure, there might be minor differences here and there, but the ones I've seen all look remarkably similar. It's like déjà vu with a side of dumplings.

Time was ticking toward 17:30, and even though the all-aboard time wasn't until 23:30, it was the last night of the cruise, and I still had packing to do. So, I hobbled back to the Pearl, muttering about the cruel gods of procrastination.

To my surprise, I discovered why I hadn't seen the crew wandering the high street in search of Wi-Fi: it was available right next to the ship! Genius, I will definitely remember this next time. I breezed past the hardworking security staff, who barely gave me a second glance, probably because I looked too bedraggled to pose any threat. Bags and cameras safely stowed in my stateroom, I made a beeline for the Summer Palace to burn through the last of my onboard dining credit.

I scored a seat with a prime view—not of the ocean, mind you, but of the couple hogging the window seat. Every time they leaned back, I caught a glimpse of the dock. Lucky me! Must be my irresistible charm because soon

I had a jolly rapport going with the waiting staff, who were fabulous, by the way.

Being the last night, I decided to go all out and ordered the Surf & Turf again, even making room for dessert. Feeling like a stuffed turkey after Thanksgiving, I finally mustered the courage to face the dreaded packing for departure.

Now, why is it that I started this 44-day adventure with one suitcase weighing precisely 23kg, and now I'm faced with a bag that feels like it's been packed by a hoarder on a shopping spree? Plus, an extra bag I bought on board that's also bursting at the seams? I blame Robbie, the Shopping Consultant, for all the gifts and bottles of champagne I'm trying to cram in. Well, I gave up on one bottle—it's going to be a liquid farewell tonight.

After a hard-fought battle, I finally got the bags packed and placed them outside for the ever-helpful Abdulla to collect. No matter how many cruises I've done with NCL, I can never understand why some people don't take advantage of this marvelous bag-packing service.

With the bags out of the way, it was time to say goodbye to all the wonderful folks I'd met on this journey, both passengers and crew, champagne in hand, of course.

I spent my last night on the magnificent Pearl in the Maltings bar with the lovely and knowledgeable Soini (pretty sure I spelt her name wrong again) and the other fantastic bar staff. Finally, I dragged myself up to my stateroom and drifted off to the land of Nod, dreaming of the next adventure.

Day 45 - Seattle – USA

The final day of my 44-day odyssey has arrived, but as they say, it's not over until you're desperately clutching your luggage at the airport. Besides, I still have one more shore excursion to squeeze in before bidding adieu to this floating buffet of joy.

Being on an NCL cruise, there are plenty of places open in the morning to grab that last, over-indulgent breakfast. As I lumbered towards the restaurant, I couldn't help but think of a fellow passenger's wise words: if you go hungry on this ship, it's your own fault. No blame game here—I fully embraced my role as the ship's resident glutton. So, off I went for one last enormous Full English breakfast, determined to eat my weight in bacon and sausages.

A huge thank you to all the hard-working chefs and galley staff who kept me fueled with such fantastic food onboard. With plenty of time before my 08:00 meeting at the Stardust Theatre, I headed back to my stateroom for a final sweep. I checked every nook and cranny—nope, I didn't leave anything behind, not even a rogue sock.

With my room clear, it was time for the emotional farewells. I must have made quite an impression because crew members were actually seeking me out to say goodbye. There were hugs all around, making me feel like the cruise's unofficial mascot.

Now, let's give a shout-out to the unsung heroes of the ship who made sure we not only arrived at the right ports but did so safely and to the housekeeping staff who kept the whole ship in pristine condition. Here are a few standouts:

- Security: Neil and his team, especially the young lady from the mountains of Peru who, found Alaska downright frosty.

- Shore Excursions: Alan and the beautiful Maria, who made sure I didn't get lost or eaten by bears.

- Housekeeping: Abdullah, the magician who made my room look like I hadn't spent the last 44 days living in it.

- Customer Service Desk: The young Spanish lady with the patience of a saint.

- Bar Service: Soini and Harold, my nightly saviours.

- Restaurant Staff: The night crew in both Garden Café and O'Sheehan's, who kept my early morning coffee addiction well-supplied.

As I sipped my farewell champagne, surrounded by my newfound cruise family, I couldn't help but feel a pang of sadness. My last night on the magnificent Pearl was spent at the Maltings bar, chatting with the lovely Soini (who I'm sure will correct my spelling again) and the other fantastic bar staff. Finally, I dragged myself up to my stateroom one last time and drifted off to the land of Nod, dreaming of my next cruise and the inevitable diet that awaited me back home.

The following morning and the time had arrived to make like a billboard one last time as the shore excursion team of Alan and Maria plastered me with enough stickers to look like a walking advertisement for today's tour: the best of Seattle, ending at the airport. This, my friends, is the best way to end a cruise—squeezing every last minute of holiday fun out of the trip while avoiding the purgatory of airport waiting lounges. Trust me, I've been there, done that, and got the "I'd-rather-watch-paint-dry" t-shirt.

After a final round of goodbyes that left me feeling like I was leaving summer camp, it was time to join the other savvy cruisers on the dock, where our eagerly waiting bags stood like loyal dogs. For some reason, I had all the security and customs staff smiling and laughing, which was a mystery, especially when Alan, whom I had last seen in the theatre, suddenly appeared near the luggage. Own up, NCL—what secret teleportation system are you hiding?

Anyway, I collected my luggage and breezed through customs with ease. Getting on the coach, however, was more of a circus. Apparently, some people think they're VIPs at a rock concert and must shove their way to the front to get their bags on first and claim prime seating. Let them have at it, I say; the coach isn't leaving without me.

So there I was, on the coach, heading for the airport, reflecting on my journey and the amazing people I'd met. The cruise had been a whirlwind of food, fun, and friendship, and as we drove away from the ship, I couldn't help but smile. Next stop: real life, but not without a ton of great memories and perhaps a few extra pounds as souvenirs.

Once on the coach, we were greeted by Father Christmas moonlighting as a summer tour guide. Okay, maybe it wasn't him, but this guy was a dead ringer for Santa Claus, complete with rosy cheeks and a jolly laugh. He was an amiable guide ready to show us the best of Seattle.

Our first stop was the iconic Seattle Space Needle. We were whisked 520 feet up to the Observation Tower via external lifts with glass fronts. If heights make you queasy, no worries—there's a nice, comforting picture of the ground on the back wall. From the top, Seattle sprawled out below us in all its glory, offering one last chance to snap a photo of the NCL Pearl docked and readying for her next voyage.

Next on our whirlwind tour was the world-famous Pike Place Market, home of the flying fish. Now, if you're as naive as I was, expecting to see actual flying fish soaring through the air like some aquatic circus, prepare for disappointment. The "flying fish" are actually the market stall holders chucking huge fish at each other as part of their sales shtick. The market itself is a riot of colors and smells, with stalls selling every kind of fish, fruit, vegetable, and snack imaginable.

This is also the birthplace of Starbucks, featuring the original logo. If you want to say you had a coffee at the first Starbucks, be prepared to join the line of caffeine pilgrims. The wait can be half an hour, which I'd argue is better spent exploring the fascinating market stalls rather than queueing for an overpriced latte.

Santa Claus gave us a couple of hours to explore before herding us back onto the coach for our trip to the airport and the end of this grand adventure.

One final tip for Seattle Airport: leave plenty of time to get through security. Seriously, it's like trying to get into a sold-out rock concert. Expect it to take at least an hour, so plan accordingly to avoid a mad dash to your gate.

With a head full of memories and a suitcase bursting at the seams (seriously, I think it's on the verge of declaring a mutiny), I boarded my flight home. Already, my mind was drifting back to the endless buffets and the gentle rocking of life at sea, dreaming of my next cruise adventure.

Final note: Huge thanks to NCL for an incredible 44 days. What started as a seven-night jaunt around the Caribbean turned into a spectacular journey through the Panama Canal and all the way to the stunning landscapes of Alaska. Shoutout to all the hardworking crew members who made every moment unforgettable. That's me signing off until next time.

I hope my misadventures have inspired you to embark on your own cruise escapade. But picking the right cruise can feel like trying to find a needle in a haystack—especially with over 300 cruise lines and more than 30,000 different cruises navigating every nook and cranny of the globe. Fear not! This short guide is here to help you steer through this minefield and select the perfect cruise for you.

Enjoy cruising, and may your journeys be filled with laughter, relaxation, and maybe just a bit of overindulgence at the buffet. Bon voyage!

So you want to go on a Cruise

The British love affair with the sea is so old, it probably predates the invention of waterproof trousers. But now, there's a new romance in town, and it's all about cruising. Yes, cruising! Every year, more Brits are jumping on these floating hotels, and the trend shows no signs of hitting the brakes anytime soon.

This surge in cruise mania means that more and more cruise lines are parking their floating paradises right here in the UK. From the petite and charming vessels of Fred Olsen to the gigantic, city-like behemoths of Royal Caribbean International, to MSC and even NCL, there's something for everyone. It's like having a never-ending buffet of cruises and destinations, all without the nightmare of dealing with airports. Unless, of course, you're one of those people who enjoy the unique thrill of airport security and in-flight peanuts.

So, let's dive into planning our first cruise adventure, shall we? We'll break it down into bite-sized pieces, because nothing says "organized fun" like a well-laid plan. Right, let's take our first steps in planning our cruise—cue the dramatic music and the confetti cannon!

Step 1 – Where Would You Like to Go

Cruise lines now cover most of the world's oceans like butter on toast. We're talking the Caribbean, Alaska, Northern Europe, the Mediterranean, the Indian Ocean, Southeast Asia, Australia & New Zealand, South America, and the Pacific. Heck, you can even cruise to the Polar Regions on special eco-friendly ships. Worried about the ice? Don't be—they've got icebreaker hulls that make Titanic look like a toy boat.

Feeling overwhelmed by the sheer number of choices? Don't panic, just stick with me. So, picking an area—sounds easy, right? Well, mostly. But here's a curveball: places like Alaska only let cruise ships in during the short summer season, usually from May to September. Because, you know, no one wants to admire glaciers in a blizzard.

Weather is another tricky beast. For instance, South America is best in our winter because it's their summer. Meanwhile, the best months to cruise Europe are in the summer because why travel all that way to shiver and curse your luck? We want to bask in glorious sunshine, not huddle under an umbrella.

Alright, we've picked where we want to go and when to go there. High five! Now, let's march on to the next step—cue the drumroll and marching band!

Step 2 – How Long

Alright, the next step in our cruise-planning adventure is deciding how long we want to float around on this giant hotel. Options range from a quick 1 or 2-night taster cruise—think of it as the tapas of cruising—to a 120-day world cruise, which is basically a semester at sea but with less studying and more cocktails.

But fear not; we've already narrowed it down to your cruising area of choice. For example, a typical Caribbean cruise is around seven days. Just remember, you'll need time to travel and meet your ship. Flights can be as unpredictable as a toddler on a sugar high, so it's best to fly the day before and spend a night near the port. The last thing you want is to be the person on the dock, waving a tearful goodbye to your departing ship, like a scene from a bad rom-com.

Shorter cruises to places like the Bahamas and the Mexican Riviera are usually 3 to 4 days. Perfect for a quick escape, but remember to tack on some extra days for travel. You might want to sandwich these mini-cruises between a land holiday, so you get the best of both worlds.

If you fancy the Baltic, you're looking at 9 to 12 days of stunning sights and maybe a few confused seagulls. South American cruises typically last 30 days or more—plenty of time to practice your tango moves and sample all the empanadas.

For those of us who are commitment-phobic, you can dip your toes in the cruising waters with a 2 to 4-day jaunt from the UK. But if you dream of sailing away to the sunny Caribbean directly from the UK, brace yourself for a minimum of 14 days—mostly because the ocean refuses to speed up for our convenience.

And for the truly adventurous, there's the option to combine cruises. Imagine a 16-day Panama Canal cruise, followed by the Mexican Riviera, Pacific Coast, and Alaska. It's like a never-ending buffet of destinations, often referred to as back-to-back cruises. So pack those extra stretchy pants and get ready to sail into the sunset—again and again and again!

Step 3 – Which Cruise line

Fantastic, we've nailed down where we're going and how long we're going to be living our best life at sea. Now, onto the next step: choosing the right Cruise Line. Get this wrong, and it could mean the difference between having the time of your life and... well, saying "it's OK" with a forced smile.

This is where things get a bit tricky. With over 300 Cruise Companies out there, picking the right one is like trying to find a needle in a haystack while blindfolded and wearing oven mitts. So, let's tackle this head-on by considering what you actually enjoy on your holiday.

Are you a thrill-seeker who wants rock climbing walls and surfing simulators on board? Or are you more of a laid-back lounger, happiest with a cocktail in one hand and a book in the other? Maybe you're a foodie dreaming of gourmet dining experiences, or perhaps you've got kids and need a cruise line that won't make you want to throw yourself overboard by day two.

Each cruise line has its own personality. Some are sophisticated and elegant, others are family-friendly fun zones, and some are like floating nightclubs. So think about what floats your boat—pun absolutely intended—and we'll narrow down the list. Now, let's dive into this sea of choices and find the perfect match for your cruising style!

Some things to Consider.

Alright, let's get into the nitty-gritty of choosing the perfect cruise line because this is where things can go from "Oh wow!" to "Oh no!" faster than you can say "All aboard."

Dress code - Are you the type who loves to strut around in your fanciest frock or your snazziest dinner suit, ready to dazzle at a glamorous night out? Some cruise lines have a delightful mix of formal, semi-formal, and informal nights that would make even James Bond do a double-take.

Or maybe you're more of a laid-back dresser, happiest in your flip-flops and Hawaiian shirt, feeling like you're always on vacation. Well, guess what? Some cruise lines have gone Freestyle with no dress code at all. Yep, you heard that right—you can rock up to dinner in your pyjamas if you really want to! Talk about taking "dining in comfort" to a whole new level.

Dining – Do you relish the idea of having set meal times at a designated table, bonding with your dinner companions as the cruise progresses? By the end, you're practically BFFs, swapping life stories and dessert tips.

Or maybe you're more of a free spirit, preferring a spontaneous approach, eating whenever the mood—and your stomach—strikes? Fear not, fellow foodie! Many cruise lines now offer Freestyle dining, where you can waltz in whenever you please.

Still, some lines stick to the traditional dining schedule because nothing says "luxury at sea," like being told when to eat your lobster bisque.

Health and Fitness – Fancy a bit of pampering at sea? Some ships boast spas bigger than my entire apartment—complete with a hot tub, saunas, and possibly their own zip code. Just a heads-up, though: you might need to book your treatments online before you even set foot on the gangway.

And let's be real, nothing screams "relaxation" like getting slathered in seaweed while you're literally at sea. It's the ultimate in nautical luxury—Poseidon himself would be jealous.

Entertainment – What's your idea of a great night out? Do you swoon for West End-style shows and big productions, the kind that make you wonder if you accidentally boarded a floating Broadway theater?

Or maybe ballroom dancing and interactive party shows are your jam, twirling and mingling like you're auditioning for "Dancing with the Stars: Cruise Edition." Perhaps you're the life of the over-the-top party scene, ready to bust a move and outshine the disco ball.

No worries if that's not your style, though. There's always a quiet corner on board where you can chill with some soothing background music, perfect for those who prefer a low-key vibe and a good book over a conga line.

Family – Traveling with the family? Look for ships with kids' clubs that will keep the little ones entertained and give you a break from playing referee. It's like shipping them off to summer camp while you lounge by the pool—everyone wins!

But if the mere thought of children running around makes you want to jump ship faster than you can say "man overboard," consider adults-only cruises or ships with fewer family-friendly amenities. Trust me, there's nothing more relaxing than knowing the only tantrum you might witness is someone missing the last shrimp at the buffet.

Extra Expenses – Do you prefer everything bundled up in one neat price, or are you fine with paying for drinks and shore excursions as you go? Some cruises offer all-inclusive packages, where you can sip on margaritas and book snorkel trips without worrying about the bill.

It's like an all-you-can-eat buffet but with more ocean and fewer questionable casseroles. On the other hand, some cruises let you pick and choose, giving you the flexibility to decide if today's budget allows for both a piña colada and a swim with dolphins or just a glass of water and a longing look at the sea.

Size – Do you relish the intimacy of smaller ships with up to 600 cruisers, where you can actually remember names and not just refer to everyone as "Hey, you!"? Or are you ready to dive into the bustling energy of larger resort ships that hold up to nearly 6,500 fellow passengers, turning every trip to the buffet into a game of human bumper cars?

It's like choosing between a cosy dinner party and a full-blown carnival—you decide if you want to be on a first-name basis with everyone or if you're ready to embrace the floating city vibe, complete with its own zip code and traffic jams.

Facilities – Are you on the hunt for state-of-the-art activities like massive water parks, ropes courses, surf simulators, and skydiving simulators? Basically, the kind of stuff that would make even Indiana Jones break a sweat?

Or are you perfectly content lounging by the pool with a good book, sipping on a drink with an umbrella in it, and pretending you're in a luxury shampoo commercial?

Whether you're an adrenaline junkie or a master of relaxation, there's a cruise ship out there that's got your name written all over it—probably in neon lights or elegant calligraphy, depending on your style.

Age – While the average age of cruisers has dropped, some ships still cater to specific age groups. Take Saga Cruises, for example—they're adults-only with a minimum age of 55, perfect for a more mature crowd who appreciate a good nap and a well-timed bingo game.

On the flip side, Carnival ships are like floating parties designed with the younger generation in mind, where the energy is high and the conga lines are never-ending.

But hey, most ships cater to a wide range of ages. Longer cruises often attract an older crowd simply because they have more time to spare and less need to rush back to reality. But remember, age is just a number.

On a cruise, you might find yourself making lifelong friends over shuffleboard or dance-offs. So whether you're 25 or 85, there's a perfect ship out there just waiting for you to come aboard and shake your groove thing!

Now, let's take a gander at some of the major cruise lines. With over 300 to choose from, we'll stick to the highlights to keep your head from spinning like a ship's propeller. So grab your captain's hat, and let's set sail through the world of cruising options!

Carnival Cruise Lines

Large Contemporary Ships

2052 - 3690 Guest

Primary Language – English

Carnival's fleet, fondly known as the "Fun Ships," is like a floating amusement park on steroids. Their ships are built with one goal in mind: to make sure that every time you walk up the gangway, you feel like you're stepping into a whole new world of fun where your inner child is free to run wild.

Kids & Teens – On a "Fun Ship," one low price covers just about everything, including Carnival's award-winning Camp Carnival children's program for ages 2-17. It's like summer camp, but without the mosquitoes and with way better food. So, you can kick back and relax, knowing you won't need to sell a kidney to cover all the expenses that usually come with travelling with kids.

Celebrity Cruises
Large Ship Premium
98 - 3046 Guests*
Primary Language – English

Welcome to the world of Celebrity Cruises, where the ships are so chic, modern, and sophisticated they'd make James Bond feel underdressed. These floating palaces consistently rank among the best in the world, and it's no wonder. Every cruiser gets to enjoy the premium experience that is a Celebrity cruise. Everything onboard is designed to engage you, pamper you, and renew you, like a luxury spa day that lasts your entire vacation.

The fleet combines cutting-edge technology with inspired style, world-class cuisine that makes your taste buds do the cha-cha, luxurious accommodations that could make a five-star hotel blush, and service so excellent you'll wonder if the crew can read your mind.

Kids & Teens– Got the family in tow? No problem! Celebrity's award-winning Family Program offers onboard entertainment and activities for children and young adults. Their four-tiered supervised youth programs are tailor-made for kids ages 3-17, with activities that are perfectly suited for each age group. So while you're being pampered and renewed, the kids can be entertained and exhausted—meaning everyone's happy and bedtime is a breeze.

Costa Cruises

Large Contemporary Ships

1244 – 4947 Guests

Primary Language – Italian (but don't worry, English is used in announcements and on printed material, so you won't accidentally end up in the engine room).

Costa Cruises boasts one of the widest choices of itineraries and ships available today. Think of it as the cruise line version of an all-you-can-eat Italian buffet—endless options and everything's delicious.

Every ship is designed to blend comfort, entertainment, and pleasure in that unmistakable Italian style. Picture yourself stepping onto your Costa Cruise ship: it's your first destination, and it's as elegant, comfortable, and beautiful as a Tuscan villa on the sea. Some ships are large and spectacular, packed with all the fun you can handle. Others are smaller, offering a more personal and intimate ambience, perfect for pretending you're a VIP.

Kids & Teens – The best things in life come in small packages, and Costa's Kids Program is no exception. They've got pizza parties, treasure hunts, face painting, and everything in between—yes, even Italian lessons. Supervised activities like these are all in a day's play for kids onboard. So, while the little ones are busy mastering the art of the perfect Margherita pizza, you can kick back and enjoy the Dolce Vita. Buon viaggio!

Cunard Line

Large Ship Luxury

1990 - 2620 Guests

Primary Language – English

Cunard takes cruising and turns it into an art form—specifically, the art of living well. On these five-star vessels, every moment is designed to make you feel like you're starring in a highbrow period drama. Guests blend music and painting with cuisine and conversation, invigorating walks with reading and relaxation, and explorations of historic landmarks with the spectacle and purity of nature.

This is the Cunard legacy: timeless elegance, exceptional service, exotic destinations, and, quite simply, a more sophisticated experience. It's like Downton Abbey at sea, but without the drama in the servant's quarters.

Kids & Teens – Now, let's talk about the kiddos. Facilities for children onboard Cunard ships aren't as extensive as some other lines, but there is a charming Play Zone filled with toys, games, and activities. Picture your little ones delighting in a soft play area while you confidently enjoy a glass of champagne, knowing they are in the best care with fully trained nursery staff. It's like having Mary Poppins on board, minus the magical carpet bag.

Disney Cruise Line

Large Contemporary Ships

2700 - 4000 Guests

Primary Language – English

Dreaming of a magical voyage across land and sea? Or perhaps a cruise to exotic island retreats? Just make a wish, and Disney will make it come true, with a sprinkle of pixie dust for good measure.

On a Disney Cruise Line vacation, adults find excitement and indulgence, children have the time of their lives, and families unite in ways only Mickey and friends can orchestrate. There's something special for everyone aboard a grand Disney cruise ship—whether it's meeting your favourite characters or simply revelling in the magic that Disney does best.

Kids & Teens – As you might expect, Disney Cruise Line ships are like floating wonderlands for children of all ages, with entertainment provided by your favourite Disney characters. Imagine your kids, ages six months through 17 years, learning and playing in larger-than-life play spaces fueled by Disney storytelling. It's like stepping into a Disney movie but without the commercial breaks.

Holland America

Large Ship Premium

835 - 2106 Guests

Primary Language – English

Holland America Line is like the Swiss Army knife of cruising—offering a plethora of options that can satisfy every traveller's appetite for exploration. Want to cruise the fjords of Norway?

Done. Fancy a jaunt around the Mediterranean? No problem. They've got more cruise and cruise tour (that's a combo of cruise and land vacations) options than you can shake a passport at. If you crave premium experiences and global adventures, Holland America is your ticket to ride, sail, and everything in between.

Kids & Teens – Now, let's talk about the little explorers. Holland America's got supervised fun on lock with Club HAL, providing a wide variety of exciting activities for kids ages 5 to 17. Think of it as Hogwarts at sea, minus the magic wands. Participating youngsters get an activity program delivered right to their stateroom and a Club HAL t-shirt—because who doesn't love free swag?

Hurtigruten Cruise Line

Niche Cruises

318 - 1000 Guests

Primary Language – English

Hurtigruten Cruises is the Indiana Jones of the high seas—minus the fedora but with all the adventure. They specialise in authentic exploration-oriented cruises that deliver expert-led journeys, taking you to the most remote, jaw-droppingly beautiful corners of the Earth. Whether you're spotting polar bears in the Arctic or penguins in Antarctica, Hurtigruten goes where few dare to tread.

Kids & Teens – Kids are welcome aboard Hurtigruten's ships, but let's keep it real: child-friendly facilities and activities arc a bit limited. And if you were thinking of bringing your toddler to meet the penguins, think again—children under five aren't allowed on Antarctic voyages for safety reasons.

But for those slightly older, this is a golden opportunity for the entire family to share the excitement of exploring some of the world's most remote and stunning destinations in a way that's both meaningful and enriching. Plus, it makes for some epic "What I Did on My Vacation" essays.

MSC Cruises

Large Contemporary

2199 - 4363 Guests

Primary Language – Varied (English, Italian, German, French, Spanish, and Brazilian Portuguese)

MSC Cruises is like the United Nations of the Seas, with the primary language onboard changing more often than a chameleon at a paint store. Whether you're chatting in English, ordering in Italian, or practising your high school French, MSC has you covered.

Their ships scream Italian style and European ambience, boasting exceptional comfort, warm hospitality, and a commitment to saving the planet one elegant voyage at a time. Picture this: marble, Swarovski crystal, walnut burl wood, and onyx, all coming together in a dazzling display of opulence that makes your grandma's best china look like Dollar Store knockoffs.

Kids & Teens – Since MSC is family-owned, they've rolled out the red carpet for your little ones. Not only do kids sail free (yes, you read that right, free!), but they also get to dive into the complimentary kids' program for ages 3-17.

The Kids Club staff are like the Mary Poppins of the sea, keeping your children entertained all day, every day. So, while you're sipping your Negroni and enjoying the Italian flair, the kids are off having the time of their lives.

Norwegian Cruise Lines

Large Contemporary

1936 - 5200 Guests

Primary Language – English

Ahoy, freedom lovers! With Norwegian Cruise Line's Freestyle Cruising, you'll find the kind of liberty usually reserved for eagles and rockstars. Imagine a cruise where you can eat when you want, wear what you want, and do what you want—without anyone giving you the side-eye.

It's like the Wild West of the high seas but with more shuffleboard and fewer saloons. NCL's Freestyle Vacation offers a smorgasbord of restaurants, a relaxed dress code (yes, you can leave the tux at home), and an endless array of activities.

Kids & Teens– If you're sailing with the next generation, you're in luck. Norwegian boasts one of the best youth programs at sea. The award-winning Splash Academy and Entourage programs now cater to children as young as six months.

Yes, you read that right—six months! They've got a complimentary kids and teens program that's split into two groups: Splash Academy for the wee ones up to 12 years old and Entourage for those moody teens from 13-17. Whether they're into arts and crafts, video games, or just trying to avoid their parents, Norwegian has got them covered.

Oceania Cruises

Mid-Size Premium

684 - 1250 Guests

Primary Language – English

Ladies and gentlemen, foodies and fancy folk gather 'round! Welcome to Oceania Cruises, the holy grail of destination cruising, where every meal feels like it's been blessed by the culinary gods. Forget your local diner—here, the five-star menus are crafted by none other than the legendary Jacques Pepin. You'll dine like royalty while sailing to award-winning destinations, sipping on complimentary soft drinks and bottled water like it's liquid gold.

Kids & Teens – Now, let's get one thing straight: Oceania Cruises welcomes guests of all ages. But if you're cruising with kids, you might want to reconsider unless your children are miniature adults who enjoy fine dining and discussing the merits of vintage wine.

There's no babysitting, no kids' clubs, and definitely no clowns making balloon animals. It's all upscale, unregimented, and unapologetically adult. So, unless your little ones enjoy a sophisticated, low-key environment, you might want to leave them with Grandma and Grandpa for this trip.

Princess Cruises

Large Premium

672 - 3560 Guests

Primary Language – English

Ahoy, future cruisers! Welcome to Princess Cruises, where "affordable luxury" isn't just a buzzword; it's a way of life. Think "big ship choice with a small ship feel," like Goldilocks' dream vacation.

Whether you're on a cosy vessel or one of their grander ships, every public space is designed to feel intimate and inviting. Decorated in a contemporary style, these ships offer an informal, relaxed atmosphere that's perfect for those of us who want to enjoy luxury without feeling like we need a monocle and a top hat.

Kids & Teens– If you've got junior cruisers in tow, Princess has got you covered. Their Kids & Off Limits Teens programs for ages 3 to 17 make family travel a breeze. These programs are a boatload of fun (pun absolutely intended), featuring everything from arts and crafts to video games, discos, movies, splash pools, and more!

It's like summer camp at sea, but with better food and no risk of mosquito bites. So, while you're soaking up the sun and sipping on a piña colada, the kids will be busy making friends and memories that'll last a lifetime.

Regent Cruises

Mid-Size Luxury

490 - 700 Guests

Primary Language – English

Welcome aboard Regent Cruises, where luxury isn't just a perk—it's the whole shebang. Imagine an ultra-luxury, all-inclusive cruise experience that doesn't just offer real value but also makes you wonder why you have ever travelled any other way.

Your cruise fare includes free airfare from select cities, gourmet meals, beverages that flow like a river, gratuities, and even shore excursions. Their ships are designed for guests numbering in the hundreds, not thousands, so you'll never feel like you're navigating a sea of strangers.

The onboard ambience is personal, accommodating, and upscale without being uptight—like a five-star hotel where you can still get away with wearing flip-flops.

Kids & Teens – If you're cruising with kids, rejoice! Regent's Club Mariner program is offered during the summer months and holiday seasons, keeping your youngsters from ages 6 to 11 and 12 to 17 entertained with activities tailored just for them.

Think of it as a summer camp on a luxury liner but with less bug spray and more gourmet ice cream. So, while you're busy indulging in all the ultra-luxury offerings, the kids will be off having their own adventure, making it a win-win for everyone.

Royal Caribbean

Large Contemporary

2076 - 5400 Guests

Primary Language – English

Ahoy there, fellow adventurers! Let me introduce you to the wacky wonderland that is Royal Caribbean International—the first floating nation known as the Nation of Why Not? Forget your troubles and hop aboard for a vacation like no other, where the motto is "Why not?" and the possibilities are as endless as the ocean itself. With diverse destinations and amenities that'll make your head spin (literally, thanks to the FlowRider surf simulator),

Royal Caribbean is the go-to choice for travellers who refuse to settle for anything less than everything. Whether you're chilling on a lounge chair or itching for an adrenaline rush in exotic locales, this is the cruise for you!

Kids & Teens – Calling all mini-adventurers! If you're between the ages of 3 and 17 and have successfully bid farewell to diapers and pull-ups, then it's time to join the excitement of the Adventure Ocean Youth Programs. These programs are like school but way more fun—think educational activities disguised as epic adventures. So, pack your sunscreen and leave the diapers at home because it's time to set sail for the ultimate voyage of discovery!

Seabourn

Yacht Style Ships

208 - 450 Guests

Primary Language – English

Ahoy, fellow seafarers! Welcome aboard Seabourn, where we take cruising to a whole new level of sophistication. Picture this: personalised service, luxurious all-suite accommodations, and superb cuisine that will make your taste buds do a happy dance. But wait, there's more!

We're talking complimentary open bars, dining where and when you please, and indulgent extras like Massage Moments on deck and beach parties with Caviar in the Surf. Because why settle for ordinary when you can sail in style?

Kids & Teens – Now, before you start packing the kiddos' swimsuits, let me stop you right there. Seabourn Cruises are strictly for the grown-ups. That's right, no kids are allowed on these adult-only ships. It's like a floating oasis of relaxation, where the only tantrums you'll encounter are from adults who missed out on dessert. But fear not, my childless friends, because the world is our oyster, and the sea is our playground.

So, now that we've narrowed down our destination and cruise length and chosen the perfect cruise line, all that's left to do is book a cabin. Easy peasy, right? Just remember to pack your sense of adventure and leave the kiddos at home—this is adulting at sea, and we're here for it!

Step 4 – Choosing the Location

Ah, the thrilling adventure of choosing the perfect location for your cruise cabin! Sounds like a breeze, right? Well, hold onto your life jacket, folks, because getting this wrong could turn your dream cruise into a Titanic-sized disaster. Here's why picking your spot on the ship is more crucial than deciding between a buffet and à la carte dining:

Position on the Ship – Strap in because we're about to navigate through the three zones of cruise ship real estate: the front, the middle, and the aft (that's fancy talk for the rear).

Front*– Ah, the front of the ship, where you can watch the world unfold before your eyes like a giant pop-up book. Sure, you might snag a balcony with killer views, but beware—these cabins are like the VIP section of a roller coaster ride. Get ready for some serious swaying and swerving, especially if the sea gets a little feisty. Motion sickness, anyone?

Middle – Welcome to the sweet spot, where the ship's motion is as steady as your grandma's knitting needles. Think of it like being in the middle of a giant see-saw—sure, there's some movement, but nothing that'll send your stomach into knots. Plus, you're just a hop, skip, and jump away from all the onboard action. Talk about convenience!

Aft or Rear of the Ship – If you're craving panoramic views and Instagram-worthy sunsets, look no further than the aft-facing cabins. Not only do you get to watch the ship reverse into port like a boss, but you'll also feel the gentle sway of the ocean beneath your feet. Just remember, not all aft cabins come with a rear view, so choose wisely and embrace the see-saw sensation.

So, there you have it, folks—choose your cabin location wisely, and you'll be sailing smooth seas ahead. Choose poorly, and, well, let's just say you'll be wishing for a life raft and a refund.

Which Deck – Ah, the age-old question: which deck is the deckiest of them all? Choosing the perfect deck on a cruise ship is like picking the perfect slice of pizza—there are countless options, and they all come with their own delicious perks. So, grab your compass and hold onto your sunhat because we're about to embark on a journey through the decks of the high seas!

Picture this: the higher you go, the closer you get to the top of the cruise ship food chain. It's like climbing Mount Everest but with more shuffleboard and less altitude sickness. And let's not forget, the closer you are to the middle, the more you'll be shelling out those hard-earned doubloons. So, which deck floats your boat? Let's break it down:

Upper Decks – Ah, the penthouse of the sea. With views that'll make your Instagram followers green with envy and prices that'll make your wallet cry, the upper decks are where the elite mingle with the seagulls. Just remember, the higher you go, the closer you are to the buffet—talk about living the high life!

Middle Decks – If you're all about that sweet spot between luxury and affordability, the middle decks are where it's at. You'll still get a taste of that upper deck glam but without the hefty price tag. Plus, you're just a hop, skip, and a shuffleboard away from all the onboard action. It's like being in the Goldilocks zone of cruising—just right!

Lower Decks – Ah, the bargain basement of the sea. Sure, you might not have a view of the captain's table, but who needs that when you're busy living your best cruise life? Embrace the cosy confines of the lower decks and save those doubloons for the souvenir shop. After all, it's not about where you sleep; it's about the memories you make along the way!

So, whether you're reaching for the stars on the upper decks, chilling in the middle deck sweet spot, or cosying up in the bargain bins of the lower decks, remember one thing: the deck you choose is just the beginning of your epic cruise adventure.

Budget – Ah, the lower decks—the land of budget-friendly bargains and bargain-friendly budgets. If you're the type who likes to stretch your sea legs without stretching your wallet, then these decks are your golden ticket to cruise paradise. Sure, you might not have a penthouse suite with a Jacuzzi and a butler named Jeeves, but who needs all that when you've got the thrifty charm of the lower decks?

Budget Bliss – Picture this: you're sailing the high seas without breaking the bank. The lower decks offer all the comforts of home without the hefty price tag. Sure, you might not have an ocean view, but who needs one when you've got the soothing hum of the ship's engines to lull you to sleep? Plus, think of all the money you'll save for souvenirs—seashell keychains, anyone?

But wait, there's more! Not only are the lower decks kind to your wallet, but they're also kind to your tired sea legs. After a long day of exploring exotic ports of call, the last thing you want is to hike up 15 decks to your cabin. With the lower decks, you're just a hop, skip, and gangplank away from your cosy cabin. No need to battle the elevator crowds or attempt the stairway to heaven—just sweet, sweet relief.

So, whether you're pinching pennies or just prefer the down-to-earth charm of the lower decks, remember one thing: budget cruising isn't just about saving money; it's about embracing the laid-back, wallet-friendly vibe of life on the high seas. Smooth sailing, my frugal friends!

Motion sickness – Ah, the age-old battle against the dreaded motion sickness—a foe as relentless as a sea captain chasing a whale-sized fish tale. But fear not, my fellow cruisers, for I come bearing tidings of great joy and minimal queasiness!

Rockin' and Rollin' – Now, picture this: you're sailing the seven seas, feeling as chipper as a sailor on shore leave. But suddenly, the waves start playing a game of Ship Shake-up, and you're left feeling like a cocktail in a blender. Fear not, my friends, for the middle of the ship is your sanctuary in this tempestuous sea of motion sickness woes. Nestled snugly in the belly of the beast, you'll find solace from the swaying and swerving that plague those poor souls on the outer decks.

Stabilisers to the Rescue! – But wait, there's more! Modern cruise ships aren't just floating palaces of luxury—they're also equipped with state-of-the-art stabilisers, the superhero of the seas.

These mighty contraptions work tirelessly to keep your ship as steady as a grandma's knitting needle, even in the roughest of waters. So, whether you're cruising through a serene sunset or weathering a stormy squall, you can rest assured knowing that motion sickness doesn't stand a chance against the marvels of modern engineering.

So, my fellow landlubbers, fear not the wrath of motion sickness, for with a strategic cabin choice and the power of stabilisers on your side, you'll sail through the high seas with nary a stomach churn in sight. Smooth sailing, my friends, and may your seas be as calm as a cucumber in a cocktail glass!

Which part of the ship will I visit most – Ah, the eternal question: which part of the ship will I call home during my nautical escapades? Well, my fellow sea voyagers, fear not, for I am here to guide you through this tumultuous sea of decision-making with the finesse of a captain navigating through a storm!

Poolside Paradise – If you fancy yourself a sun-soaking, cocktail-sipping, poolside prince or princess, then look no further than the pool deck for your cabin abode. Picture this: you're lounging on a deck chair, feeling the gentle spray of the ocean breeze, and suddenly, a waiter appears with a tray of frosty beverages. Ah, the life of luxury awaits you on the pool deck, my friends.

Bar-Hopping Bonanza – Now, if your idea of a good time involves hopping from one bar to the next like a tipsy kangaroo, then set your sights on a deck lower down towards the middle of the ship. Why, you ask? Well, my dear cruisers, that's where the heart of the action lies! With bars and dining rooms aplenty, you'll be swaying to the rhythm of the ship's movement while sipping on your favourite libations. Just remember to hold onto your drink tight when the ship decides to do its sideways shuffle—wouldn't want your martini ending up in the lap of the captain!

So, whether you're basking in the sun by the pool or swaying to the ship's rhythm in the midst of a bar-hopping extravaganza, rest assured that there's a deck for every sailor's fancy. Bon voyage, my friends, and may your cruise be filled with laughter, libations, and plenty of memorable moments!

Physical Ability – Ahoy there, fellow cruisers! Let's talk about the one thing that could make strolling down those endless corridors feel like a marathon: physical ability. Now, if you're not exactly keen on trekking down the never-ending hallways of the ship or if your legs have decided to go on strike, fear not! I've got just the solution for you.

The Lifts! Ah, the magical contraptions that whisk you away to your desired destination with just the press of a button. But here's the kicker: they're not just located in one spot; oh no, they're strategically scattered throughout the ship like treasure chests waiting to be discovered. You'll find these lifelines—pun intended—either at the front, middle or back of the ship, ready to transport you to your deck of dreams.

So, if the mere thought of traversing those corridors has your legs protesting louder than a crew of mutinous pirates, fear not! Just snag yourself a cabin closer to the lifts and let those trusty elevators do all the legwork for you. After all, why break a sweat when you can break a smile as you glide effortlessly to your destination? Smooth sailing, my friends, and may your cruise be as effortless as a ride in those magical floating boxes of wonder!

Ahoy, fellow adventurers!

Strap on your sea legs because we're about to navigate through the treacherous waters of cabin selection. Now, choosing the perfect cabin is like picking the juiciest slice of pineapple from a tropical buffet—there's a lot to consider, and if you choose wrong, you might end up with a sour taste in your mouth.

Above and Below the Main Theatre: Picture this: you're trying to catch some shut-eye, but all you hear above you is the thunderous applause from the evening's theatrical masterpiece. Below, the rhythmic stomping of dance numbers turns your ceiling into a makeshift dance floor. Note to self: avoid these areas unless you fancy a nightly serenade of show tunes.

Near All-Night Bars: Ah, the siren song of late-night revelry! But beware, my friends, for those party animals can turn a quiet corridor into a cacophony of cheers and clinking glasses well past the witching hour. Unless you're one of them, then by all means, party on!

Next to the Lifts: Sure, it sounds convenient to have the lifts right at your doorstep, but imagine the incessant ding-ding-ding as they ferry passengers to and fro all night long. It's like having your own personal elevator symphony—minus the harmony.

The Mysterious Blank Spaces: If the deck plan resembles a game of Battleship with large blank areas, you might be unwittingly sailing into the realm of crew service zones. Prepare for a cacophony of clanging machinery and bustling crew members working around the clock.

Under the Main Dining Room: While it may seem peaceful during dinner hours, come nighttime, you'll be treated to a symphony of scraping chairs and clattering cutlery as the hard-working crew transforms the dining area back to its daytime glory.

On the Lower Decks: Watch out for those ominous blank spaces on the deck plan—they could be hiding anything from noisy machinery to the ship's laundry room. Unless you enjoy the soothing lullaby of industrial washers, steer clear!

So, my fellow adventurers, heed this advice: aim for a cabin sandwiched between decks to buffer yourself from the noise. And remember, while the majority may strive for quiet nights, there's always a rogue wave of noise lurking just around the corner. Bon voyage, and may your cabin be as peaceful as a hammock on a deserted island!

Step 5 – Choosing the Right Cabin Type

Ahoy, fellow cruisers! We're on the home stretch now, but there is just one more hurdle to leap over before we can officially set sail: choosing our cabin. But fear not, for I come bearing the treasure map to navigate these choppy cabin waters.

Now, picture this: you're standing at the crossroads of cabin categorisation, with options aplenty and confusion galore. Inside, Ocean View, Balcony, Mini-Suite, Suites—sounds straightforward, right? Wrong! Each of these categories comes with its own labyrinth of sub-categories, like cabins with a view, cabins with a balcony, cabins with a mini-bar, and so on. It's like trying to choose a flavour of ice cream in a gelato shop with 30 different options—it's enough to make your head spin!

And let's not forget, my fellow adventurers, that not all ships are cut from the same sailcloth. Oh no, some ships like to play the high roller game, offering standard cabins that are fancier than a peacock in a top hat. Take Regent and Seabourn, for instance—they've set the bar so high that even their standard cabins feel like a luxury penthouse suite. Talk about setting the bar (or, should I say, deck) high!

But fear not, brave souls, for I shall guide you through the murky waters of cabin selection, one category at a time. So buckle up, grab your compass, and let's chart a course through the wild world of cruise ship cabins!

Inside cabin – Ah, the elusive inside cabin—like a hidden treasure chest buried deep within the bowels of the ship. These cosy little nooks are tucked away from the prying eyes of the sea and offer a snug haven for weary travellers.

Picture this: you step into your inside cabin, and what do you see? Darkness. Complete and utter darkness. But fear not, my fellow adventurers, for this is where the magic happens. With no windows to distract you, you're free to immerse yourself in the blissful embrace of ship life.

Now, these inside cabins may be small, but they're mighty! They can squeeze in up to four brave souls, although I wouldn't recommend it unless you're all on very friendly terms. And speaking of terms, let's clear up a few mysteries, shall we?

First up, we have the French Balcony—a whimsical name for a cabin that lacks the actual balcony part. It's like ordering a croissant and getting a baguette instead. But fear not, for Royal Caribbean has conjured up a solution: the Virtual Balcony. Picture this—a wall that magically transforms into a window, complete with panoramic views of the high seas. It's like having your own private IMAX theatre, minus the popcorn.

But wait, there's more! Some lucky souls may find themselves with an inside cabin facing the Central Boardwalk—a bustling hub of activity and excitement. But beware, my friends, for with great views comes great responsibility. Forget to draw the curtains, and you might unwittingly give your fellow cruisers a show they won't soon forget. So, remember to keep those curtains closed unless you're feeling particularly adventurous!

Ocean View Cabins – Ah, the ocean view cabins—where the sea meets your window and waves hello in the most picturesque way possible. But wait, there's more than meets the eye (pun intended)! Let's dive into the different flavours of ocean-view cabins:

First up, we have the Port Hole View. Think of it as a tiny peephole to the outside world, strategically placed to let in just the right amount of natural light. Sure, you might not get the panoramic views of a penthouse suite, but hey, who needs that when you've got a porthole, right?

Next on the list is the Picture Window View. Ah, now we're talking! Picture this: a large, square window that serves as your personal portal to paradise. With more natural light than a disco ball at noon, you can soak in the sights of the high seas without even leaving your cabin. It's like having front-row seats to the greatest show on Earth, or rather, on water!

But hold onto your life jackets, folks, because we've got the Obstructed or Restricted View cabins. Now, these are for the true adventurers among us—those who don't mind a little obstruction in their view. Whether it's a partial or full blockade by a lifeboat or the ship itself, you'll still get a glimpse of the outside world.

Plus, think of it as a bonus feature: you'll always know exactly where the lifeboats are in case of emergency. Just remember, no matter how tempted you are, that window isn't going anywhere—it's strictly for admiring the view, not for trying to squeeze through during a daring escape attempt!

Balcony Cabins – Ah, the balcony cabins—the VIP seats of the cruising world, where you can sip your morning coffee with a side of sea breeze or catch the sunset like a boss. It's like having your own slice of paradise with a railing!

But wait, there's more to these balconies than meets the eye (and the railing)! Let's step out onto the comedic balcony and explore:

First up, we have the Standard Balcony cabins. Picture this: a spacious room with a side dish of outdoor luxury. These babies come with a separate sitting area, making them the envy of all other cabins. Plus, with those sliding patio doors, you can let the fresh air sweep in like a Hollywood star making a grand entrance.

Then, we have the Family Balcony cabins—a.k.a. the "party size" option. These bad boys are bigger than your average balcony cabin, perfect for accommodating the whole family. And hey, if you need a little extra space, just slide open the adjoining door to the next cabin (or keep it locked if you're not in the mood for surprise guests).

And let's not forget about the Obstructed View Balcony cabins. Sure, you might not get the panoramic vista of your dreams, thanks to a sneaky lifeboat or ship part blocking the way. But hey, who needs unobstructed views when you've got a balcony to call your own?

Just remember, in case of emergency, the balcony isn't your shortcut to a lifeboat getaway—sorry, no balcony bungee jumping allowed!

Mini-Suite – Ah, the Mini-Suite—where size really does matter! These bad boys are like the penthouses of the sea, boasting a larger-than-life sitting area and enough space to host a sofa bed slumber party. It's the perfect place to stretch out and live your best cruise life!

And guess what? No obstructed views here, folks! These suites come with all the perks, including a balcony for those scenic ocean views. But hey, always double-check to make sure there's nothing blocking your view—unless you're into the whole "ship part obstacle course" vibe.

But wait, there's more! Some cruise lines are taking luxury to a whole new level with Spa suites. That's right; you get access to the ship's spa, which is included in the price. So, while everyone else is busy lounging by the pool, you'll be getting pampered like royalty. It's like a vacation within a vacation—cue the relaxation!

Suites – Ah, the Suites—where the rich and fabulous go to live out their wildest cruise fantasies! These bad boys are like floating palaces, with enough space to make your landlubber friends green with envy.

Picture this: up to three separate bedrooms, spread out over two glorious levels, all yours to rule with an iron fist (or a plush robe, your call). And guess what? You get your very own butler, ready to cater to your every whim. Need a towel folded into an origami swan? Done. Craving a midnight snack? Voilà! Your butler's got your back.

But wait, there's more! These suites come with a balcony so big you could throw a block party. And if that's not enough, some even have a hot tub—because why not turn your cruise into a full-blown spa retreat?

So, if you're ready to cruise like royalty, the Suites are where it's at. Just remember to wave down to us peasants from your balcony throne!

The Posh Cabins

Ah, behold the Posh Cabins—the crème de la crème of cruise accommodations! It's like having your own little slice of luxury paradise within the floating paradise of a cruise ship.

So, picture this: you're lounging in your opulent cabin, sipping on a fancy cocktail, when suddenly, your personal butler appears like a genie from a designer bottle, ready to grant your every wish. Need a pillow fluffed? Consider it done. Craving a midnight snack? Presto! Your butler's got it covered.

But wait, there's more! These Posh Cabins are part of a secret society known as the Ship within a Ship concept. It's like the VIP lounge of the high seas, accessible only to those lucky enough to score a ticket to this exclusive club. And let me tell you, they don't skimp on the perks. Separate dining area? Check. Private bar? You betcha.

So, if you're looking to elevate your cruise experience from "meh" to "oh la la," look no further than the Posh Cabins, just be prepared to never want to leave the lap of luxury!

Step 6 Choosing the right cabin for you.

Congratulations on sticking with us through this cruise comedy extravaganza! Now, we're on the brink of the penultimate step: choosing the perfect cabin for you. With a boatload (pun intended) of options—30 to be exact—picking the right one can feel like navigating a maze of luxury and confusion.

But fear not, intrepid cruiser! We're here to guide you through this labyrinth of cabin choices with all the finesse of a drunken sailor on shore leave. So buckle up (or maybe just fasten your floaties) as we embark on this hilarious voyage of cabin selection.

How much time will I spend in the room – Ah, the eternal question: How much quality time will I actually spend in this floating abode? Are you the type to flit about the ship like a social butterfly, only retreating to your cabin for a quick wardrobe change and a snooze? Or do you envision cosy evenings spent sipping cocktails on your private balcony, watching the sunset and plotting your next onboard adventure?

Let's face it, folks, size matters—even on the high seas! From the snug embrace of an inside cabin (more like a closet, really) to the airy expanse of a suite big enough to host your own dance party, there's a cabin size for every cruising personality. And yes, some suites are so spacious you could fit your entire neighbourhood in there (just think of the block party potential)!

So, before you set sail on this comedy of cabin errors, ask yourself: How much room do I need to spread my metaphorical sea legs? Because let's be real, nobody wants to feel like a sardine in a tin can when you're supposed to be living the high life on the open ocean!

What's your Budget – Ah, the eternal question: What's your budget, darling? Are you ready to live it up like a high roller or pinch those pennies like there's no tomorrow? If you're all about sailing on a shoestring, then cosying up in an inside cabin is your ticket to frugal fabulousness.

Let's be honest, folks, who needs a window when you've got dreams as big as the ocean? Save those dollars for the real star of the show—like unlimited buffets and souvenir cocktail umbrellas! Plus, who needs natural light when you can glow from the inside out with sheer excitement?

So, if you're all about keeping that bank account afloat while still cruising in style, remember: It's what's on the inside that counts! And trust me, with an inside cabin, you'll have money left over for all the fun stuff—like cheesy vacation shirts and tacky souvenirs that will haunt you forever.

Do I need a Full View – Ah, the eternal question of the view: to see or not to see, that is the cabin dilemma! Do you really need a full view of the ocean's majesty, or are you cool with a little obstruction here and there? Because let's face it, folks, who needs a pristine panorama when you can have a quirky, obstructed view for half the price?

Picture this: you're sipping your morning coffee on your balcony, admiring the sunrise, when suddenly—boom!—there's a lifeboat blocking your view like a nosy neighbour's hedge. But hey, who needs unobstructed vistas when you can have a slice of nautical mystery right outside your window?

So, if you're all about embracing life's little obstacles and saving some cash in the process, then go ahead and book that obstructed-view cabin. Who knows, maybe that lifeboat will become your new favourite conversation starter at the onboard cocktail parties!

Do You Need Outside Space – Ah, the eternal question of outdoor space: to balcony or not to balcony, that is the question! Do you really need a little slice of open air heaven to step out onto and bask in the sea breeze, or are you cool with admiring the view from behind a pane of glass?

Let's break it down, shall we? If your idea of a perfect cruise involves more deckside adventures than cabin cosiness, then maybe you can skip the balcony and opt for a cabin with a view and a roof over your head. After all, who needs a balcony when you're too busy living it up at the buffet or hitting the dance floor?

But hey, if you're the kind of person who dreams of sipping martinis on your private balcony as the sun sets over the horizon, then by all means, splurge on that balcony cabin! Just be prepared to spend more time admiring the ocean from your perch than exploring the onboard amenities. Decisions, decisions!

The Size of your Party – Ah, the age-old dilemma of cruising with a party of four! Picture this: you're all crammed into an inside cabin like sardines in a can, trying to wriggle into your evening attire without elbowing each other in the face. It's a battle royale for mirror space, and don't even get me started on the jostling for bathroom time!

Sure, the idea of cosying up together in a budget-friendly cabin might sound like a hoot at first, but when push comes to shove (literally), you might find yourself longing for a little more elbow room.

That's where the suite life comes in, my friend! With enough space to swing a cat—or at least a small penguin—you can spread out, relax, and even enjoy a bit of peace and quiet away from the chaos of your fellow travellers.

So, unless you're all best buddies with a penchant for close quarters and communal living, consider splurging on a suite or adjoining cabins. Trust me, your sanity—and your elbows—will thank you for it!

Is the concierge level right for me? Ah, the allure of the concierge level! It's like stepping into a realm where your every whim is catered to with the finesse of a magician pulling rabbits out of hats—except, in this case, it's more like pulling extra fluffy pillows out of the closet.

Imagine waltzing onto the ship like a VIP, bypassing the queues with a nonchalant wave of your hand, and settling into a cosy lounge where your every desire is anticipated before you even voice it. Need a dinner reservation? Consider it done. Want to book a shore excursion? Easy peasy lemon squeezy. Craving a specific type of pillow to cradle your weary head? Say no more, my friend!

But before you go booking that swanky concierge-level cabin, ask yourself: Is this the right fit for me? Sure, you'll be living the high life, but do you really need priority boarding when you can turn waiting in line into an impromptu dance party? Do you crave a pillow menu, or are you content with whatever fluffiness fate throws your way?

Remember, it's your cruise, so choose the cabin that speaks to your inner cruise connoisseur. Whether you're lounging in luxury or kicking back in cosy comfort, make sure it's a voyage you'll remember for all the right reasons!

The Final Step – Book your cruise

Well, look at you, all set to sail the seven seas like a seasoned captain! You've cracked the code to crafting your dream cruise holiday, and boy, does it feel good.

You've plotted your course to paradise, decided how long you'll be living the high life on the high seas, and even picked the perfect cruise line to carry you away into the sunset. Plus, you've mastered the art of cabin selection, deck determination, and finding the ideal floating abode for your seafaring escapades.

Now, you stand at the crossroads of cruise greatness. You could dive headfirst into the vast ocean of internet searches, navigating through a sea of cruise deals and ship specs, hoping to find the perfect voyage for your newfound expertise. Or, you could take the shortcut to cruise bliss and ring up one of those mystical Travel Consultants, those wizards of wanderlust, who can whisk you away on the cruise of your dreams faster than you can say "anchors aweigh"!

So, what's it gonna be, sailor? Will you chart your own course through the digital waves, or will you entrust your voyage to the capable hands of a Travel Consultant? The choice is yours, but either way, smooth sailing awaits!

Cruise Terminology

Ahoy there, landlubbers! We've finally set foot on the magnificent vessel that will carry us to our wildest nautical dreams. And let me tell you, it's a ship, not a measly little dinghy. Calling this majestic floating palace a "boat" is like calling a lion a "kitty" – it just doesn't do it justice!

Now, as we embark on this grand adventure, you might find yourself feeling a bit lost in the sea of nautical jargon. Fear not, my fellow seafarers, for I'm here to steer you through the choppy waters of cruise terminology.

ABOARD

The opposite of being ashore. This delightful word simply means being on the ship, soaking in all its splendour and glory. So, get ready to embrace the salty air and the gentle rocking of the waves as we navigate the high seas together!

ABREAST

No, it's not a typo for "a feast" – although let's be honest, that would be quite fitting for a cruise. Instead, it means sailing alongside another ship. But don't go looking for this phenomenon in the buffet restaurant – you're more likely to find it out on the open deck, where the only thing on the menu is breathtaking ocean views!

ACCOMMODATION

the sacred sanctuary where weary cruisers seek refuge after a hard day's partying – or, let's be real, after realising it was their own wobbly legs, not the ship, causing the sway. Yes, it's where dreams meet reality, where the magic happens (or where you try to make sense of last night's karaoke performance). Cruise lines call it a stateroom or suite, but let's not sugarcoat it – it's your humble abode on the high seas, complete with ocean views and the occasional bump in the night.

ADD ON

The sneaky little charges magically appear on your bill faster than you can say, "all-you-can-eat buffet." From airfare to transfers to shore excursions, these babies have a knack for turning a budget-friendly cruise into a wallet-emptying extravaganza. And let's not forget the holy grail of add-ons

– the Beverage Package. Rumour has it there's even a Soft Drinks Package for those who prefer their fizz without the buzz.

AFT

Also known as the back of the ship, or as I like to call it, the blunt end. It's the yin to the front's yang, the place where you'll find serenity, solitude, and maybe a few less seasick passengers. So, next time you're feeling lost on the ship, just remember – head aft, and you'll never be bowled over by the crowds again!

AIR & SEA (Fly-Cruise)

for those who prefer their cruises without the hassle of sprouting gills and swimming to the ship. Because let's face it, as fun as it sounds, doing the doggy paddle across the Atlantic isn't everyone's idea of a good time. With this nifty package, you get the whole shebang – cruise price, airfare, and even a chauffeur-style transfer to and from the ship. It's like a one-stop shop for all your seafaring needs!

ASHORE

the promised land for weary sailors tired of being cooped up on the high seas. Ah, the sweet embrace of dry land, where the Wi-Fi flows freely like the ocean breeze. Yes, my friends, if you ever find yourself in need of a little internet fix, just follow the crew. They'll lead you straight to the nearest hotspot faster than you can say, "Ship ahoy!"

BAGGAGE ALLOWANCE

The cruel, ever-shrinking limit on our seafaring swag. On a fly cruise, it's like playing a high-stakes game of suitcase Tetris, where every pair of socks and novelty hat counts towards your airline's strict baggage policy. And let's not forget the post-cruise conundrum, where you're left scratching your head, wondering why your suitcase resembles a bursting pinata. Spoiler alert: it's not just the souvenir trinkets weighing you down; those complimentary bottles of bubbly might have something to do with it!

BEAM

No, not the kind you use to construct pirate ships, but the nautical term for the ship's width. Picture yourself standing next to the bar, then sashaying across to the other side. Congratulations, you've just walked across the beam! Navy buffs might add that it's the ship's widest point, but we prefer to think of it as a stylish bar-hopping exercise.

BEARING

Ah, bearing – the mysterious art of not getting lost at sea. If you ever spot the ship doing a funky figure-eight dance, don't panic; the captain isn't hitting the rum too hard. They're just recalibrating the compass to ensure we're headed in the right direction. Trust me, the crew knows where they're going... probably. After all, a good bearing is the key to avoiding unplanned detours to deserted islands or encounters with giant squids.

BERTH

Whether it's the cosy bed in your stateroom or the designated docking spot at the port, it's a term loaded with potential for misunderstanding. And speaking of misunderstandings, if you hear what sounds like a feline vocalising its displeasure at a karaoke night, do yourself a favour and give that venue a wide berth. Trust me, no one needs to witness the auditory assault of a tone-deaf rendition of "My Heart Will Go On" after a few too many piña coladas.

CABIN

Ah, the humble cabin – or, as I like to call it, the luxury hovel where dreams come to sleep! On the high seas, the fancier you are, the fancier your digs become. Suddenly, your "cabin" morphs into a "stateroom" or even a "suite" – because nothing says opulence like swapping out a regular old bed for a king-sized throne of comfort!

CATEGORY

Now, let's talk categories – not the kind that involves tabby cats or cheesy reality TV, but the classification of your floating abode. It's all about location, size, amenities, and, of course, how much moolah you're willing to part with. Think of it as a game of "Cabin Cash Clash," where the posher you are, the higher the category climbs. Just remember, while you're busy splurging on your digs, you might miss out on the real fun – like that midnight buffet or the conga line on the Lido deck!

CRUISE FARE

Next up, we have the cruise fare – the cold, hard cash you shell out for the privilege of sailing the seven seas. But hold onto your life jackets, folks, because this price tag doesn't include all the sneaky extras like taxes, port charges, airfare, and the obligatory tip for the towel animal artist who transforms your bed into a menagerie of folded cloth critters.

CRUISETOUR

The cruisetour – the indecisive vacationer's dilemma. Can't choose between a cruise or a land-based adventure? Why not have both? It's like trying to decide between pizza and tacos, so you just throw everything into a blender and hope for the best. Whether you opt for the pre or post-cruise option, just remember: you're in for a whirlwind of maritime madness followed by a dash of terra firma tomfoolery!

DEBARKATION

Ah, debarkation – the grand exit from the floating fun factory! Whether you're bidding adieu to a port of call or reluctantly disembarking at the end of your journey, it's time to track down your trusty baggage. But beware, those mischievous House Elves have taken over baggage duty, and your luggage is probably enjoying a wild ride on the conveyor belts, living its best life while you're left waiting at the dock like a landlocked landlubber!

DECK

Now, let's talk decks – no, not the kind you shuffle cards on, but the levels of the ship that keep you from taking an unexpected dip in the briny deep. You'll find them lurking beneath your feet, supporting your sea legs as you navigate the maritime maze of bars and restaurants. Did I mention bars? Because, let's face it, who needs a compass when you've got a barometer of booze to guide your way?

DECK PLAN

The treasure map of the ship! It's like a giant game of connect-the-dots, where each dot represents a tantalising hotspot of revelry. But beware, there are blank gaps on this map that can lead to perilous pitfalls – like accidentally stumbling into the crew's quarters or, worse, the karaoke lounge during amateur hour!

DEPOSIT

Now, onto deposits – no, not the kind you find in your pockets after a night of raucous revelry, but the partial payment required to secure your spot on the ship. It's like putting a down payment on a floating palace of pleasure, ensuring that you'll have a cosy cabin to rest your weary head after a day of high-seas hijinks. Just remember, this deposit won't get you first dibs at the bar – that's what your winning smile and generous tip are for!

DRAFT

Not the kind you send to the Navy, but the measurement from the waterline to the lowest point of the ship's keel. It's like the ship's version of checking the depth of your cocktail glass, ensuring you've got just the right amount of liquid oxygen to fuel your maritime adventures. So, bottoms up, my seafaring friend, and may your draft be deep and your voyage be smooth sailing!

EMBARKATION

The grand entrance onto the floating pleasure palace! It's like running the gauntlet past the paparazzi, except instead of flashing cameras, you're dodging the relentless pack hounds known as cruise ship photographers. They'll snap your pic quicker than you can say "cheese," leaving you with more souvenir photos than you know what to do with!

FINAL PAYMENT

Now, onto final payment – the moment when you kiss your hard-earned cash goodbye and hand it over to your ever-so-helpful travel agent. It's like a high-stakes game of financial roulette, where the only guarantee is that your wallet will be lighter by the end of it. And forget about trying to pay in livestock or other assorted critters – these days, cruise lines are only interested in cold, hard currency. So leave your sheep at home and bring your wallet instead!

FIRST SEATING

Ah, first seating – where you get to dine like royalty at the appointed hour, surrounded by the same merry band of shipmates for the duration of your voyage. It's like being part of an exclusive club, except instead of secret handshakes, you get unlimited breadsticks and a guaranteed seat at the captain's table. But if all this rigmarole sounds like too much effort, you can always go freestyle and dine whenever and wherever your heart desires. Just be prepared to fend off the hungry hordes of hangry cruisers vying for a table!

FORWARD

The pointy end of the ship that's as sharp as your wit and as sleek as a sardine slicing through the sea. If you ever find yourself lost on board, just follow the fishes on the carpet – after all, when's the last time you saw a fish swim backwards? So point your compass towards adventure and set sail for the forward frontier, where the only thing sharper than the ship's bow is your sense of humour!

GANGWAY

Ah, the gangway – that precarious passage between ship and shore, where you must navigate the treacherous waters of the Pack Hounds, otherwise known as cruise ship photographers. They lie in wait, ready to pounce with their flashy cameras and cheesy poses, determined to capture your most awkward moments for posterity!

GRATUITIES

And then there are the gratuities – those sneaky little envelopes of appreciation that magically transform into a top-up for the ship's crew wages. On land, it might be called a bribe, but on the high seas, it's just good old-fashioned gratitude. Just be sure to slip those envelopes discreetly unless you want to be mistaken for a shady dealmaker instead of a generous soul!

GUARANTEES

Ah, guarantees – the cruise line's ingenious solution for filling those less-than-desirable cabins that nobody else wants to touch with a ten-foot pole. From the dancefloor dwellers to the lifeboat loiterers, these cabins offer a unique blend of adventure and inconvenience. But fear not, for with a guarantee comes the promise of at least a slightly less terrible cabin, complete with the possibility of an extra tea bag or two to sweeten the deal!

GUEST RELATIONS/GUEST SERVICES

Your one-stop shop for all things complaint-related on the high seas. Whether you're upset about the lack of towel animals or the abundance of karaoke, these brave souls are here to take your grievances with a smile. And if they're not busy fielding complaints, they might even help you with useful stuff like directions or booking your next massage. Just don't forget to thank them with a hefty gratuity on your way out!

HULL

That looming mass of metal that surrounds you like a protective shell, or, if you're unlucky enough to be staring at it while at sea, a desperate cry for help. You see, the hull is what keeps the ocean where it belongs – outside the ship! So, if you find yourself gazing at it from the main deck down to the keel, it might be time to grab a lifeboat and start paddling!

INSIDE STATEROOM

Now, let's talk about inside staterooms – those cosy little cabins that lack the luxury of portholes, windows, or balconies. They're the perfect excuse to stay in bed all day on a sea day, claiming you were just waiting for it to get light outside. After all, who needs sunlight when you've got room service and endless episodes of "Shipwrecked and Bored"?

MIDSHIP

The middle ground between the pointy end and the blunt end of the ship. If you're not quite sure where you are on the ship, just aim for the middle, and you're bound to hit midship sooner or later. It's like the sweet spot of the sea, where the waves rock you gently to sleep without veering too far off course.

OCEANVIEW STATEROOM

Now, let's talk about oceanview staterooms – the inside cabins' slightly more glamorous cousin. They may not have the excuse of sleeping in, but they do come with the added bonus of a window to let in the light. It's like having a tiny slice of the ocean right outside your door without the hassle of actually having to go outside!

OCEANVIEW STATEROOM WITH VERANDA

The pinnacle of onboard luxury for us common folk. These outside staterooms come with their very own balcony, where you can sit and watch the world go by or hide from that couple you got stuck with at dinner. You know the ones – they followed you everywhere, like a bad case of seasickness, and now they want to exchange email addresses. Ah, the joys of cruising!

PORT

Port – not the drink, but the left side of the ship when facing forward. Just to clarify, that's the way the ship is pointing, not the way you're looking. Because if you're facing backwards, the left side magically becomes the right side. Confused yet? Welcome to the wonderful world of maritime directions!

SAILING TIME

Now, sailing time – the exact hour when the ship bids adieu to the dock and sets sail for adventure. It's also the perfect opportunity to play a riveting game of "Spot the Pier Runners." These are the folks who forgot what time the ship leaves because, let's be honest, nobody thought to write it on their hands. Cue the frantic sprinting and panicked waving as they desperately try to catch the ship before it disappears over the horizon.

SECOND SEATING

Second seating – like first seating, but with a side of patience. You see, you're not allowed to eat until all the ravenous ruffians from first seating have stuffed their faces and vacated the dining room. It's like waiting for the dessert cart to finally make its way to your table, except it's the entire meal.

SHORE EXCURSION

Ah, shore excursions – the organised tours where you blindly follow a guide around like a lost puppy. They'll lead you through bustling markets, ancient ruins, and tourist traps galore, all while sporting a shiny badge that screams, "Hey, look at me, I'm a tourist!" Because apparently, the locals wouldn't have guessed otherwise. And don't forget the extra charge for the privilege of being herded like cattle!

STARBOARD

Starboard – the right side of the ship when facing forward. Unless, of course, you're facing the blunt end, in which case it becomes the post side. Confused? Just remember, fish always swim forward, and you'll be fine.

TENDER

Ah, the tender – the not-so-glamorous cousin of the cruise ship. Picture this: you're all dressed up in your finest vacation attire, ready to hit the town, and suddenly, you find yourself herded onto a tiny boat bobbing in the water like a cork. That's right, folks, welcome aboard the tender! It's like the Uber of the sea, except instead of a smooth ride, you get rocked and rolled like a theme park attraction.

TRANSFERS

The magical journey from ship to shore and back again. It's like a real-life game of musical chairs, except instead of chairs, you're shuffling between modes of transportation. From airports to hotels to who-knows-where, it's a whirlwind adventure of confusion and chaos. Just try not to get lost in the shuffle – or end up on the wrong bus to Timbuktu!

Ah, my fellow seafarers, fear not, for the ocean of cruising lingo is deep and vast, like a bottomless buffet of words waiting to be devoured! These terms are just the tip of the iceberg, the appetisers before the main course of maritime madness. So grab your life jackets and hold onto your hats because we're about to embark on a voyage of linguistic hilarity!

Published in 2024 by
Steve Barker
Copyright © 2024 Steve Barker
All rights reserved.
ISBN:
All rights reserved.

First Edition: May 2024

Disclaimer:

The information in this book is provided for general informational purposes only. The author and publisher have made every effort to ensure the accuracy of the information herein. However, they assume no responsibility for errors, inaccuracies, omissions, or any inconsistency herein. The reader assumes all responsibility for the use of this information. The author and publisher disclaim any liability, loss, or risk taken by individuals who directly or indirectly act on the information contained in this book.

You can read a selection of my books at Green Cat Books
https://www.green-cat.shop/steve-barker